Ethics at the Edges of Law

Ethics at the Edges of Law

Christian Moralists and American Legal Thought

CATHLEEN KAVENY

OXFORD
UNIVERSITY PRESS

OXFORD
UNIVERSITY PRESS

Oxford University Press is a department of the University of Oxford. It furthers the University's objective of excellence in research, scholarship, and education by publishing worldwide. Oxford is a registered trade mark of Oxford University Press in the UK and certain other countries.

Published in the United States of America by Oxford University Press
198 Madison Avenue, New York, NY 10016, United States of America.

Library of Congress Cataloging-in-Publication Data
Names: Kaveny, Cathleen, author.
Title: Ethics at the edges of law : Christian moralists and American legal thought / Cathleen Kaveny.
Description: New York, NY, United States of America : Oxford University Press, [2018] | Includes bibliographical references.
Identifiers: LCCN 2017000779 | ISBN 9780190612290 |
ISBN 9780190612306 | ISBN 9780190612313 | ISBN 9780190612320
Subjects: LCSH: Christian ethics. | Christian sociology—Catholic Church. | Catholic Church—Doctrines. | Law—United States. | Law and ethics.
Classification: LCC BJ1251 .K275 2018 | DDC 241/.2—dc23
LC record available at https://lccn.loc.gov/2017000779

To the
Religion Department Lounge
1879 Hall
Princeton University

Contents

Preface

THIS BOOK IS dedicated to a place, not to a person: the Religion Department Lounge at Princeton University. But it is a place that has fostered a rare and precious set of relations among the persons who have been fortunate enough to encounter one another there. It is a place that has facilitated challenging yet mutually respectful conversations about important political, moral, cultural, and religious issues among people with very different belief systems and experiences. It is a place that stands as the counterpoint and antidote to the culture wars.

The Lounge is also the place where I discovered my own vocation to teaching and scholarship thirty years ago. As a sophomore fascinated with questions of faith, morality, and politics, I wandered into the Lounge after a precept (discussion section) in 1879 Hall, where the Religion Department was housed. It was a large, bright space located near the departmental offices and across a narrow hall from the seminar room. Faculty, graduate students, and several excessively bold undergraduates like me would drift in before or after class and grab a cup of strong coffee. Sometimes, we would take a seat on the hideous green leatherette sectional sofa that provided the focal point of the room. We would read the newspaper, catch up with paperwork, or chat about the weekend.

Inevitably, however, most of us were drawn into the Lounge's informal daily seminar, which usually began in late morning and continued through lunchtime into the early afternoon. Often the text was the day's edition of the *New York Times*. Paul Ramsey, who had read the *Times* cover to cover early that morning, would call our attention to an editorial or news story on a matter of domestic policy, foreign policy, or constitutional jurisprudence that merited his searching critique. Jeffrey Stout and Victor Preller would challenge his analysis and put forward alternative viewpoints. Eminent historians John Gager, John Wilson, and Martha Himmelfarb often joined in the discussion, along with graduate students who would go on to distinguished careers of their own: Randy Balmer, Mark Cladis, Steve Crocco, Joe Incandela, Dan Nelson, Tim Renick, and Buzzy Teiser were frequent denizens of the Lounge in the early eighties. Scott Davis, a recent graduate, regularly graced the room with his genial demeanor and razor-sharp analytic abilities. And Lorraine Fuhrmann miraculously managed to contribute to the discussions while simultaneously keeping the Religion Department running smoothly.

And so I wandered into this august company as an undergraduate. Other undergraduates were equally adventuresome; I think in particular of Cristie Traina, Gene Rogers, and Ann Mongoven. We all had the good fortune of enrolling in an astounding seminar on Barth and Rahner that Bill Werpehowski taught as a visiting professor in the spring of 1982. That seminar was intellectual catnip. We all went on to doctoral work in religious studies.

No one stood on ceremony in the Lounge—a kinder and less pretentious group of people would be hard to imagine. At the same time, no quarter was given for bad arguments—even to sophomores. I vividly remember a long conversation about legalized abortion in which Preller told me I needed a more nuanced perspective on the relationship of law and morality, and directed me to go read Thomas Aquinas's treatise on law. I have been reading and rereading Aquinas on law ever since. And I have repeatedly recalled Ramsey's offhand remark that if he could do it all again, he would earn a law degree along with a doctorate in ethics; it was that remark that first set me on my own quest to integrate the study of these two fields. Stout's analysis of what it means to reason critically within a tradition has radically shaped my approach to both law and Christian ethics.

The ongoing, informal Lounge seminar modeled the practice of truly collaborative intellectual engagement. During my senior year, the morality of nuclear deterrence was a pressing question in applied ethics; it was also the topic of my senior thesis. The Lounge hosted innumerable conversations on whether the conditional intention to use nuclear weapons as part of a deterrence policy was ethically acceptable. These conversations pondered various views of the nature of intention, the difference between intended effects and those that are merely foreseen, and whether it is immoral to threaten what it is immoral to do. The intellectual culture of the Lounge demanded that we interpret each other's positions charitably, that we enter into each other's arguments to improve them before formulating our own critiques, and that we honestly admit the limits of our own viewpoints, even as we continued to defend them as the most adequate given the alternatives. In short, Lounge discussions were a practicum in the ethics of discourse.

It is my sincere hope that my engagements with the thinkers I discuss *in Ethics at the Edges of Law: Christian Moralists and American Legal Thought* are faithful to the spirit of the Lounge. Both the title and the structure of the book are gestures of deep respect to Paul Ramsey, who served as advisor to my senior thesis along with the preternaturally wise Jeff Stout. My title is a nod to Ramsey's important work on medical ethics, *Ethics at the Edges of Life: Medical and Legal Intersections.*[1] The structure I adopt is modeled on his volume *Nine Modern Moralists,*[2] in which he developed his own thought in searching conversation with a diverse group of contemporary thinkers.

Ramsey famously said: "The highest tribute one can pay any thinker, or any body of writing, is to wrestle with it."[3] Readers may observe that my chapter devoted to his thought is significantly more critical than those dedicated to other thinkers, who have also been my important teachers and colleagues. The point of my critique is to facilitate a conversation between the earlier Ramsey and the later Ramsey on the relationship between law and Christian ethics. The earlier Ramsey was open to the idea that the secular law could be a worthy conversation partner, while the later Ramsey took a much dimmer view. Supreme Court decisions such as *Roe v. Wade*[4] shook his confidence in the fundamental capacity of the American legal system to grasp basic moral truths.

As readers of this book will see, I believe the earlier Ramsey has the better of this argument. Now, as then, there is much to criticize in the deliverances of American courts, particularly the Supreme Court. For example, in *Citizens United v. Federal Election Commission* (2010),[5] the Court protected the liberty of corporations to make donations to political candidates as an aspect of the constitutional right to free speech. In so doing, it pushed those without money or power to the margins of the American public square, with disastrous effects for democratic deliberation.

Both *Roe* and *Citizens United* can be justly criticized for their judicial overreaching. Yet neither case, in my view, disqualifies the American legal system as a whole from being a fruitful conversation partner for Christian ethicists. It simply means that the conversation must be conducted in the searching, rigorous, but open manner modeled not only by Paul Ramsey but also by all the other thinkers I have been privileged to engage with in *Ethics at the Edges of Law.*

Acknowledgments

THE CHAPTERS IN *Ethics at the Edges of Law: Christian Moralists and American Legal Thought* wrestle with the writings of important contemporary scholars in the field of Christian ethics, all of whom have taught me a great deal about fundamental questions of love and justice. I thank my interlocutors for the opportunity to engage their ideas and benefit from their wisdom, not only in print but also in many face-to-face conversations over the years.

I would also like to extend my appreciation to colleagues at Duke University, Princeton University, St. John's University, the University of St. Thomas, the University of Virginia, and Yale University for inviting me to try out some of my ideas in conferences and colloquia they organized. Special thanks to friends at the University of Notre Dame (where I taught for many years) and Boston College (my new home) for helping me think more deeply about the intersection of theology and law, especially Lisa Sowle Cahill, John Finnis, James Keenan, John Paris, John Robinson, and Vincent Rougeau. I benefited enormously from the generosity of John Coughlin, Michael Perry, and Jonathan Rothchild, who graciously provided incisive comments on the entire manuscript. I am also indebted to William Werpehowski for his wise advice. Lu Ann Nate, my assistant at Notre Dame, was extremely helpful in the early days of the project. Daniel DiLeo, a graduate student in theological ethics at Boston College, provided insightful suggestions as I brought the manuscript to completion. Some of the chapters in this book are revised versions of my previously published essays, reworked to contribute to a coherent whole. They are: "Listening for the Future in the Voices of the Past: John T. Noonan, Jr. on Love and Power in Human History," *Journal of Law and Religion* 11, no. 1 (1994): 203–27, "A Response to John T. Noonan, Jr.," *Proceedings of the Catholic Theological Society of America* 54 (1999): 57–64, and "Development of Catholic Moral Doctrine: Probing the Subtext," *University of St. Thomas Law Journal* 1, no. 1 (2003): 234–52 (chapter 1); "Hauerwas and the Law: Framing a Productive Conversation,"

Law and Contemporary Problems 75, no. 4 (2012): 135–60 (chapter 2); "Between Example and Doctrine: Contract Law and Common Morality," *Journal of Religious Ethics* 33, no. 4 (2005): 669–95 (chapter 3); "Erastian and High Church Approaches to the Law: the Jurisprudential Categories of Robert E. Rodes, Jr.," *Journal of Law and Religion* 22, no. 2 (2007): 405–32 (chapter 7); "Mercy, Justice, and Law: Can Legal Concepts Help Foster New Life?," in George Augustin, ed., *Marriage and Family: Relics of the Past or Promise of the Future?* (Mahwah, NJ: Paulist Press, 2015), 75–106 and "Mercy for the Remarried: What the Church Can Learn from Civil Law," *Commonweal*, August 14, 2015. (chapter 8); and "What is Legalism? Engelhardt and Grisez on the Misuse of Law in Christian Ethics," *The Thomist* 72, no. 3 (2008): 443–85 (chapter 9). All citations to Scripture are from the New Revised Standard Version, as accessed on the website BibleGateway.

I am very grateful to Cynthia Read, my editor at Oxford University Press, for her support and patience. And I extend my heartfelt appreciation to my friends and family for their encouragement—and their sustained forbearance—as I brought this manuscript to completion.

Introduction

RELIGIOUS ETHICS IS not a hermetically sealed discipline. Moralists working within specific religious traditions regularly interact with fields such as theology, biblical studies, history, the sciences, and the social sciences. Yet many religious ethicists consider the discipline of philosophy a privileged conversation partner. They treat philosophy not merely as a source of helpful background information or empirical facts but also as a potential locus of true moral insight. They turn to great works in philosophy for helpful ways of exploring and articulating the meaning of human dignity, the ethical import of human actions, and the relationship between individuals and the community. And they are right to do so. But philosophy should not be the only privileged conversation partner.

In *Ethics at the Edges of Law: Christian Moralists and American Legal Thought*, I make a case that religious ethicists profitably might treat the field of law in much the same way that it does philosophy. Law, in a sense, is applied and enculturated philosophy. It not only articulates but also puts into practice fundamental normative judgments about why human beings are important, what counts as human flourishing, and how we should live our lives together. In putting those judgments into practice, it also tests them. What seems like a good idea for organizing society in a seminar room may prove to be utterly disastrous when actually implemented. At the very least, implementation may reveal significant flaws or gaps in the corresponding theory.

Making my case will entail disabusing my readers of some common misperceptions. For example, many ethicists tend to assume that law is primarily of instrumental value rather than epistemic value to those interested in systematic moral reflection. They tend, in other words, to treat the law as a mechanism that may be used to implement the public policy directives settled on by religious or philosophical ethicists after vigorous and open discussion. Moralists evaluate practices such as abortion, euthanasia, or same-sex relations, or they scrutinize natural and social phenomena such as climate change and economic inequality. The law enters the picture only after the serious ethical analysis has been completed, as a means to enforce its deliverances.

Many moralists, in short, do not perceive the legal tradition as a source of insight for their process of moral discernment. I will encourage them to broaden their field of vision. The legal tradition can in fact help them explore a wide variety of theoretical commitments, ranging from the role of narrative in ethics, to the relationship of rules and exceptions, to the place of compassion for victims in personal and communal relations. Moreover, legal decisions raise sharp questions of social justice and fundamental fairness, in ways that might advance or hone both the theoretical and the applied reflections of religious ethicists.

Making my case will also entail moving beyond assertion to demonstration. The nine chapters in this book are meant to illustrate how engagement with the law can illuminate and extend the work of important contemporary religious moralists on a range of topics. The figures I have chosen to engage represent some variety and breadth with within the realm of Christian ethics, which is my own specialty within the broader field of religious ethics. Some are Protestants (Outka, Hauerwas, Ramsey); some are Catholics (Noonan, Farley, Rodes, Kasper, and Grisez). One critically engages Christian ethics from the perspective of nonbeliever (Stout), and another belongs to the Orthodox tradition (Engelhardt). Some are theological progressives (Farley and Kasper), some are conservative (Ramsey and Grisez). Some emphasize the importance of a distinctively Christian morality (Hauerwas, Engelhardt), while others press for a more universal perspective (Outka, Farley). Taken together, they constitute a range of important figures in Christian theology and ethics over the past fifty years. At the same time, of course, I do not wish to pretend that these figures comprehensively represent the increasingly expansive field of religious ethics. I can only encourage other scholars with interest and expertise in fields such as Jewish ethics, Islamic ethics, and African-American ethics to consider treating secular law as a conversation partner. I have much to learn from them.

The argument of *Ethics at the Edges of Law* is developed in three parts. The book moves from a discussion of how engagement with secular law can illuminate the general methodological commitments of Christian ethicists (part I), to a consideration of how the meaning of the key theological concepts of love, justice, and sin can be sharpened in conversation with legal cases and doctrines (part II), to an examination of how legal concepts and categories can shed light on current problems and controversies in Christian ethics (part III). Taken as a whole, the book aims to demonstrate the substantive contributions that engagement with the law can make to important discussions in different facets of the field.

Part I: Narratives and Norms

The first part of *Ethics at the Edges of Law* shows how grappling with legal concepts and cases may assist Christian ethicists in addressing three important methodological questions. First, how does a historically constituted normative tradition (legal or theological) construct a moral worldview through the development of characteristic narratives, characters, and norms? Second, how exactly are norms made, critiqued, and developed within a tradition? Third, how do Christians think about the relationship between Christian ethics and common morality? The three chapters in this section approach these questions from different angles.

Chapter 1, "Tradition and Development," serves as the foundation for the book. Focusing on the work of legal scholar and Catholic moral theologian John T. Noonan Jr., the chapter knits together Alasdair MacIntyre's narrative-based tradition theory, which is an important methodological strand in contemporary Christian ethics, with common law reasoning, which is the characteristic methodological commitment of the Anglo-American legal system. Drawing upon Noonan's work, it shows how a richly detailed historical account can reveal both continuities and discontinuities in doctrinal development in both law and Christian ethics. The chapter also shows how legal cases illuminate the tension between promoting individual flourishing and protecting the common good—a difficult and enduring problem for Christian social ethics.

Chapter 2, "Creation and Covenant," shifts the focus to an important strand of Protestant ethics represented by Stanley Hauerwas. The first chapter explored how the common law is a useful conversation partner for moralists such as John Noonan. Yet Noonan writes from the Catholic tradition, which emphasizes points of commonality between Catholic moral norms and common morality. Can the common law also prove helpful to Protestant ethicists such as Stanley Hauerwas, who stress the distinctiveness of Christian ethics and challenge Christian communities to resist the temptation to adopt prevailing secular value systems? I suggest that it can. The common law is a useful place for ethicists who emphasize distinctive Christian claims to engage contemporary secular morality, precisely because its methodology is inductive, epistemologically humble, and case-centered. Drawing on key concepts from contract law (which I have taught for two decades now), I argue that there is room for the sort of ad hoc correlations between Christian ethics and secular morality that both Hauerwas and Karl Barth should find congenial.

Chapter 3, "Examples and Rules," further expands the conversation to include Jeffrey Stout, one of the most acute critics of contemporary Christian ethics. Writing within the tradition of American democratic pragmatism, Stout has carried on a sustained dialogue with a range of important figures in Christian ethics, including MacIntyre and Hauerwas. I suggest that Stout's analysis could be enriched if he took the American common law as an additional conversation partner, for two reasons. First, the common law treats the relationship between rules and facts, narrative and character, and certitude and skepticism in ways in that Stout might find congenial. Second, common law deftly addresses other questions that are of interest to democratic theorists, such as the relationship between secular insights and religious insights in the public square, or the nature of political authority.

Part II: Love, Justice, and Law

Part II of *Ethics at the Edges of Law* grapples with the relationship between Christian love and the norms of justice, a relationship that has been a dominant concern in the field of Christian ethics for the better part of a century. What does love of neighbor demand? Does it require simply "equal regard"—the application of impersonal rules to all persons, who are equally made in the image and likeness of God? Is it permissible for neighbor love to take into account particular strengths and vulnerabilities in applying the norms of justice to particular people? Or does such a practice violate the demands of equal concern and fairness? Important facets of these enduring questions in Christian ethics are illuminated in the work of common law judges, who are required to do justice to the specific parties before them while also formulating binding legal rules to guide those who face similar situations in the future.

Chapter 4, "Neighbor Love and Legal Precedent," engages the recent scholarship of Gene Outka, the dean of contemporary Christiane ethicists writing on the relationship of love and justice. By placing his ideas in conversation with an intriguing Wisconsin Supreme Court case involving the break-up of a couple who held themselves out as legally married without actually having gone through the ceremony, the chapter explores the tension between our obligations of special care for the particular neighbors before us, on the one hand, and the demand for equal regard for all neighbors, near and distant, on the other.

Chapter 5, "Compassionate Respect and Victims' Voices," inaugurates a dialogue between the writings of feminist theologian Margaret Farley on love and justice and the controversy surrounding the use of victim impact statements in criminal sentencing. That debate instantiates the tension between love's call for particularized justice and the demands of fairness for general norms. It also raises the question of how far justice (or love) can depart from equal regard. Victim impact statements regularly include moving accounts of grief, anger, and loss. Yet their widespread use in sentencing can have troublesome consequences. It risks suggesting, for example, that the murder of a much admired pillar of the city should be punished more severely than the murder of a homeless person.

Chapter 6, "Covenant Fidelity and Culture Wars," grapples with the evolving and sometimes contradictory ways in which Paul Ramsey approaches secular law in his efforts to work out the relationship of love and justice. Over the course of three decades, Ramsey moves from treating the law as a locus of rich perspectives on the concrete requirements of that relationship, to viewing the law a more or less neutral field ripe for the application of Christian norms, to seeing the law as the menacing subject of a hostile takeover by secular liberal values inimical to Christian commitments. This last stage, in my view, is harbinger of the manner in which many socially conservative culture warriors have now come to view the law. That perspective is inadequate, I think, for reasons that are ultimately more theological than jurisprudential: Ramsey never fully confronts the question of how law should respond to the phenomenon of human sinfulness.

Part III: Legal Categories and Theological Problems

The third and final part of *Ethics at the Edges of Law* moves from substantive to methodological questions. My goal in this part is to show how particular legal categories and legal doctrines can help shed light on current theological debates.

Chapter 7, "Juridical Insights and Theological Disputes," highlights the methodological contributions of Robert E. Rodes Jr. Writing at the intersection of law and theology, Rodes shows how conceptual tools designed to distinguish between different types of legal statements can also shed light on knotty theological and ethical problems. Moreover, by offering us ways of reframing conflicts like the one between religious liberty and same-sex marriage, Rodes may help us quell the culture wars that have divided the society for the past fifty years.

Chapter 8, "Second Chances and Statutes of Limitations," explores how particular legal concepts can assist in resolving contemporary disputes in theological ethics. Cardinal Walter Kasper has argued that the principle of mercy suggests that in some situations, Catholics who divorced and remarried without first obtaining an annulment should be allowed to receive communion. His opponents have rejected that argument, claiming that such persons are committing adultery, in violation of the vows they made in their first marriages. Using secular legal tools such as the statute of limitations and the distinction between a completed and a continuing offense, I attempt to strengthen Kasper's argument by showing how we can avoid thinking of people in second marriages as engaged in a continuing offense against their first marriages. They can, therefore, repent of any wrongs committed against their first spouse, and receive communion without being treated as if they were in a continuing state of mortal sin.

The final chapter, "Legalism and Christian Ethics," concludes the book by tackling directly what I believe is a nagging objection to the use of secular law as a conversation partner in Christian ethics: the worry that too close a relationship to the methods and concerns of law risks falling into a "legalism" that obscures the Good News of the Gospel. Although Germain Grisez and H. Tristram Engelhardt Jr. both condemn "legalism," close analysis shows that they mean opposite things by the term. I conclude that labeling an ethics as "legalistic" is too imprecise a critique, and needs to be replaced by more specific challenges and concerns. When properly addressed, these challenges and concerns do not impede the use of law as a constructive conversation partner for Christian ethics.

A Word about Methodology

Throughout this introduction, I have been speaking about the possibilities of constructive engagement between Christian ethics and the law. Yet the category of "law," no less than that of "Christian ethics," is a general term. There are many different types of legal norms and many different ways of categorizing law. One can distinguish between criminal law, which concerns norms whose violation is seen as an attack on the whole community, and civil law, which regulates the behavior between and among members of that community. One can differentiate between federal law and state law, as well as between common law and statutory law. Just as Christian ethicists work in different subspecialties, so do legal scholars; their work includes fields such as administrative law, constitutional law, corporate law, international law, tax law, and trusts and estates. Just as Christian ethicists operate with different foundational commitments, so do legal theorists and judges. Some see the fundamental point of legal norms as maximizing economic efficiency, while others maintain that its purpose is to protect and expand the sphere of individual freedom. Just as Christian ethicists adopt different methodologies, so do lawyers and legal scholars. Some are strict constuctionists, emphasizing the "letter" of the law, while others are comfortable allowing the "spirit" of the law to develop organically over time.

In making a case for a more constructive and fruitful relationship between Christian ethics and law, I cannot do justice to all areas or perspectives in legal studies, any more than I can do justice to all areas or perspectives in Christian ethics. At the same time, I am committed to engaging legal matters with some particularity, rather than remaining on the level of generalities. So, I have repeatedly drawn from the areas of law I know best: the common law of contracts, which I have taught to first-year law students for over two decades, aspects of criminal law that are related to my longstanding interest in the relationship of mercy and justice, and facets of criminal procedure that help define distinct human acts for purposes of moral and legal analysis.

I hope all these points of contact between law and Christian ethics are fruitful and interesting. At the same time, the last thing I want to do is imply that the legal topics and cases I draw on here exhaust the possibilities for engagement. My earnest hope is that other scholars will build many additional bridges, showing how concepts and cases from tort law, insurance regulation, property law, and many other legal fields can both enrich and challenge the ongoing work of Christian ethics.

Ethics at the Edges of Law

PART I

Narratives and Norms

1

Tradition and Development

Engaging John T. Noonan Jr.

WITH THE PUBLICATION of *After Virtue* in 1981, Alasdair Maclntyre revolutionized the study of post-Enlightenment moral philosophy by insisting that it repent of its current pretensions to a view from eternity and confess its temporal roots in the long and motley history of human reflection about the good life.[1] Almost a quarter of a century earlier, John T. Noonan Jr., a young Harvard-trained legal scholar who also possessed a doctorate in philosophy from Catholic University, had waged a similar battle against the widespread misconception of the medieval concept of usury as monolithic, self-contained, and immutable.[2] Noonan's writings, in my view, help show how both Anglo-American law and Roman Catholic moral theology have actually functioned as living traditions in the manner described by Alasdair MacIntyre: each is "an historically extended, socially embodied argument, and an argument precisely in part about the goods which constitute that tradition."[3]

Working with medieval authors who were themselves largely insensitive to the idea of historicity, and writing in the context of a pre-Vatican II Catholicism still imbued with the abstract and ahistorical spirit of nineteenth century neo-Thomism, Noonan demonstrated in his first book that the concept of usury was in fact a fusion of concrete theological, ethical, economic, and legal concerns that were not stagnant but, rather, organically developing. In so doing, he gave Catholic Christianity a more adequate conception of its past. More than that, he gestured optimistically toward its future. Tracing how the absolute prohibition of usury, defined as any lending of money at interest, was circumscribed, attenuated, and finally abandoned by succeeding generations of moral theologians and canon lawyers, Noonan underscored that the Roman Catholic Church could and did change its mind about important moral issues that were held to implicate unalterable strictures of the natural law. Revealing that an increased willingness on the part of moralists to acknowledge that the moral experience of Christians professionally involved in the practices of commerce and banking had fueled the evolution of the usury doctrine in past centuries, Noonan nourished the hope for a stronger voice of lay experience in ecclesial discussions of moral issues throughout the years to come.

Written during the Second Vatican Council (and before *Humanae vitae*[4] was issued), Noonan's second magisterial study, *Contraception: A History of Its Treatment by the Catholic Theologians and Canonists*,[5] incorporated and extended both of these insights. Since that time, Noonan's work on such topics as the canon law of marriage,[6] slavery,[7] bribery,[8] and religious liberty[9] has consistently embodied the conviction that moral teachings and religious doctrines must not be divorced from the historical and social context engendering them. Prodigious in learning, as well as graceful and often witty in style, his books draw upon sources both ancient and modern, composed in several languages, and cutting across the disciplines of theology, philosophy, history, and law.

My purpose in this chapter is not primarily to distill into capsule form the conclusions Noonan reaches in each of his detailed tomes. Indeed, it would violate Noonan's own historical sensibilities to suggest that these conclusions can be wrenched without distortion from his discussion of the particular episodes that give them shape and substance. Metaphorically speaking, my aim is, rather, to look for a moment at the mirror itself, instead of the reflection placed before our gaze. In the conviction that they cannot fail to influence his perspective, and our perspective through his, I hope to highlight some of Noonan's own normative commitments regarding such fundamental issues as epistemology, theological anthropology, and the relation of love, justice, and law.

In so doing, I also hope to indicate several ways in which Noonan's legal sensibilities and use of legal materials might offer some direction for present and future discussions in theological ethics. More specifically, Noonan's work not only assists theologians and ethicists in thinking more generally about their intellectual heritage as a MacIntyrean tradition, but also provides more detailed guidance about how argumentation proceeds regarding the nature and relative ranking of the goods carried forward through history by the tradition. His writings also take seriously the tension between honoring the particularity of each person's life circumstances, on the one hand, and formulating generally applicable norms that promote the common good, on the other hand. In Christian ethics, this tension has been explored as a matter of the relationship between love and justice.

Multifaceted Historicity in Making Doctrine

Why is it so important for Noonan to situate his moral analysis historically? First, as with MacIntyre, Noonan's stance presupposes an epistemological outlook. Knowledge in general, and moral knowledge in particular, is both sought after and articulated in particular times and places. Over the years, Noonan's construal of what counts as adequately situating a moral concept or practice has consistently expanded. While interdisciplinary in character, his first book is best characterized as a history of ideas. Noonan's primary concern is to trace the development of the moral concept of usury through the treatises of the theologians and canon lawyers who discuss it; his consideration of the actual social and economic circumstances in which the doctrine was forged and applied lacks detail and plays a subsidiary role.

Contraception expands the database of which Noonan takes account in at least two ways. First, he pays more attention to questions of a concrete nature: what sort of person practices contraception, under what social and familial circumstances, and by what means. Second, he sketches the polemical context in which the doctrine developed so as better to illuminate both its impetus and its ultimate purpose. For example, it is only in light of Augustine's experience with the anti-procreative ethic of the Manichees that we can accurately grasp the saint's unwavering conviction that all contraceptive practices (including the "rhythm method") count as sinful violations of the primary procreative purpose of marriage.[10] Notwithstanding its attention to social situation and political or doctrinal controversy, *Contraception*, like the usury book, is still best described as intellectual history. Noonan's fundamental stress still falls upon the development of doctrine. Despite their importance, the historical background and social context appear not as proper centers of attention in themselves but as the indispensable prerequisites to proper understanding of moral ideas.

By contrast, Noonan's next book, *Power to Dissolve*,[11] reveals a marked shift in concern. Aptly subtitled "Lawyers and Marriages in the Courts of the Roman Curia," the book is not focused on the development of canonical teachings about marriage and annulment, but more broadly on the moral practices that those teachings foster and the living system of canon law in which they take their place. More specifically, Noonan refuses to separate the ideas and ideals of canon law from the way in which they were formulated by and applied to particular *human persons* in the context of human institutions. Consequently, the book is organized around six specific cases, which are annulment petitions brought before the Roman ecclesiastical courts between 1653 and 1923. Each case presents the Curia with the unavoidable task of ranking the priority of various commitments of the tradition that stand in mutual tension, such as between the theologically driven affirmation of the possibility of a valid, intentionally virginal marriage (as typified in the Catholic tradition by that of Mary and Joseph) and the more practically minded Augustinian view that persons contracting marriage must be open to the good of procreation.[12] Following their often serpentine courses through different layers of ecclesiastical bureaucracy, Noonan shows how the final disposition of each case depends as much upon the individual quirks of the persons involved as upon more abstract and impersonal doctrinal exigencies.

Noonan's subsequent massive historical studies—a treatise on bribery,[13] and both a casebook[14] and a monograph[15] on religious liberty—manifest his increasing dexterity in reflecting the development of moral and legal movements through the prism of individual lives and choices. One might say that Noonan's insistence upon situating moral concepts not only in a rough social context but even more precisely within the lives of particular persons, bespeaks an epistemological commitment to historical specificity that surpasses even that of MacIntyre. Yet his commitment to such specificity is not merely epistemological. It is a necessary entailment of his theological anthropology, and the conception of human obligations to one and other which it generates.

For Noonan, the study of ethics, law, and theology are historical enterprises because the *persons* who engage in these activities are historical beings. Moreover, because human nature is essentially social, and human society also moves within time, he recognizes that those of us who are living today stand in community and conversation with the dead. The shape of our minds and hearts is informed by the ideas and purposes of our forebears, much as the shape of our bodies is informed by their genetic material. We manifest our fidelity to the persons of the past not in slavish repetition of old formulas but rather in sensitively attempting to discern the core purposes of traditional doctrine and in creatively applying it to a new situation. Such a process requires us both to understand and to judge our predecessors. In sifting through their thought, we must separate insights of enduring value from the rough bundle of time-bound presuppositions and failures of will and vision that trap them.

This demythologizing exercise is by no means easy, nor untouched by ambiguity. The best and most holy of persons can remain tragically constrained by their context. For example, while praising Pope Benedict XIV as a man of "intelligence seasoned by experience and joined to goodness,"[16] Noonan also hints of the rigid order constricting the pope's mind by depicting his world in terms of the yearbook issued at that time by the Roman Curia. Concluding with a flourish his detailed and ironic catalog of the odd scraps of information contained in the yearbook, Noonan writes: "This hieratic structure on the horarium of Italy, which opened with the date of the creation of the world, continued with the dates of the creation of the cardinals, and closed with the schedule of committee meetings of the Inquisition, was the universe of Prospero Lambertini, in which he lived, for which, perforce, he spoke as Pope."[17]

Noonan struggles against treating the past as a mythical golden age. He also, however, resists the temptation to portray the great sins of bygone eras as performed by monsters, not human beings. True, Noonan does take poetic satisfaction in the fact that the mean-spirited Bishop of Beauvais responsible for condemning Joan of Arc to the stake bore the name "Pierre Cauchon," or "Peter Pig,"[18] and that the bribe-taking Roman praetor painted by Cicero as so foul, cruel, greedy, and lustful in his corruption that he bordered on the inhuman was known as "Verres," or "Hog."[19] Yet Noonan cautions that we can never know if the Hog of Cicero's account ever actually existed; Cicero, after all, was an expert orator charged with the role of prosecuting attorney, and his more colorful accusations should be interpreted accordingly.

In Noonan's accounts, even fundamentally admirable persons appear as agents of banal and dishonorable behavior. Sir Francis Bacon was a taker of bribes, John Quincy Adams a giver of them. However, most wrongdoing, even in its more spectacular forms, is performed by persons whose character is an ordinary blend of good and evil. Samuel Pepys, one of Noonan's most intriguing and industrious practitioners of graft, acted as clerk to the British Naval Board in the mid-seventeenth century and "received from those interested in his official actions animals, clothing, food, furniture, silverware, cash and sex."[20] Meticulously recording these transactions in his private journal, gleefully totaling his net worth on New Year's Eve 1664, and showering God with heartfelt praise for the increase,

Pepys unwittingly furnishes posterity with incontrovertible evidence of his own greed, corruption, and lubriciousness.

Yet even while reprinting particularly damning excerpts from the journal, Noonan is at pains to prevent his readers from consigning Pepys to a moral realm too far removed from the one in which we locate ourselves. Pepys, "though he committed adultery, loved his wife," and "though he was in the pay of the Navy's suppliers and the king's contractors, loved the Navy and served the king."[21] Evoking "the complexity of [Pepys's] consciousness," Noonan traces the path of self-deception by which he quelled his inner misgivings. "Before his inner judge he customarily claimed to observe two rules: No one was hurt by what he took. What he got was voluntarily given."[22] Insisting that we recognize the ambiguity that characterizes each human heart, Noonan forestalls our initial instinct to recoil against Pepys and his corruptions as repulsive, alien, and therefore irrelevant to us. Rather, we are absorbed by Pepys's rationalizations and are led to wonder under what circumstances we ourselves might have done the same thing. To acknowledge our continuing community with Pepys and others like him is to give such persons their due in justice and in charity. No less significantly, it can also force us to exercise greater vigilance regarding the myriad ways in which self-deception goes hand in hand with sin in our own lives. Chronicling the histories of bribe-takers and bribe-givers, ecclesiastical bureaucrats long dead and American politicians still living, Noonan deftly traces a map of the pitfalls facing all of us who struggle to conduct our own lives with moral seriousness.

Noonan's focus on the lives and choices of individuals also implies an anthropology that resonates deeply with the Catholic personalism developed earlier in the twentieth century, and accords most strikingly with what David Hollenbach has called the "personalist communitarianism"[23] of Jacques Maritain.[24] For both Maritain and Noonan, each human person, gifted with both intelligence and will, and possessed of "spiritual superexistence through knowledge and through love,"[25] demands the utmost respect in the arrangement of temporal matters. As Maritain puts it, every human being is "thus in some fashion a whole, not merely a part"[26] of a larger entity. Yet this does not mean that persons are atomistic, isolated individuals; Maritain goes on to say that "[t]he person is a whole, but he is not a closed whole, he is an *open* whole," blessedly open toward other persons for "communications of intelligence and love."[27] Persons, then, are essentially social and created to live together in societies organized by the rule of law. Yet it also implies that the common good can be no straightforward utilitarian calculus that undercuts the sanctity of the individual persons constituting the community. The common good "is therefore common *to the whole and to the parts,* which are in themselves wholes, since the very notion of *person* means totality; it is common to the whole and to the parts, over which it flows back and which must all benefit from it."[28]

Every student of Christian ethics is familiar with the internal tensions that Maritain's personalist communitarianism engenders. Individuals are essentially and ultimately valuable, yet the exigencies of community organization often require impersonal rules, laws, and institutions that cannot afford to take into account the needs of particular persons. What, then, is the proper relationship between the personal love possible between individuals and the less personal justice necessary to order their lives together? Furthermore, how can either love or justice be borne within the abstract and sometimes rigid categories of law? Each human being is a unique creature of God, yet shares with other persons similar capacities and needs. In case of conflict, does love for other persons give priority to the unique aspects of individuals, or to their common human characteristics? Confounding in themselves, these questions are further obscured by the blot of human sin and failure upon individual and social life.

Much of John Noonan's work can be viewed as an attempt to investigate these tensions as they have arisen not only in ethical theory but also in real life. His work demonstrates that the legal realm offers a plethora of case studies against which ethicists can examine, test, and refine their theological and moral commitments. In *Persons and Masks of the Law,* Noonan reflects: "The central problem . . . of the legal enterprise is the relation of love to power. We can often apply force to those we do not see, but we cannot, I think, love them. Only in the response of person to person can Augustine's sublime fusion be achieved, in which justice is defined as 'love serving only the one loved.'"[29] Like Maritain and other Thomists, Noonan believes that the power of law is necessary for social existence, not only to restrain wrongdoers but also to channel human energies toward cooperative relationships, and to teach the basic values of the society.[30] Standing at the heart of any legal system are two entities: rules and persons. For Noonan, the legal "process is rightly understood only if rules and persons are seen as equally essential components, every rule depending on persons to frame, apply, and undergo it, every person using rules."[31] Grave moral dangers arise from letting go of either component. On the one hand, the abandonment of impartially formulated rules can produce "monsters" that strangle justice with favoritism. On the other hand, the subsumption of persons into the inexorable impersonality of rules can be ruthless.

Noonan's book on bribery exhaustively probes the former problem: a bribe comprises "an inducement improperly influencing the performance of a public function meant to be gratuitously exercised."[32] A bribe-taking judge prostitutes justice and tramples upon impartiality. In reproachful contrast to judicial graft and as the paradigmatic just judge, the God of the Book of Deuteronomy and of the apostle Paul eschews *prosōpolempsia* (which literally means "face-lifting")—that is, corrupt respect of persons.[33] Justice must be impartial. Acknowledging the necessity of the impersonal rules that give form to institutions serving purposes beyond the individual, and recognizing the need for human beings to participate in these institutions by playing socially defined roles, Noonan affirms such impartiality.

Yet in other writings, he stresses that at least as much damage has been inflicted throughout history by neglect of the individual persons interacting by necessity or by choice with the coercive power of the legal system. A major culprit is the use of rules to construct *masks*, or "ways of classifying individual human beings so that their humanity is hidden and disavowed."[34] Playing on the ambiguity of the Latin term *persona*, Noonan explores several ways in which the American legal system has allowed masks (*personae*) to be used to conceal persons (*personae*) in both his *Persons and Masks of the Law* and *The Antelope*.

The latter book provides a case study in one of the most deadly and efficient uses of legal terms to obscure humanity: the subsumption of enslaved Africans and their descendants under the category of "property." The *Antelope* was a ship captured off the coast of Florida by American agents in 1820, with about 280 Africans on board destined for the slave markets.[35] At the time, it had been illegal for over ten years to import slaves anywhere into the United States, and the president had recently acquired power to ensure the "safekeeping, support and removal beyond the United States" of Africans taken on captured ships. Despite these facts, over one hundred Africans from the ship died, many of neglect or mistreatment, and nearly forty were enslaved.[36] Only about 120 of them were finally deemed free persons, and were put on ships to Liberia seven years after their capture.[37] Noonan tells the tale of the political machinations, the bureaucratic ennui, the petty calculations, and the self-delusion that enabled, for instance, men like Judge William Davies and Justice William Johnson to "overcome" their personal revulsion to slavery long enough to uphold its legality under international law and decide that foreign slave traders should be allowed to recover their "property" in the courts of the United States.[38]

According to Noonan, the masks that trigger moral catastrophes such as that befalling the *Antelope* are of two kinds: masks imposed on others, such as "property" in the case of slaves, and masks impressed upon on oneself, such as "the court" and "the law" in the case of judges rendering opinions.[39] Practically and morally, they are deeply interconnected. Practically, it is only by secreting their own human feeling under impersonal masks that such fundamentally decent persons as Holmes, Cardozo, Wythe, and Jefferson could bear to place such dehumanizing masks on the faces of those over whom they exercised power. From a moral perspective, however, the two types of masking are deeply interrelated; to mask another, in fact, is also to mask oneself. For Noonan, as for Maritain, it is at the essence of personhood to relate with knowledge and love to other persons. Consequently, to treat another as less than human also denigrates one's own humanity.

One crucial question that Noonan's writings raise without fully answering is how to differentiate between judicial attention to claimants that wrongfully "lifts up faces" and attention that pays rightful regard to the "particular flesh and blood and consciousness"[40] standing before the bench. When does attention to the specific details of the lives of particular persons facilitate a just result, and when does it impede such a result? For example, in the vast majority of cases, the comparative financial status of the litigants appears both immaterial to any legal dispute between them and irrelevant to their status as persons. Indeed, as Noonan emphasizes, to favor a particular petitioner because she is powerful and rich clearly seems to violate judicial impartiality. But what about giving special concern to the *poor*? Consider Noonan's assessment of Judge Benjamin Cardozo's decision in the most famous tort case of the twentieth century, *Palsgraf v. Long Island Railroad.*[41] A forty-three-year-old mother doing janitorial work to support her three children, Helen Palsgraf was injured in a freak accident involving a railroad employee while waiting for a train to the beach. She sued the railroad for negligence. Cardozo not only denied her claim for damages but also ordered her to pay both her own and the railroad's court costs, a sum which would have amounted to more than her annual income and which the railroad could have collected by selling her personalty. Of Cardozo's imposition of costs, Noonan argues that "[o]nly a judge who did not see who was before him could have decreed such a result."[42] Under New York rules of practice, assessing costs was a matter of judicial discretion. It is hard not to blame a judge who imposes costs upon a poor plaintiff bringing a good-faith, colorable claim against a rich corporate defendant. In fact, since the law explicitly gave Cardozo discretion in this matter, one could even argue that his decision to levy costs on Helen Palsgraf was as much a failure in applying rules as it was blindness in assessing persons.

But Noonan does not address as forthrightly the question that highlights the tension between respect for rules and regard for individual persons. Should Cardozo have taken account of Helen Palsgraf's poverty and the railroad's great wealth in actually deciding the case? More specifically, does Noonan's construal of respect for persons imply that in the last analysis, Helen Palsgraf should have won her lawsuit against the Long Island Railroad? He does not explicitly say, but hints that his answer would be in the affirmative. Assuming for a moment that this is so, a more subtle question presents itself. Precisely *why* does respect for persons require her to win? Such respect could focus on two different aspects of Helen Palsgraf: the specific details of her own unique life or the features of her existence that she possesses in common with many other persons. Noonan does not always distinguish between the two.

On the one hand, does Noonan think Cardozo should have given decisive weight to the *specific* difficulties of Helen Palsgraf's *particular* life, such as the fact that she was the sole support of her children and already worked two jobs? The considerable effort Noonan devotes to fleshing out impersonal law reports with the details about her background supports this position, as does his emphasis on the need for a love-informed justice that concentrates on the needs of concrete individuals. On the other hand, certain of his remarks suggest that extending Mrs. Palsgraf such special consideration would have given too automatic a preference to *this* David over *this* Goliath.[43] Perhaps, then, respecting Mrs. Palsgraf as a person entails taking account not of the aspects of her life that are *specific* to her but of the more *generalizable* fact of her poverty and lack of social power. If this had been Cardozo's approach, he would have focused not on the actual troubles of Mrs. Palsgraf but on the more general social problems embodied in them.

This is not a moot point in our common law system where judges make law, and where the opinions of those sitting on higher courts have precedential weight. His position of power gave Cardozo both the freedom and the responsibility to shape social policy through the legal framework he developed in deciding this case. For example, Cardozo could have decided that the railroad had an obligation to pay damages to persons like Helen Palsgraf, since it could easily treat the amount as an operating cost that could be distributed among all its passengers through slightly higher ticket prices. That way, no one customer would be forced to bear the brunt of an unfortunate accident.

Noonan may well believe that respecting Mrs. Palsgraf as a person means taking account of the generalizable features of her situation, such as her poverty and social powerlessness. Criticizing Cardozo's failure to address the issues of social justice raised by the case, he locates its source in Cardozo's inability to see the *persons* standing before his bench.[44] But to adopt this construal of responsibility toward persons would begin to blur the distinction between respect for persons and regard for impersonal rules that Noonan wants to maintain. To talk about precedent and the more generalizable features of persons' lives is to begin to talk about *rules* again, albeit fairly specific ones. If the objection to Cardozo's opinion is not so much that he failed to attend to Mrs. Palsgraf's particular troubles but to the more general feature of her social status, why not say that Cardozo articulated the *rule* of tort law in an unjust fashion?

While Noonan does not provide a method for elucidating the knotty problems raised in *Persons and Masks of the Law*, one can read him as recommending a *model* of sorts in *Bribes*. Suggesting that the Western viewpoint on bribery has been profoundly influenced by its dominant religious traditions, he points to a paradox historically abiding at the very heart of Christianity: the simultaneous merciful favor and just judgment of God, who in Jesus Christ both condemned our sin and brought us back from its penalty. Noonan writes:

> Only a consciousness committed to the mystery of Christian particularism—that God chose this people, this virgin, these apostles, these converts, this Church—could have insisted so fiercely that God acts gratuitously. Only a consciousness committed to the requirements of an impartial judge could have felt so keenly the force of the cry that God is a just Judge. Only the mystery that the Judge is also the Repurchaser, the Redeemer, the Giver of himself could have made beliefs in impartiality and in favor bearable.[45]

Assuming that Noonan affirms the Christology just described, what light can be shed on the tensions within his version of personalist communitarianism? I offer three observations, all of which flow much from my sense that Noonan conceives Christian ethics as fundamentally a matter of *imitatio Christi*.[46] First, since the relation between Christ's power as impersonal judge and his personal love as savior is ultimately a theological mystery, we cannot expect to work out its ethical implications in a fully systematic way. Second, we can, however, note that when God's impartiality is set aside in the Bible, it is set aside on behalf of the weak. "God is just, impartial, and simultaneously the champion of the underdog."[47] This consideration implies that in the process of making social rules, which necessarily involves classifying persons in general terms, we should grant prima facie legitimacy to categories designed to protect the poor and socially vulnerable. Human persons have an ultimate reality that human rules do not. So does human pain. The sight of it should force a judge at least to reconsider the adequacy of the categories used by any given rule to classify persons. Third and finally, divine mercy and judgment are ultimately focused on each person in all her individuality. This fact intimates that no matter how sensitive a rule or category might be to general features of human need, earthly judges can never afford to ignore the particularity of the person standing before them. In the end, if a judge must err, it is better to do so in favor of the person rather than the rule. Equity trumps law.

Creativity, Not Magic, in Developing Doctrine

While discussing the credibility of the canonical practice of granting annulments, Noonan draws an intriguing distinction between creativity and magic in the development of doctrine. "Magic, the whisking away of difficulties by a nod, the replacement of reality by illusion, is, however, but one step away from creativity, the transformation of a situation by energetic innovation. Like magic, creativity connotes spontaneity and freedom from iron law, but it also implies labor and increase by organic development."[48] Noonan's distinction, of course, applies as much to ethics as it does to canon law. In what follows, I would like to explore three areas in which his work might help contemporary Christian ethics turn toward creativity and away from magic as it faces the challenges of postmodernity. For Roman Catholics, of course, these challenges are inseparable from the controversies arising after the Second Vatican Council.

The year 1991 marked the centennial of Pope Leo XIII's encyclical *Rerum novarum*,[49] widely lauded as inaugurating modern Roman Catholic social teaching decisively proclaimed by *Gaudium et spes*, the Second Vatican Council's Pastoral Constitution on the Church in the Modern World.[50] Examining the substantial body of scholarly literature on social justice that has grown up since Vatican II, an unwary reader might conclude that the Catholic tradition was uninterested in such issues before the late nineteenth century. John Noonan's work on usury demonstrates that such a conclusion would be erroneous. While the prohibition of usury, taken most stringently to mean all lending of money at interest, was greatly tempered over the centuries, its stable (although often unrecognized) core "were the desires to prevent exploitation of the poor and to discourage riskless profit."[51]

The object of considerable attention on the part of theologians, canonists, prelates and businessmen between the twelfth and eighteenth centuries, the church's teaching on usury has all but been forgotten (except perhaps as an example of the church's ability to change its mind about moral issues).[52] Usury receives passing attention in many important contemporary works on social justice[53] or recent histories of Catholic moral theology. Their authors do not claim, of course, that no theoretical or practical interest in questions of social justice existed between the biblical or patristic eras and the time of Leo XIII. They have simply delimited their topic in such a way that the medieval discussion of usury falls outside of it.[54] Moreover, Catholic moralists are not unique in this regard. Usury has been a widely ignored topic in Christian ethics more generally, despite the fact that many of the norms have their roots in pre-Reformation sources.

I would like to suggest that reintegrating this aspect of scholastic thought into contemporary scholarly consciousness could alleviate an unhelpful competition that has arisen between the twin aims of the Second Vatican Council: *aggiornamento* (modernization) and *ressourcement* (historical retrieval). According to Joseph DiNoia, for example, the American tendency to give unqualified priority to *aggiornamento* unfortunately resulted in a conception of Vatican II as "representing a sharp break" with previous centuries, particularly the scholastic era, and thus undercut the impetus for retrieving the panoply of riches in the tradition.[55] DiNoia's own thesis can be expressed with the maxim "*Ressourcement* without *aggiornamento* is empty. *Aggiornamento* without *ressourcement* is blind." Noonan's work on usury illuminates ways in which the fruits of *ressourcement* and *aggiornamento* can be complementary. That complementariness is important for Catholic Christians, of course, in light of the developments of the Second Vatican Council. It is also, however, important for other Christians as well, to the extent that they hold themselves responsible for making the enduring insights of the tradition freshly applicable to new eras and new questions.

Noonan calls the scholastic analysis of usury "the only detailed and comprehensive philosophical effort in history to explore the requirements of justice in the credit operations central to commercial life."[56] The early Christian tradition's "immensely important shift from treating usury as a sin of uncharitableness or avarice to treating it as a sin of injustice"[57] bears the same moral claim as the U.S. Bishops' demand for a restructuring of international banking practices to improve the lot of Third World countries thirty years ago, and the recent and repeated condemnations of unbridled capitalism on the part of Pope Francis.[58] The later scholastic tradition's efforts to circumscribe the absolute prohibition against usury in light of the experience of Christian merchants in Europe exhibits a common kernel of insight with the emphasis of liberation theologians upon the unity of theory and practice in the struggle for justice in South America. Of course, the historical and political contexts of these theological and ethical reflections diverge dramatically. So do the philosophical tools they employ. But even as Christians affirm the necessity for those living in different times and places to respond to the Gospel with their own "freshness," the same Spirit calls us into the "continuity" of eternal community with one another through Christ.[59] Supporting that belief, John Noonan's work can foster the discernment of new patterns of unity and difference in Christian moral thinking.

John Noonan concludes his 1965 edition of *Contraception* with an optimistic note about the possibility of change in the church's prohibition against artificial methods of birth control. Having demonstrated in the volume that at the center of ecclesiastical teaching were the "values of procreation, education, life, personality and love," he argues that "About these values a wall had been built; the wall could be removed when it became a prison rather than a bulwark."[60] Issued three years after Noonan's book was published, the papal encyclical *Humanae vitae* did not remove the wall. Noonan's reaction to the encyclical is contained in an article entitled "Natural Law, the Teaching of the Church and the Regulation of the Rhythm of Human Fecundity," which has been appended to the enlarged edition of *Contraception*.[61]

In a polarized church, where the only acceptable options were either "dissent" or "assent" to magisterial teaching on contraception, Noonan's response provoked puzzlement from both sides.[62] On the one hand, Noonan began with the claim that "the time for debate over doctrine itself is past.... The time now is to understand the encyclical and to answer questions within its framework."[63] Those who opposed *Humanae vitae* could have feared that Noonan is abandoning the fruits of his intellectually groundbreaking and liberating work in favor of submission to the magisterium. On the other hand, the practical import of the appended article is that contraceptive practices must be avoided only a small portion of every month. Those who supported *Humanae vitae* could have seen this as an attempt to evade the strictures set down by Pope Paul VI.

How, then, should Noonan's appendix be perceived? Was it "dissent from" or "assent to" magisterial teaching? It was neither, and it was both—at least according to the way these terms are commonly understood. The article exemplifies a distinctively legal mode of reasoning that fruitfully transcends the rigidity of both categories. First published in the *American Journal of Jurisprudence* in 1980, it reads like the brief of a lawyer whose argument is circumscribed but not ultimately undone by the existence of an authoritative and possibly opposing decision written by an eminent judge.[64] Without questioning the authority of *Humanae vitae,* Noonan interprets it in such a fashion that the bulk of his book's argument survives intact.

Consider his strategy. First, having announced his good faith in attempting to work within the confines of the encyclical, he forestalls any attempt to interpret it in light of the purposes of those opposed to the Second Vatican Council. He insists that *Humanae vitae* be read together with *Gaudium et spes*. Second, he stresses the considerable development of doctrine that *was* ratified by the encyclical and supported by his own historical study: personalism, the expression of conjugal love as a purpose of marital intercourse, and the duty of married couples to make a responsible judgment about the proper size of their families. Finally, under the heading "Clarifications" of doctrine, Noonan considers three case studies designed to test the flexibility within the boundaries of *Humanae vitae*. In the third, noting that "nature" implies "normalcy" in Catholic thought, Noonan suggests that the strictures of the encyclical do not prevent a married couple from using contraceptives on all but the prudently estimated four days each month when it is normally probable for intercourse to lead to procreation. After considering possible arguments against his position, Noonan concludes by noting that "it is scarcely an objection that the scope of a law should be narrow. In general, Christians have been called to liberty. . . . Do we worship God less because we are called to worship him formally only one day in seven?"[65]

Thus in the appendix, Noonan offers a vision of *Humanae vitae* that is continuous in essence, if not in all details, with the developing personalist values he highlights in the main body of *Contraception*. Moreover, his interpretation of the encyclical could facilitate the choice of any future pope to lift its prohibitions by enabling that choice to be viewed as a further development of doctrine, rather than as a reversal of it. These observations should satisfy those tempted to charge him with capitulating to magisterial pressures.

What of the opposite criticism—that he does not show sufficient *obsequium* for the teaching authority of the church? First, the attention and intellectual energy that Noonan expends upon the encyclical testifies to the respect in which he holds it. His painstaking efforts to trace the encyclical's argument and its implications appropriately evoke the root word of *obsequium (sequor,* "to follow"). And second, Noonan's response to *Humanae vitae* has precedent within the tradition; it echoes, for example, some of the interaction between the magisterium and the theologians regarding the doctrine on usury. Of these earlier attempts to interpret papal pronouncements narrowly, Noonan writes "If the legislator allows a legalistic and close interpretation of his law, it is scarcely the part of others to challenge his liberality; and in such a case, it is not discreditable for an interpreter of the law to insist that it not be extended beyond the cases it formally proscribes."[66] Finally, the larger purposes in light of which Noonan interprets the encyclical are not alien to it but instead are drawn from its very core. It strikes me that the fresh reading of tradition, which is both loyal to tradition and responsive to contemporary needs, is part of what Pope Francis has modeled since assuming the Petrine office.

While it would be fruitful to explore in detail the ways in which Noonan's mode of argumentation differs from more common approaches in Christian ethics, I have space here only to highlight two of the more distinctive features of legal argument. First and foremost, legal argument is *advocacy*, not only of a particular conclusion or result but also of a certain way of viewing the world that supports and surrounds it. Thus the form of the best arguments at law is not a disinterested attempt to balance the data yielded by discretely treated scholarly or legal sources. This is not to say that attention to crucial materials need not be incorporated into the argument; it is merely to note that admitting they must be accounted for tells nothing about the mode of their presence. A dissection can inform us that the human body is composed of given percentages of various elements; that does not mean we can mechanically mix those elements and obtain life. Analogously, a truly excellent legal brief does not merely compile evidence but also proposes a vision of reality (or at least that portion of reality which is in dispute) that is more complete and compelling than the vision offered by the opposition. It is an exercise in aesthetics as much as in organization, a task for rhetoric no less than for logic.[67]

Second, the fact that legal argument is oriented toward achieving a certain practical result for one's client means that the way lawyers approach authoritative sources differs from that of many scholars. For example, when confronted with an authoritative ecclesiastical pronouncement, many academic ethicists would see their task as twofold. First, they would strive to pin down its meaning as objectively and precisely as possible, and second, they would attempt to *respond* to that clearly fixed interpretation of the pronouncement. By contrast, the dominant question for a lawyer is not what *to say* to a controlling opinion, but what *to do* with it.

In her efforts, the lawyer does not merely respond to a fixed and predetermined construal of the opinion but also actually helps shape its interpretation. The opinion, itself one word in the continuing conversation of law, provides the raw material and the framework that enable the lawyer to exercise both creativity and judgment in proposing the next word. Some purposes are emphasized, some phrasing borrowed; other elements are downplayed or marginalized.

Thus the authority of the opinion is not a command for deference imposed upon the lawyer's mind like an extrinsic force. Rather, the opinion's authority lies in the fact that it becomes intrinsically incorporated into the lawyer's thought processes, reciprocally influencing and influenced by them.

Taken together, these points suggest that what Noonan does in his appendix is advocate a way in which *Humanae vitae* can be better incorporated into the vision of the church described in *Contraception* than into that proposed by those who oppose development of doctrine in the area of marriage and birth control. Rather than slaying the tiger, he tames it. Particularly in times of great tension between "progressive" and "conservative" Catholics, Noonan's lawyerly approach may suggest new tacks to Catholic theologians striving for faithful creativity within their tradition.

Arguing about Doctrinal Development

The accounts that John Noonan has given of how the church's moral teaching has evolved have been challenged, either implicitly or explicitly, with respect to virtually every topic he has treated. No one denies, of course, that the church's response is not in every respect the same on these topics as it was hundreds or even thousands of years ago. Yet it would be fair to say that other thinkers seem to be at greater pains than Judge Noonan to stress continuities in the teaching, as well as to minimize the nature and degree of the change that has occurred.[68] In so doing, some thinkers challenge his reading of key texts,[69] while others take issue with his emphasis on change over continuity in church teaching.[70] In some cases, the author takes pains to show that the substantial change that has occurred, and the continuing changes that Noonan advocates, will not require the church to alter irreformable teaching,[71] while in other cases the author argues that any change that seems to be warranted by Noonan's work will fly in the face of irreformable teaching.[72]

In my view, readers trying to come to grips with the work of Noonan and his implicit and explicit critics should not be surprised if they experience a mounting sense of frustration and unease in pondering the issues at stake. First, and most important, very few of us have the expertise necessary to evaluate Noonan's historical scholarship, much of which involves archival and manuscript work. Confronted with learned challenges to his reading of a particular text, or the broader import of that text in its social context, most readers will find themselves experiencing an uncertainty analogous to that which jurors face when confronted with eyewitnesses giving conflicting accounts of the same event.[73]

Second, when reading the literature around development of moral doctrine, it is difficult to avoid the sense that the relevant issues have not been properly defined or joined. Many of the conversation partners seem to be talking past (or around) one another, rather than mounting direct criticisms of one another. Perhaps the source of this problem is inherent in the notion of "development" itself, which must involve some combination of the notion of change and the notion of continuity. On the one hand, without any change whatsoever, one does not have development—one has mere stasis; on the other, if there is no identifiable continuity, one does not have development, but only raw difference. Consequently, one party in the discussion can emphasize the change while the other emphasizes the continuity, without their positions being directly contradictory.

Third, when combined, the first two sources of frustration augment a third source in the mind of the reader. It is impossible to read the relevant literature without a growing sense that many of the participants believe that something very important is at stake that goes beyond the correct resolution of the particular cases Noonan discusses. The burgeoning literature on the development of moral doctrine conveys the impression that the concept of "development" itself is the theological equivalent of nuclear energy—acknowledged by all as a powerful and potentially helpful tool in theory, but intensely feared by some as dangerous and even deadly in practice.

In the remainder of this chapter, I would like to do something to alleviate the sense of frustration and unease that now swirls around John Noonan's work. I will try to develop a framework that will facilitate not agreement but at least a real joining of the issue on the part of those who wish to debate the nature and extent of doctrinal development within the realm of the church's teaching on moral issues. I will also attempt to make explicit some of the reasons why some might approach with such anxiety the discussion of development in the church's moral teaching. By drawing upon analogies with the legal tradition, I hope to indicate some ways in which their anxiety may be assuaged.

The sense that the discussants are frequently talking past one another in their conversations about the development of doctrine is, in my view, due to two major factors. First, as I noted previously, the term "development" incorporates both continuity and change. One party can emphasize change while the other emphasizes continuity without there actually being a disagreement between the two parties regarding the set of true claims that can be made about what happened to the church's moral teaching over the course of time. Second, in evaluating continuity and change, we need to pay attention to what we mean by the "church's moral teaching." We need to see that with respect to any moral question, questions of similarity and difference can be asked on three distinct levels: (1) the permitted or prohibited act itself; (2) the pattern of justification for a moral judgment, as seen within the broader normative vision advocated by the church; and (3) its coherence with authoritative magisterial teaching.[74] What looks like a significant change on one level may not appear to be so significant on another level. Focusing on one level, one party can argue for dramatic difference in church teaching on a particular question; tacitly changing the focus to a different level, another party can argue that continuity in teaching is more pronounced than different.

Consider the first level, tightly focused on the permitted or prohibited act itself: According to Judge Noonan's analysis, in the case of usury, what was prohibited (lending money at interest) became permitted. In the case of marriage, what was impossible (e.g., certain types of sacramental marriage) became possible. With slavery, what was permitted (owning slaves) became prohibited. In the case of religious toleration, what was required (persecution of heretics) became prohibited. Finally, with capital punishment, what was permitted (and perhaps encouraged) is now discouraged, and perhaps on its way to being forbidden.[75] On this level, the biggest change seems to be in the context of religious toleration: acts that were once required are now forbidden. Capital punishment, in contrast, seems not particularly problematic: moving from "permitted" to "discouraged" does not seem to be that great a change.

But things look different on the second level. This level involves the internal logic of principle and justification: How great a change in the internal structure of the tradition's thought is required to accommodate the change in practice? In the case of usury, what was initially treated as a universal exceptionless moral norm became understood as a culture-dependent exceptionless moral norm. That is, the claim that "lending money at interest is always wrong" became modified to read "in pre-capitalist cultures, lending money is always wrong."

The death penalty, however, presents a much tougher case of conflicting commitments on the level of theory. The church formerly taught that, in and of itself, it was a positive good for the state to take the life of a guilty person, furthering the common good by removing a diseased member from the body of the community, restoring the balance of justice through retribution, and honoring the guilty person's free will by holding him or her accountable for his or her actions. In Pope John Paul II's encyclical *Evangelium vitae*,[76] it appears that the intentional taking of human life, even that of a guilty person, in and of itself can be detrimental to the common good because it erodes a "culture of life" that values all human persons. Capital punishment can be justified only as a last resort if the community cannot otherwise provide for its protection. Here, one theoretical understanding of the actions that further the common good (which emphasizes retributive justice) seems now to be replaced by another (which emphasizes the sanctity of life) at the same level of importance.

The third and final level on which change can be analyzed is that of official church teaching. Which developments seem to involve the greatest upheaval in the settled and authoritative teaching of the magisterium? On this level, it appears that the most radical development can be found in the case of usury. As Noonan recounts in his *Theological Studies* article on development of doctrine, the categorical prohibition of usury, understood to encompass any profit on a loan, was "enunciated by popes, expressed by three ecumenical councils, proclaimed by bishops, and taught unanimously by theologians."[77] The fact that it was at least arguable that the condemnation of usury was infallibly taught is demonstrated by the argumentative nuance and analytical delicacy marshaled by the esteemed Jesuit moralist Arthur Vermeersch to address this question in the 1913 edition of the *Catholic Encyclopedia.*[78] He maintains, for example, that Pope Benedict XIV's condemnation of usury in his 1745 encyclical *Vix pervenit* was not infallible because it was addressed only to the Italian bishops and not to the universal church, and that the 1836 decree of the Holy Office extending it to the universal church did not make it infallible because "such a declaration could not give to a document an infallible character which it otherwise did not possess."[79]

Why is it important to pay attention to the levels at which change—or the continuity—is found with respect to particular moral questions with regard to which development is said to occur? First, as I noted, it is important to do so in order to ensure that the participants in the debate about the nature or extent of development are in fact talking about the *same thing.*

Second, paying explicit attention to the level at which change occurs is a necessary prelude to analyzing how the levels interrelate, or more precisely, how locating change at one level affects the degree to which change is said to have occurred at another level. For example, consider the case of usury. If one argues that what to all appearances looks like a universal exceptionless moral norm ("Lending money at interest is always wrong") should in fact be interpreted as a context-dependent exceptionless moral norm ("In pre-capitalist economies, lending money at interest is always wrong"), then one can interpret the proposition affirmed by magisterial teaching implicitly to include the qualification as to context.[80] More specifically, one could argue that what they (pope, bishops, ecumenical council) *really* intended to say, what they *meant,* was that "lending money at interest is always wrong in a context in which there is no market where money could be productive for its owner if it is not lent out" (i.e., in the context of a pre-capitalist culture). By locating the change at the second level, by showing how the proposition in question—the condemnation of usury—was once understood as a universal exceptionless moral norm and then came in time to be recognized as a context-dependent moral norm, one can maintain that little or no doctrinally significant change occurred on the third level, that of magisterial teaching.

Third and finally, as I will explore in more detail, significant changes at one level may raise different questions or problems for members of the church community than significant changes at a different level. We will only make progress in our discussion of the nature and conditions of true development of the church's moral doctrine if we succeed in putting the question into a broader perspective, perhaps shedding light on the dark and diffuse threat that a significant number of people believe to be posed by either the fact that development has occurred or the increased attention given to its occurrence in scholarly and popular discussions.

Noonan himself has been quite reticent to explore the implications of his studies of doctrinal development on moral issues for contemporary questions. Many of his scholarly critics, moreover, have shown the same reticence: they take on the particular issues Noonan puts forward as candidates for development, emphasizing continuity rather than change, instead of systematically exploring what is at stake in the discussion.[81] What is obscured by the reticence of academic debate, however, is made patently clear by the market of ideas on the Internet: A search for the terms "Noonan" and "development of doctrine" revealed, among other things, two interesting articles.

First, an article published in the year 2000 in the *Independent Gay Forum* attempted to use Noonan's work as a basis for predicting change in the church's teaching on homosexual relationships. Paul Varnell wrote: "As church historian John Noonan points out, the Vatican reversed its view of usury when loans and credit became part of everyday commercial life and it was forced to examine 'the experience of otherwise decent Christians who were bankers and who claimed that banking was compatible with Christianity.'"[82] In the same way, Varnell claims, the Vatican will feel the increased pressure to rethink its view of homosexuality for the same reason—the growing presence in the Catholic Church of "otherwise decent Christians" who claim that homosexuality "is compatible with Christianity."[83] In a 2013 interview, Pope Francis was asked about his view of homosexual priests. He did not emphasize that their desires were "intrinsically disordered," as the tradition has long held. Instead, he focused on the person, not a sexual desire viewed in abstraction. Pope Francis told reporters on the papal plane: "If someone is gay and he searches for the Lord and has good will, who am I to judge?"[84]

The author of the second essay, Patrick O'Neil, would no doubt view the claims made in the first essay as confirmation of his worst fears. In his essay, "A Response to John T. Noonan, Jr. Concerning the Development of Catholic Moral Doctrine," O'Neil is admirably forthright about his concerns regarding the potential impact of Noonan's work in this area:

> On account of the moral assault against the Church which rages today, therefore, Noonan's piece is both timely and potentially dangerous—dangerous because anything which opens a potential for doubt about the authority and reliability of the Church's teachings on moral matters will be exploited at once and ruthlessly by those who wish to undermine the Church's opposition to abortion, artificial birth control, divorce, what are euphemistically called "alternative life styles" (including gay marriage), euthanasia, premarital sex and "trial marriage," artificial insemination, in-vitro fertilization, surrogate motherhood, etc.[85]

The comments of Paul Varnell and Patrick O'Neil are mirror images of each other. Both believe that Noonan's work contributes to a situation in which wholesale reconsideration and revision of the church's moral teaching will immediately take place, particularly on the most controverted issues of our day. Progressives such as Varnell believe that such a situation is to be welcomed, while conservatives, such as O'Neil, look upon it with dismay, if not dread.

In my view, however, the hopes of the progressives and the fears of the conservatives are both significantly exaggerated, at least in the degree to which they are based in Noonan's own work. In seeing how this is the case, it is important to keep some sense of historical perspective. Noonan's work in general covers the two-thousand-year history of Christianity, particularly as that history has been instantiated in the Roman Catholic Church. The changes that Noonan described in the teaching on usury and slavery took place over centuries, against the backdrop of changing political and economic contexts far beyond the control of any one individual. They were not brought about by sudden fiat; in fact, I have no doubt that both progressives and conservatives would agree that the change with respect to the latter practice took too long to occur.

As we saw in the case of usury, even an apparently absolute claim—for example, "Lending money at interest is always wrong"—can be contextualized by later interpreters. They can do so by attempting to minimize the authority with which the claim was made (as did Vermeersch with respect to usury),[86] or by arguing that despite its seemingly absolute nature, the force of the claim depended upon a number of tacit background assumptions (i.e., the existence of a pre-capitalist society), which the makers of the claim could not have been expected to acknowledge. Later interpreters can carefully parse the language of the relevant teaching, distinguishing the facts of the current case to the facts assumed to be operative at the time the teaching was issued. In short, they can behave rather like lawyers do in the common law tradition, highlighting and extending favorable precedent, and distinguishing or downplaying unfavorable precedent, in order to support or advance the interpretation they deem best.

Moreover, to the extent doctrinal development will occur on controverted issues, it will occur by highlighting continuities between older positions and newer ones. For example, should the Catholic Church shift its teaching on same-sex marriage, it will likely do so by highlighting the tradition's longstanding affirmation of the importance of mutual support and help in a marriage, and noting that such support is also possible in the case of same-sex couples. It will also likely point out that while the good of procreation is important, it is not paramount. Older couples who are known to be infertile can enter into sacramental marriages. Moreover, a younger couple who unexpectedly discovers that one party is not able to have children cannot obtain an annulment on that ground.

In my view, a choice between rigid certainty and utter arbitrariness is a false choice with respect to a rich, living tradition such as Catholic teaching on moral issues. Yet I know from experience that it is an attractive false choice. I have encountered the issue many times, not as a theology professor but as a professor who teaches contracts to first-year law students. Anyone who has offered a big "common law" class to beginning law students, or who once was a law student him- or herself, will no doubt remember the scenario under which they arise. Negotiating the pull toward certainty, on the one hand, and toward arbitrariness, on the other, is a necessary step in the professionalization of lawyers. It is, however, only a preliminary step. Success as a law student, and ultimately as a lawyer, depends upon recognizing the deep inadequacy of approaching legal reasoning in terms of the dichotomy between utter certainty and utter arbitrariness.

In their first year in law school, students are commonly admonished that they must now learn to "think like a lawyer." That rather vague phrase refers to two basic components of training in the legal profession. First, students must relinquish a method of learning a subject matter that they followed in high school and college. They enter law school assuming that they will be taught the "answers"—that is, a set of true facts about the applicable law in a particular jurisdiction. And they are, of course, taught some true facts. The point of law school, however, is not the answers but, rather, the questions. More specifically, the first-year law curriculum does not teach students a discreet set of rules and facts to be regurgitated on an exam, but a series of ways of thinking and arguing, a series of ways of identifying and approaching relevant questions within a certain normative context. In other words, law students are not taught to be passive recipients of knowledge; rather, they are taught to be active participants in an ongoing practice. To become such participants they must learn to identify which sources of authority have more weight than others with respect to particular questions (e.g., an opinion from the Supreme Court on a federal question) and which rules and principles are fundamental (e.g., the "mailbox rule" is not a fundamental rule, but an auxiliary rule facilitating orderly application of the fundamental principle *pacta sunt servanda)*. Part of the socialization process involves learning which scholars and judges have acquired authority about the nature of the practice, because their work has consistently proven to be helpful in preserving and advancing the legal tradition.[87]

Second, fledgling lawyers must acquire a set of competencies. They must absorb the appropriate habits of attention and thought, the unstated criteria by which relevant information is sorted from irrelevant in formation, and the acceptable patterns of argument and inference. A "good lawyer" is a lawyer who has internalized these habits, criteria, and patterns. More than that, however, he or she has developed the capacity to appreciate what (borrowing from Alasdair Maclntyre) I will call the "goods internal to the practice"[88] of law. External goods such as money, prestige, and power are earned by and through the practice of law, but they are not its heart. Rather, the practice of law is a means to those goods; other means work just as well (and sometimes better). In contrast, the goods internal to the practice of law are intrinsic to that practice, achievable only by those who have learned to value the practice for the values it inherently embodies. They include the facilitation of just relationships among the members of society, including the just resolution of what John Finnis has called society's "co-ordination problems."[89] As Alasdair Maclntyre has pointed out:

> A practice involves standards of excellence and obedience to rules as well as the achievement of goods. To enter into a practice is to

> accept the authority of those standards and the inadequacy of my own performance as judged by them. It is to subject my own attitudes, choices, preferences and tastes to the standards which currently and partially define the practice.[90]

It is only the excellent practitioners of the practice, only the *virtuous* practitioners of the practice,[91] who are capable of so judging, who are capable of assessing better or worse instantiations of the goods internal to it, and who are capable of discerning which course of action best promotes those goods in hard cases.

In the first year of law school, therefore, men and women embark upon the path of becoming virtuous in the practice of law. The initial step upon that path plunges them into a massive intellectual and existential uncertainty. They fear that there is no right answer, that everything is up for grabs, that any position can be defended or attacked, that arbitrariness rules the day. They see no rhyme or reason to the decisions that are made, to the way cases are resolved. Their fears, in other words, are extremely similar to the fears expressed by Professor O'Neil and other conservatives with respect to the development of the church's moral doctrine.

Yet most students move beyond that step. The next phase in the development of a budding lawyer generally involves embracing the ambiguity—embracing it a little too enthusiastically, in fact. Students reach for the other extreme, maintaining there is no outcome that is better or worse than any other, no argument that is better or worse than any other, no policy that the tradition cannot be stretched to accommodate. Their vision, in other words, sound a lot like those of Paul Varnell and other progressives with respect to the seemingly unlimited potential for change of the church's doctrine on moral issues.

As some of them painfully learn on their final exams, however, the fact that they *can* make an argument using certain sources or defending a certain revision in certain positions does not mean that a person competent to recognize the goods internal to the practice of law (e.g., their professor) will recognize their arguments as sound. The point of the first semester of law school is to teach students that studying law is about learning what it means to make arguments within the context of a living tradition. The point of the remaining two and a half years is to teach them that one argument is not necessarily as good as another, and to teach them how to recognize good arguments. In large part, this is done by exposing them to the best of the common law tradition, in all its depth and breadth. For example, by reading opinions by Learned Hand and Benjamin Cardozo, law students absorb a vision of the field of torts or contracts through the eyes of its masters. Ideally, by the end of their legal education, law students will have transcended both the fear of radical uncertainty and the embrace of skepticism. They will have taken their place as members of the ancient and venerable guild of lawyers, having internalized its important standards and thereby become competent to argue in good faith for its ongoing extension and revision.

It strikes me that the deep worries about the development of doctrine within the realm of Catholic moral theology are in large part attributable to the ways in which education in moral theology is no longer like legal education. Before the Second Vatican Council, there was a clear path of professionalization, of socialization, for those who wished to become Catholic moral theologians. All moral theologians were priests, all studied much the same curriculum, all learned to assign the same degrees of authority to certain texts, and all internalized the criteria by which better or worse arguments were assessed. One could say that their education taught them to "think like a moral theologian" in much the same way that one can still say that legal education teaches students to "think like a lawyer."

But all of that changed after the Second Vatican Council. Lay persons in general, and women in particular, began going into the field. Not only did they no longer receive seminary degrees but it was also the case that many of them no longer studied at Catholic universities. At the same time, Catholic schools began hiring persons trained at Yale, Chicago, and Princeton, in addition to (or sometimes instead of) the Gregorian or Leuven. In many ways this broadening was salutary; it brought different experiences, different backgrounds, and different expertise to bear on the complicated field of human action.

Yet an unwelcome by-product of the salutary expansion of the field of moral theology has been the loss of a common canon that characterizes the field, or a common set of sensibilities that characterize its practitioners. Practically speaking, no one defines a person as a Catholic moral theologian except the person him or herself. There is no required curriculum. Not all contemporary Catholic moral theologians will think the same texts are relevant, not all will give similar weight to a similar set of courses. Not all moral theologians will identify the same set of goods as internal to the practice, and not all will pick out the same qualities as essential to a competent practitioner of the field. Furthermore, if matters were not complicated enough, it seems as if there may in fact be two distinct, if sometimes overlapping, practices within the general discipline. Some Catholics who focus their academic work on moral matters consider themselves moral theologians, whose task it is to carry on and develop the Catholic tradition of moral reflection within the context of the church. Other Catholics, however, primarily identify themselves as Christian ethicists—they tend to see their audience as primarily the secular academy and their topics of research as the questions considered important by that audience. The goods internal to these two practices are not identical; for example, a personal commitment to the Catholic faith is essential for a Catholic moral theologian, not necessarily for a Christian ethicist.[92]

The culture wars in the Catholic Church have meant that the concern about the coherent practice of the discipline of moral theology has become too narrowly focused on the "bottom-line" positions people hold. The questions that seem to many people relevant to ask of moral theologians have been focused almost exclusively on outcome: Do you or do you not defend magisterial teaching on abortion, contraception, and homosexuality (if the questioner is a conservative Catholic) or on capital punishment, immigration law, and economic justice (if the questioner is a liberal Catholic)?

Yet this outcome-oriented approach may not be the most helpful way to deal with the current situation. It misleadingly suggests that the complexity of the Catholic tradition can be reduced to a multiple-choice test. But it cannot be so reduced, any more than being a good lawyer can be reduced to achieving a passing score on the bar exam. The Catholic moral tradition is multidimensional; it cannot ignore (1) the integral relationship of systematic theology, liturgical theology, and moral theology; (2) the source of all theology in Holy Scripture; (3) the foundation of scripture and tradition in the triune God, as revealed to us most perfectly in the person and work of the Redeemer, Jesus Christ; and (4) the bedrock assumption that the God who creates and the God who redeems are one and the same, which is reflected in the Catholic belief in the capacity of human reason and reflection to discern, however imperfectly, the requirements of the natural law.

What would be a better approach to deal with the current situation? In my view, the process of legal education and socialization provides a helpful model. Different law schools inculcate different approaches while ensuring that all law students have read the same basic canon and acquired the same basic skills of legal reason. Graduate schools in moral theology could attempt to achieve analogous goals. Such an education would focus more on sources, methods, and intellectual and moral habits than on bottom-line positions. It would critically examine the primary texts that leading moralists draw from, the thinkers they hold up as insightful, and the care, attention, and respect they give to the tradition as a whole. In so doing, such an approach would attempt to create the basis for a common conversation, albeit one that is richer and more diverse than it was before the Second Vatican Council.

Moral Progress and Conflicting Traditions

John Noonan has not only engaged controversial issues with Roman Catholic theological circles, he has also not hesitated to engage neuralgic questions with American society. In fact, Noonan has been a forceful participant in the difficult and divisive debate about abortion.[93] From his perspective, advocacy of a pro-life position is profoundly consistent with the moral lessons of history explored in his other writings; he sees the attitude toward the unborn entailed by most pro-choice stances as yet another example of the dehumanizing masks that human persons are capable of throwing over one another's countenances.

Needless to say, Noonan's pro-life writings have provoked vigorous disagreement. While I will not rehearse the familiar shape of the abortion debate here, I would like to highlight one criticism that is particularly telling in Noonan's own terms. Feminist ethicist Beverly Wildung Harrison objects that in *A Private Choice,*[94] his only book-length work on abortion, Noonan frequently refers to the pregnant woman by the equivalent Latin term *gravida.*[95] In effect, she charges Noonan with employing depersonalizing masks of his own—masks which conceal the pained faces of women confronting crisis pregnancies under the weight of an imposing Latin term.

Despite their many deep and intractable disagreements, Noonan should be able to affirm wholeheartedly that part of Harrison's agenda which is expressed in the dedication of her book in gratitude "for the *particularity* of women's lives" (emphasis mine). Noonan's great strength as an ethicist has always been his refusal to turn a blind eye to the complexities and ambiguities that moral obligations generate as they are instantiated in the lives of actual human beings. Showing us time and again that the moral life is rarely the easiest life, he does not often ignore the human tragedy which that fact can involve. It is thus even more unfortunate that in some respects his writings on abortion have a curiously abstract quality about them. Concentrating upon repersonalizing the *unborn,* Noonan does not attend as closely as he might to the difficulties facing *female* persons with problem pregnancies, nor to the tragedy that in our society those most likely to pay the cost of acting morally with regard to unborn life are those least able to afford it.

Noonan's other writings suggest that there was a way for him to have addressed this criticism. He could have written a book on abortion that was structured in terms of the "case" method of moral analysis he employs so effectively in *Power to Dissolve* and most of his later works. This is not to say that if Noonan viewed abortion through the prism of individual lives and choices he would change his mind about its ultimate moral status. He might, however, have conveyed a deeper and ultimately more persuasive sense of the true dimensions of the difficulties that can surround the demand for it.

Yet if Noonan were to have written such a book in the past forty years, the contemporary situation regarding abortion might force him to make hard methodological and substantive theological choices he had not yet faced. Noonan's writings reflect not only a notion of development of doctrine within the church, but a conception of the relation between "church" and "world" that resonates deeply with the teachings of the Second Vatican Council and its theological progenitors (for example, John Henry Newman, Karl Rahner, John Courtney Murray). Humanity has moved from a static to an evolutionary conception of its own history that exemplifies the promise of real moral progress. The development of the church is not isolated; rather, it is intimately related to this promise. Vatican II proclaims that in Christ "can be found the key, the focal point and the goal" of human beings and of human history.[96]

Accordingly, Noonan's confidence in the development of Catholic teaching on such issues as usury and marital sexuality was matched by a similar belief in the positive moral trajectory of the secular world regarding such matters as slavery and bribery. On the whole, neither realm can be said to lead consistently or to follow slowly behind; Noonan highlights the interweaving of secular and religious motives on the sometimes tortuous path of moral growth. This close and ultimately harmonious relation between the developing moral vision of the church and true human wisdom long allowed Noonan to remain fruitfully ambiguous about the ultimate epistemological warrants in the natural-law ethics espoused by the Catholic tradition. He succinctly summarized the two basic options in his first book: "On the one hand, any act prohibited by the Christian tradition could be treated as if it were evil by nature, not by positive law. On the other hand, any act not naturally demonstrable as evil could be considered as not prohibited by Christian teaching."[97] As long as Noonan perceived there to be no ultimate conflict between the best insights of humanity and those of the Roman Catholic Church, he did not have to make any choice, but could allow the insights developed in the two realms to play off each other in the history of moral development. Yet the protracted nature of the abortion debate has rendered such a strategy more difficult to maintain.

Assume, as seems very possible, that the Catholic Church's teaching will remain strongly pro-life, while the broader secular consensus settles firmly around a coherent and rigorous pro-choice perspective that in all good faith cannot acknowledge the full personhood of the unborn. From Noonan's perspective such a situation would begin to call into question the compatibility of moral reasoning from a humanistic perspective, and that done from the vantage of the Roman Catholic tradition. Moreover, it would threatens the perception of an evolution of moral sensibility in both realms. What would be his possible responses to these pressures?

On the one hand, Noonan could attempt to preserve the ultimate compatibility of the insights of the church with those of the wider world by taking a longer and more complicated view of moral development. This could be done in two ways. The less likely course would be for Noonan to rethink his position on abortion. Concluding that the broad secular consensus and the not inconsiderable opinion of Christians like Beverly Harrison had the better viewpoint, he could trust that the church would also revise its own opinion in time. In effect, this would be to assimilate the abortion issue to his views on usury and contraception. More likely, however, would be for Noonan to contend that the church's perspective on unborn life will ultimately prevail in the wider society, although it may take a very long time.

Moral development does not preclude human choice. At times, as in the case of the secular attitude toward abortion, such choices can be tragically wrong, thereby greatly hindering but not ultimately destroying the possibility for growth in moral insight. Thus Noonan could maintain the hope for long-term moral improvement in the case of abortion much as in the case of racial equality. However, while this hope might have been credible in the 1970s, when Noonan wrote his abortion books, it has become increasingly less as time passes without any sign of a shift in moral sensibilities.

On the other hand, Noonan could take a much more radical methodological route. He could give up the possibility of ultimate and developing concordance between the best deliverances of faith and those of secular reason on the abortion question, and by implication, on a whole host of other issues. He could acknowledge that as the post-Christian, post-modern era wears on, the residual effects of Constantinean Christian morality on the wider culture will wear thin. Taking this approach immediately implicates matters at the forefront of contemporary theology. Questions of ecclesiology present themselves. Will the church in a post-Christian era inevitably be sectarian? Does sectarianism imply separatism? So do problems in the theology of history. If we give up the notion of a positively evolving human morality, can we still maintain the notion of development of doctrine within the church? Is not that notion, particularly as explicated in the Second Vatican Council, intimately connected with making the light of Christ ever more visible to the nations? Finally, issues at the heart of moral theology must be faced, particularly those implicating the traditional Catholic commitment to a natural-law approach. As noted, it is theoretically possible to maintain that the strictures of natural-law ethic are *ontologically* valid for all human beings while simultaneously asserting that only a small portion of humanity (i.e., Christians) have significant *epistemological* access to it. Yet practically speaking, does not such a stance retain only the shell of a natural-law approach, while abandoning its central purposes and advantages? If Catholic thought must leave behind its natural law tradition, would it be better to do so more forthrightly? Moreover, with what should it be replaced?

These are large questions, much easier raised than answered. They also seem quite far afield from the issue with which we started this section—the much narrower topic of Noonan's writings on abortion. Yet if abortion is in fact a moral crisis for contemporary Christianity, as well as for the wider American community, its ultimate resolution will not leave fundamental substantive and methodological commitments untouched. If Noonan's histories teach us anything, it is that a true moral crisis inevitably brings theological, ethical, political, and legal changes in its wake.

John Noonan's relative optimism about the concordance between the best deliverances of secular wisdom and the deepest truths of Christian morality tends to be more characteristic of Roman Catholic moralists than Protestants, who often have a more lively sense of the effects of original sin upon the capacity of all human beings both to recognize and to follow the path of moral truth. Is there a way for Protestant ethicists more suspicious of the insights of the secular world to engage insights from the legal tradition in a constructive manner? The next chapter makes a case that there is such a way, taking the thought of Stanley Hauerwas as a case study.

2

Creation and Covenant

Engaging Stanley Hauerwas

THE PURPOSE OF this chapter is to show how the secular law can engage the work of Stanley Hauerwas, and by extension, the work of other moralists who take a dim view of the overlap of secular moral reasoning and Christian morality. When I discussed this project with colleagues specializing in Christian theological ethics, they were interested, even intrigued. Truth be told, however, they were also rather skeptical. Why the skepticism? It is universally acknowledged that Hauerwas's work has actively engaged with academics, pastors, doctors, and—yes—even lawyers. Furthermore, no one would deny that arguments rooted in the Christian theological tradition have made their way into American law over the years. Indeed, in 1892, a Supreme Court opinion unself-consciously proclaimed that "this is a Christian nation."[1]

"A Christian nation"? Many Christian theologians indebted to Stanley Hauerwas would say that *this* is the problem in a nutshell. Throughout his career, Hauerwas has tirelessly protested all efforts to embed Christianity, as either an intellectual system or a social group, into the framework of worldly power. Such efforts, in his view, inevitably corrupt the thought and the practices of Christians, twisting both toward the goal of sustaining the kingdoms of this world, rather than building the kingdom of God that was inaugurated by the life, death, and resurrection of Jesus Christ. Unlike the "peaceable kingdom" of Jesus, earthly kingdoms are inherently built on violence—not only the violence of warfare but also the threats of coercive force that ultimately and undeniably back any system of positive law.[2] The law, in other words, describes and implements the operating system of the strikingly unpeaceable secular world. Upon what basis could Hauerwas possibly engage it?

Like lawyers, theologians are not generally content to raise only one objection to a project or proposal. Those schooled in divinity would also point out that Hauerwas has vociferously articulated additional concerns about Christian involvement in the particular type of secular polity the United States has become since 1892—a modern liberal democracy. Hauerwas maintains that the United States has generated a political discussion that presses all citizens to adopt a first-order moral and political framework meant to be neutral among competing worldviews, and then calls upon them to recast their particular religious beliefs in terms of that neutral framework when they enter the public square. According to Hauerwas, playing this game saps Christians of the confidence they need to proclaim the good news of the Gospel to all nations in their own, distinctive, first-order language. They need to remember that the main purpose of the Christian community is to testify to the distinctive story of God's salvific intervention in history through Jesus Christ. Ultimately—Hauerwas insists—the Christian story *judges*, it is not *judged by*, secular standards of epistemology and ethics. To hold otherwise is to sell short both the Christian community and the world itself, for the Christian message is true for the world too, though it knows it not.

Is there, then, a way in which the type of theology Stanley Hauerwas finds congenial can engage American law? I would like to explore this question in this chapter. More specifically, my plan is as follows: Drawing primarily upon Hauerwas's Gifford Lectures, the first section will explicate his view of the nature and purpose of Christian theology, as well as the dangers he believes it to face in the contemporary American context. The purpose of this section is to clarify the theological challenges any adequate Hauerwasian engagement with the American legal system will need to meet. Taking into account these clarifications, the second section then will sketch a normative framework for the engagement of theology with the secular law that Hauerwas would, I hope, recognize as legitimate. The centerpiece of this framework is Karl Barth's account of the relationship of covenant and creation, and the possibilities for ad hoc engagement of theology and secular disciplines that it enables, according to the perceptive interpretations of Barth offered by Hans Frei and William Werphehowski.

In the third section, I will turn from broader issues of theological method to more particular questions of the relationship of theological ethics to law. I will draw upon Paul Ramsey's engagement with the thought of Jacques Maritain and Edmond Cahn to suggest that the common law tradition, in which legal and moral norms are articulated and applied in the context of concrete cases, can provide a fruitful basis for an ad hoc conversation between theology done in a Hauerwasian way and the secular legal system. Hauerwas is often called a narrative theologian, precisely because he resists treating moral norms in isolation from character, narrative, and tradition. For this reason, he has a natural conversation partner in the common law. The common law, however, is a vast domain. Where should the conversation begin? I will suggest that contract law—the body of statutes and cases dealing with making and enforcing promises—might serve as a natural starting point, given the historical and normative overlap between the notion of "covenant" and that of "contract."

My own theological framework is somewhat different from Hauerwas's. I approach questions of political theology from a stance more like John Noonan's, which tends to recognize more continuities between nature and grace, and therefore more possibilities for natural theology and natural ethics (sometimes called natural law) than Hauerwas ordinarily acknowledges. In what follows, I am writing, so to speak, as Hauerwas's theological lawyer and advocate, not in my own name. By putting myself in his shoes, I am attempting to develop a position that justifies Christian engagement with the secular law in a way that is consistent with his fundamental theological premises—which are not in every case my own. Why engage in such an exercise? Because grappling closely with Hauerwas's perspectives on the relationship of the church to the world is a fruitful exercise for Christians of all stripes. Moreover, it is a mistake to avoid the challenges his work poses to competing strands of Christian political thought by dismissing him as a "sectarian" whose perspective has no real point of contact with political life in a broader, pluralistic society. Before Christians of other viewpoints can responsibly engage a Hauerwasian vision of the relationship of theology and law, we need to work out his position as carefully and sympathetically as possible.

Hauerwas on Theology, Church, and World

Stanley Hauerwas is a staggeringly prolific writer. He has offered perceptive reflections on a range of key topics at the intersection of theology and ethics. In part because so much of his writing has taken the form of occasional essays, it can be difficult to formulate an accurate and comprehensive account of his overall approach to theology, ethics, and contemporary culture. My own strategy will be to draw upon his Gifford Lectures, *With the Grain of the Universe: The Church's Witness and Natural Theology*,[3] in constructing such an account because it offers his most extensive treatment of the relationship of the church and the world.

Like most of Hauerwas's work, *With the Grain of the Universe* is dialogical; he develops his own views about the proper relationship of Christian theology to broader secular philosophical and political currents in conversation with three prior Gifford lecturers: William James, Reinhold Niebuhr, and Karl Barth. James, Niebuhr, and Barth, of course, were and remain key figures in their own right. For example, Barack Obama's well-publicized admiration for Niebuhr influenced his decision making regarding both foreign and domestic policy.[4] Although it is certainly worthwhile to consider whether Hauerwas's interpretation of their writings is accurate, let me emphasize that doing so is beyond the scope of this project. My goal is to glean Hauerwas's position, as he articulates it in conversation with them, in order to build a platform for engaging the law from there. My aim is not to defend James, Niebuhr, or Barth against any purported misinterpretations of them by Hauerwas.

What, then, is Hauerwas's argument in *With the Grain of the Universe*? Centrally, he contends that the project of the Gifford Lectures—to develop a natural theology, an understanding of God, humanity, and morality that is intelligible and defensible on grounds fully independent from the complete and vigorous account of reality offered by Christianity—is a serious mistake. Hauerwas thinks it is wrongheaded for *anyone* to try to develop a natural theology, because he is convinced that the goal of producing a context-free foundation for knowledge, or a context-independent account of morality, is thoroughly misguided. Moreover, he believes it is a terrible misfire for *Christians* to pursue this strategy, because the epistemological and moral power of their tradition is inextricably entwined with the very particular story of God's intervention in the history contained in the Bible. In short, Hauerwas thinks Christians who go the way of natural theology are selling their birthright for a mess of pottage.

Hauerwas devotes the first two chapters of his book to William James, concentrating centrally but not exclusively on the views James developed in his own Gifford Lectures, which became *The Varieties of Religious Experience*.[5] He takes James to represent both the harbinger and the progenitor of modern secular liberal democratic attitudes toward Christianity. Hauerwas argues that James's work was infused with an ulterior political purpose: to reshape religion in general and Christianity in particular, so as to support the emerging liberal, democratic *polis* in the United States and elsewhere. He charges that James "thinks democracy is not just a social and political arrangement but the very character of the emerging universe."[6] According to Hauerwas, Christianity threatened to impede what James saw as cosmic progress:

> What really bothered James was not that Christianity seemed to entail false views about the world, but that Christianity challenged the moral and political arrangements necessary to sustain the human project without God. James was profoundly right to see Christianity as the enemy of the world he hoped was being born. That James's world has come into being, a world about which he had some misgivings, makes it all the more important to attend to this aspect of his thought. Many Christians today want the world James wanted, while assuming that they can continue to have the Christian God. But James was right to think that you cannot have both.[7]

To suit and serve the emerging democratic world, James attempted to soften and reframe the hard, distinctive claims of Christianity. In fact, Hauerwas charges that James virtually evacuated the religious content from Christianity, leaving only a shell containing a disguised humanism.

More specifically, Hauerwas identifies three specific problems with James's thought from a Christian perspective. First, influenced by Ralph Waldo Emerson, James frames religious belief as essentially a matter for individuals in their solitariness, rather than a communal matter. According to Hauerwas, this approach wrongly discounts the primacy of communities of believers as the context in which individuals learn the language and grammar of faith.

Second, James separates religious feelings from convictions about religious truths, identifying the former with religious belief and discounting the latter. This separation, according to Hauerwas, wrongly suggests that feelings are separable from the religious propositions that support them.[8] In Hauerwas's view, James's account fails to do justice to the intellectual content of Christianity, and neglects to highlight the degree to which religious affections are shaped by that content.

Third, James fails to recognize the irreducible particularity of Christian claims, reconceptualizing Christianity as simply one example of the more common human phenomenon of "religion." Hauerwas notes that for James, religions are characterized by their sets of "over-beliefs"—philosophical and theological formulas that cannot be proven and that are also not justified on the basis of James's pragmatic theory of knowledge.[9] Moreover—and this is key—because over-beliefs are not pragmatically justified, they cannot serve as a basis for acting, or at least acting in ways that affect the interests of those who do not share the beliefs. Hauerwas opposes James on both counts. He rejects James's claim that Christian beliefs are not pragmatically justified—justified, that is, by their place in a broad network of workable assertions about how the world operates. He also, therefore, repudiates the implication that Christian beliefs can have no bearing upon one's actions in the public sphere of politics and public policy, but instead must be relegated to the realm of private interests and pursuits.[10]

In a nutshell, then, Hauerwas argues that a central aim for William James was to resize Christianity to fit the nascent liberal democratic project, which can admit of no moral authority higher than human consensus. In Hauerwas's view, James's conceptual Procrustean bed would ultimately prove lethal to Christian belief and community. Hauerwas laments that not all Christians living then were able to see the effects of James's views on their communities of faith. Moreover, Hauerwas contends that Christians living in our own time are equally blind to the harm caused by James's successors: the economists, philosophers, and public intellectuals who defend America's emphasis on economic freedom in the era of globalized capitalism. I can only imagine what Hauerwas would say about the fascination with Ayn Rand expressed by many leaders of the religious right, such as Glenn Beck and Rush Limbaugh. That admiration is not limited to pundits; it was also shared by powerful legislators, such as Paul Ryan (R-Wisc.), a practicing Roman Catholic who has chaired the House Budget Committee.[11] Moreover, I doubt that Hauerwas would be either sympathetic to or shocked by the hostility that conservative Catholic commentator George Weigel expressed regarding a document from the Vatican under Pope Benedict XVI calling for the establishment of a global economic authority.[12] That hostility on the part of American political conservatives has only grown with the papacy of Francis, who tirelessly castigates the excesses of capitalism for its brutality to the poor and marginalized.[13]

What would theology look like if it capitulated to the demands of William James and his ilk to resize Christianity to fit comfortably within the epistemological and political constraints of liberal democracy? To answer this question, Hauerwas turns to Reinhold Niebuhr, arguably the towering figure of twentieth-century American Protestantism. In Hauerwas's estimation, Niebuhr's normative commitments are uncomfortably close to James's; he maintains that "Niebuhr's Gifford Lectures are but a Christianized version of James's account of religious experience."[14] Moreover, Hauerwas believes Niebuhr's ultimate purpose was, like James's, to reconfigure Christianity in a way that would be useful to prevailing American commitments to individualism and the exercise of national power in order to protect America's ideological and economic interests. Hauerwas charges that "[t]he animating center of Niebuhr's life and work was the crafting of an account of liberal Christianity acceptable to a liberal culture and politics."[15]

What, in Hauerwas's view, was Niebuhr's key methodological mistake? It was to relativize Christian claims about God's way of acting in the world by treating them as metaphorical statements about more fundamental, common human experiences and longings. By attempting to make Christianity more widely appealing and accessible, Niebuhr drained it of its distinctive content and power. Hauerwas charges that "[f]or Niebuhr, Christ and the cross are not realities limited to the specific revelation found in Christianity; rather they are symbols of the tensions we must endure as people who expect history to be fulfilled, who expect a 'Christ.' Just as sin describes our nature, so Christ and the cross describe our destiny."[16]

For Hauerwas, Niebuhr treats Christianity as merely one instantiation of a common human phenomenon, which can be appreciated and understood apart from Christian claims, albeit maybe not as easily or as well. In the end, Hauerwas doubts "we have anything more in Niebuhr than a complex humanism disguised in the language of the Christian faith."[17]

Hauerwas acknowledges, of course, that most people do not think of Niebuhr as a *liberal* because of his emphasis on human sin in his ethical and political writings. Many previous Christian public intellectuals on the American scene, such as Walter Rauschenbusch, a key figure in the "Social Gospel Movement," were far more optimistic about the capacity of human beings to improve their collective moral lot. Hauerwas responds by calling his readers' attention to the distinction between theological liberalism and political liberalism. Niebuhr is a *theological liberal,* because the ultimate ground and test of his theological claims is human experience. Moreover, his *political conservatism* is firmly rooted in his theological liberalism; in Niebuhr's view, common human experience shows that human beings cannot avoid the exercise of political responsibility, sometimes by exerting military force even in morally murky situations. It is futile and dangerous for nations to pursue or expect pure justice in their military endeavors. In most cases, relative justice is all that can be expected. For Hauerwas, the decisive weight that theological liberalism gives to common human experience supports a policy of war-making as the only "realistic" response to political and military threats. Hauerwas writes,

> Niebuhr's ethics and his theology were of a piece. His theology sought to make Christian belief intelligible within the naturalistic presumptions that he thought were a prerequisite of modern science. His ethics sought to make Christian belief intelligible and even useful within the presuppositions of political liberalism. Theological liberals after Niebuhr often want his theology without his ethics; and political conservatives, like the "atheists for Niebuhr," often want his ethics without his theology. Yet Niebuhr, I think, rightly saw that you cannot have one without the other.[18]

Sorting through Hauerwas's criticism of Niebuhr's theological method is important here because it will help us avoid analogous methodological mistakes in constructing a Hauerwasian theological approach to American law. Hauerwas, for example, does not object to Niebuhr's emphasis on the pervasiveness of sin in human life. He strongly rejects, however, Niebuhr's account of how sin can be perceived, identified, and defined. What is that account? Niebuhr's fundamental methodological decision is to begin with general human experience, focusing on the lived contradiction between finiteness and freedom, and then to identify that contradiction with the experience of original sin. From there, Niebuhr goes on to defend Christianity as the best way of understanding and responding to general human experience, even as he revises the content of Christianity in the process. In other words, Niebuhr first articulates a general human problem, and then he proposes a Christian account of sin and redemption as both an explanation and a solution to that problem.[19]

In Hauerwas's judgment, then, the key flaw in Niebuhr's strategy is its *directionality*: In fact, he would say that, from an epistemological perspective, Niebuhr's approach is entirely backward. According to Hauerwas, persons must *first* be transformed by the redemptive story of the Bible before they can recognize sin *as* sin—as the breach in the relationship between God and humanity, between God and oneself, that Christ died to overcome. No twentieth-century theologian, in Hauerwas's estimation, proclaimed this point more firmly than Karl Barth.

According to Hauerwas, the chief achievement of Karl Barth is that he accurately grasped the proper directionality required to know the truth about "the nature and destiny of man" (to borrow from Niebuhr); it is a directionality that moves from church to world, rather than from world to church.[20] In the order of the biblical narrative, sin precedes redemption. In the epistemological order, however, the reverse is true. Redemption precedes sin, because we can know sin for what it is only if we know it from the vantage point provided by faithful witness to the redemptive activity of God. We are able to accurately interpret the beginning of the biblical narrative of salvation—the fall—only in light of the end, the resurrection of Jesus. Barth clearly proclaimed that Scripture is the primary source of knowledge about God and God's relationship to humanity. He also recognized that Christians cannot learn to read Scripture on their own, but must learn to do so in the context of a believing and worshiping community—the church. Shaped by this ecclesiastically transmitted knowledge, Christians can then interpret the situation in the world correctly; for the story of Scripture actually applies to all people, although not everyone acknowledges it.

Hauerwas emphasizes that the core message of Barth is simple; Barth himself summarized it as "Jesus loves me, this I know, for the Bible tells me so."[21] Why then did Barth write the fourteen immense volumes of the *Church Dogmatics*? That work is a mighty effort, Hauerwas would say, to reverse the powerful currents of theological liberalism, not only (or even primarily) by mounting a syllogistic argument against those currents but also by comprehensively modeling sound theological reflection. What might that be? According to Barth, practicing good theology is not an abstract academic exercise but, rather, a practical endeavor in service to the church's saving pedagogy. According to Hauerwas, "[t]he *Church Dogmatics*, with its unending and confident display of Christian speech, is Barth's attempt to train us to be a people capable of truthful witness to the God who alone is the truth."[22] Faithful witness—Hauerwas's understanding of the central Christian activity—requires transformation of the speaker, not only of the speech. Barth trains Christians to see correctly by building up, through sheer volume and repetition, a rich account of how the church and world look from the confident perspective of those who believe in the life, death, and resurrection of Jesus Christ.

Despite its length, Hauerwas argues that Barth's *Church Dogmatics* is not rightly considered systematic theology—an exhaustive account and orderly arrangement of true propositions about God and humanity from the Christian perspective. Hauerwas thinks this is a virtue, not a vice of the work. Theology is not a desiccated academic *topos* but, rather, the free response of a believer to the claims of the living God. One problem with systematic theology, from his view, is that it wrongly constricts the believer's response; another is that it futilely attempts to chain God to a preconceived organizational or philosophical structure. Furthermore, precisely because theology is properly construed as a written reflection of an ongoing relationship between God and his people, theology can have no formal beginning or end in the way systematic accounts of any merely academic subject necessarily have.

For Barth, theology's natural structure is narrative, reflecting the narrative structure of the biblical account of creation, sin, and redemption through the life, death, and resurrection of Jesus of Nazareth. Theology is properly seen as an ongoing attempt to retell the biblical story of God and humanity from various angles and perspectives:

> "Who and what Jesus Christ is, is something which can only be told, not a system which can be considered and described." The gospel, according to Barth, is just that simple, but because it is just that simple it requires a complex telling, since we are telling a story about the beginning of all beginnings whose end has come and yet is still to come.[23]

Accordingly, Barth's métier is not syllogistic argument, as both Hauerwas and Hans Frei[24] have noted. Hauerwas, however, points out something that Frei did not grasp: not all argument, understood loosely as persuasive speech, takes the forms of syllogistic argument. According to Hauerwas, "as Barth uses it, the language of the church is itself already an argument just to the extent that his descriptions and redescriptions cannot help but challenge our normal way of seeing the world."[25] Here, I think, is a strong point of contact between Hauerwas and the common law. The "facts" of the case both in lawyers' briefs and in court opinions are not neutral. Some elements are highlighted, whereas others are downplayed. If a brief or opinion is well written, the narrative of the controversy naturally suggests that the action the narrator asks of the audience is the next logical and suitable step in the story. The gravitational force of a plaintiff's lawyer in a closing argument in a tort case can push the jury toward awarding generous damages to compensate the plaintiff for the wrong he suffered. The gravitational force of the facts presented in an appellate opinion can prompt the legal community toward accepting the decision as a sound specification of the requirements of justice. Hauerwas and Barth would say that the gravitational force in the biblical narratives pushes believers toward repentance, gratitude, and witness to the power of God's mercy.

In the Reformed tradition out of which Karl Barth writes, gratitude is the first and proper response of the Christian who realizes that he is forgiven because Christ died and rose again. Other good works, the works of sanctification, are concrete signs of our gratitude and joy at our redemption. For Hauerwas,

> [o]ur participation in God's revelation consists in our offering thanks; such is the very condition of our speaking truthfully about God and ourselves. In every aspect of our lives, we cannot try to be anything other than a grateful response to God's revelation. As Barth says: "The work of the knowledge of God as man's participation in the veracity of the revelation of God certainly involves a witness, a question and a summons to all other works. But it takes place as such, as human work, with the same unpretentiousness with which they must take place, and alone can take place as good works."[26]

For both Barth and Hauerwas, truthful witness to the story of redemption is the central element of Christian ethics. Neither thinks that this witness will be easily accepted—even the joyful, noncoercive testimony that Barth thinks will be a fruit of God's gracious movement of the human heart. Barth maintains that a true Christian will be considered by the world to be "a strangely human person."[27] Perhaps too vividly, Barth suggests (and Hauerwas agrees) that "what the 'world perceives when it hears the witness of the Christian is the opinion of a fanatic who has obviously broken his bridges and burned his boats behind him and demands that it should do the same.' "[28]

Why bother, then? Why should Christians witness to those who scorn their message? Because the message is true for them, too, despite their resistance. For Hauerwas and Barth, "[t]he truth that makes Christians distinct is not a truth that is peculiar to them. It is not *their* truth but *the* truth for anyone."[29] They both agree that the vocation of a Christian, which can take different forms in different social contexts,

> "implies a responsibility of every man and thus compels the Christian to see and understand not only himself but also the non-Christian in his responsibility, and to address him in terms of it."

> The Christian, in other words, cannot address the non-Christian on the basis of a general or human responsibility interpreted as the responsibility to conscience or to supposed or real orders and forces of the cosmos. Rather, every person is to be addressed as one who exists and stands in the light of Jesus Christ.[30]

For Hauerwas, as for Barth, Christians must speak to the world out of the truth of the Gospel. Not every person believes in Jesus Christ, but Jesus Christ died and rose again for every person. That, I think, is the key both to Hauerwas's resistance to and engagement with the world beyond the church.

Creation, Covenant, and Law

According to Hauerwas, then, the primary task of Christian theology is not to recast its claims in the language of the secular world in general, or secular liberal democracy in particular, but confidently to proclaim the truth it bears in its own language—the language of Scripture and the church's prayer-filled reflection on Scripture over the centuries. Given the primacy of the kerygmatic role of theology, for what reason—and on what basis—would it engage secular law?

Before we turn to these questions, some terminological clarification is necessary. What exactly does Hauerwas mean by "church"? And what, in his view, is its relationship to the "world"? Although they are terms Hauerwas uses frequently, he does not grace us with full explanations of their meaning in his Gifford Lectures. Both terms, of course, have long histories in Christian thought. Some (for example, Roman Catholics) frequently have used the term "church" to refer to the institutional structure of their religious community, which is deeply embedded in worldly structures. Others (for example, the American Puritans) have used it centrally to refer to the "elect"—those who have evidently been saved from eternal damnation by divine decree. Some Christian religious groups (for example, the Amish) have set up distinctive communities apart from the larger world or with limited interaction with it (the Mennonites). Other Christians, such as Catholics and mainline Protestants, have not viewed faithfulness to the Gospel as requiring withdrawal from the world.[31]

What about Hauerwas? Sorting through the full meaning and implications of his ecclesiology is not an easy task. Apparent tensions, if not outright contradictions, are easy to identify. Why, for example, does a theologian who emphasizes the distinctiveness of Christian claims and highlights the inimical nature of liberal democratic society to Christianity find himself in *Time* magazine as America's best theologian?[32] How can Hauerwas see both John Howard Yoder, a Mennonite, and Pope John Paul II as theological heroes, when they would have deep disagreements about morality (for example, the moral legitimacy of war), worship, and church membership (for example, the role of baptism)? He does not say. It is not clear, in other words, what robust definition of "church" he could offer that would encompass both men.

While Hauerwas may on some level presuppose that there is a sociological group called "church," in which both Yoder and John Paul II can be counted as members, he does not give us a way to identify that group, nor any reason for confidence that all its members will recognize one another as belonging to it. They may, of course, belong to the "invisible church" that will be gathered around Christ at the end of time. But what about a visible ecclesiology for here and now?

I would like to propose that many of these definitional challenges can be ameliorated, if not resolved, by treating Hauerwas as largely working with a *functionalist* rather than an *essentialist* ecclesiology. I think that for Hauerwas, "church" points primarily to what we *do*—Christians give thanks to God in worship and witness to God's saving activity in truth—rather than who we *are*. To put it another way, within his framework, "church" should be understood as more of a verb than a noun; it is a distinct activity, rather than a distinct membership group. If this is the case, then Hauerwas does not need to draw sharp boundaries between various branches of Christianity, labeling some true churches and some false. *Both* Yoder and John Paul II *enact* (rather than *belong to*) the one true church when and to the extent they are truly witnessing to the biblical story of salvation.

Furthermore, by adopting a functionalist conception of church, Hauerwas does not need to act as a sectarian to sharply divide Christians from the world in every respect in order to preserve its distinctive message. Witnessing is an activity that can take place anywhere, as the account of St. Paul's witness to the Athenians evinces.[33] Paul did not protect the Christian message from encounters with cosmopolitanism; in fact, he embraced such encounters. After preaching against idolatry in the marketplace (agora) and the synagogue, and debating Jews and Epicurean and Stoic philosophers, Paul was invited to speak at the Areopagus, a region of Athens on the Acropolis that at one time comprised temples, associated cultural activities and facilities, and the supreme Athenian council (their supreme court).[34] There, Paul preached the Gospel message in terms the Athenians could understand, proclaiming to them that the "unknown God" they worshiped was in fact the God who would raise them from the dead.

I suggest we think of the "world" in Hauerwasian terms as analogous to Athens, the agora, and the Aereopagus—as the locus of joint *activity* for all people, including those people who do not know that Jesus died for their sins. For Hauerwas, they are the people who need to hear the truth about themselves, which they can only do if Christians work and live and profess their faith in their midst. To the extent that Christians are incompletely converted—and all Christians are that—they need to receive the same message.

Moreover, interpreting the distinction between church and world in this functionalist rather than essentialist manner allows us to push Hauerwas's framework constructively, in a way that may help clarify the relationship between two sets of terms that are key for our discussion. At times, it can appear that Hauerwas thinks the relationship between church and world is analogous to the relationship between theology and liberal democratic politics and philosophy:

> *The Church is to the World as Theology is to Liberal Democratic Political Philosophy*

Furthermore, it sometimes appears that Hauerwas is willing to turn these analogical relationships sideways, so the relationship between the church and theology, on the one hand, is analogous to that between the world and liberal democratic politics and philosophy:

> *The Church is to Theology as the World is to Liberal Democratic Political Philosophy*

Presuming that Hauerwas accepts the account of the relationship of the church to the world described above, he would do well to reject both analogies. The church's fundamental role, in his view, is to witness to the world. The task of theology, however, is not to witness to liberal democratic political philosophy. Furthermore, flipping the analogy on its side entails even more relational distortions. The point of theology, as Hauerwas understands it, is to help the church recover its kerygmatic voice. Theology's task consists primarily of redescription of the web of Christian commitments, and secondarily of offering critical, internal reflection on the current practices and challenges faced by the church. Liberal democratic political philosophy does not function in the same way for the world that theology (in Hauerwas's view) does for the church. To suggest that it does is to make two mistakes: (1) to reduce the world to the American state, and (2) to assume that the normative commitments of the American state are largely captured and reflected by liberal democratic political philosophy.

But the world—the broader practices and activities in which Americans and others live their lives—includes far more than the apparatuses of the state. And liberal democratic philosophers are not philosopher-kings, with the power to transform American society in the manner in which they wish to do. They sell their ideological wares in the agora and on the Areopagus, just like everyone else—including theologians. Religious language is far from on the wane in American political speech. In 2011, for example, Texas Governor Rick Perry hosted a stadium-size day of fasting and prayer,[35] which echoed the day of fasts that New England Puritan divines held at the behest of the state in the seventeenth century in order to ensure national prosperity through obedience to divine law.[36]

The intricate web of state and federal law clearly and directly shapes the activity of the agora and the Areopagus—including the activity of political theorists. For example, it is in large part because of the Supreme Court's broad interpretation of the First Amendment right to free speech that even radical denunciations of American policy are not generally suppressible or punishable as sedition. Precisely because it immediately and sometimes coercively influences behavior, the law has a far more direct role than academic political theory in expressing, shaping, and teaching the values of our political society. Political theorists of all stripes may make their proposals, but it is the lawmakers who make the ultimate dispositions. I do not deny that it is important for theologians to pay attention to philosopher John Rawls's account of the "difference principle," which sketches the framework for a theory of distributive justice.[37] It is equally if not more important, however, for them to examine the theory of distributive justice that is coercively implemented through the tax code.

When most people think of legal norms, they think of the requirements and prohibitions of the criminal code. Lawyers know, however, that what the law enables and encourages, or impedes and discourages, is at least as important as what it straightforwardly requires or prohibits under the threat of penal sanctions. The law has a channeling function, highlighting certain activities as worthwhile (for example, home ownership) and marking clear paths that can lead to achieving them. Much of the law curriculum, in fact, deals with bodies of law that are essentially positive in function: contract law, corporate law, property, and constitutional law are all meant to enable the orderly interaction of human beings with one another. As John Finnis has often said, a major point of the law is to solve "coordination problems"—not always to say no, but frequently to say how and when certain activities may take place.[38]

Moreover, the web of law does not manifest, at either the state or the federal level, the coherence of systematic political theory. Particularly in common law countries such as the United States, the law is not like a suburban McMansion built all at once six months ago; rather, it is like an old farmhouse with additions and renovations from different periods clinging together in a rough and wary harmony. Liberal legal theory may be systematic, ahistorical, and thematically coherent, but the law of the United States of America—federal law and the law of the fifty states—most definitely is not.[39] It is, to borrow from Jeffrey Stout's borrowing from Claude Lévi-Strauss, a "*bricolage*."[40] We see coherence and functionality, but we also see tension, and sometimes even contradiction. We see development—or devolution—over time.[41] This is particularly true of the common law tradition, which grows over time as an accretion of decisions made in the context of particular cases. The common law does not entirely shuck off the past, but it does highlight some aspects while playing down others.

I think Hauerwas's own approach to theology, which eschews systematic reflection and places a high priority on narrative, would find a natural conversation partner in American case law. It is the compilation of narratives of actual controversies, which was settled by the judicial articulation of a governing rule "in the prism of the case."[42] Norm and narrative are interrelated in the common law; law students do not learn merely how to apply the rule to the facts but also how to appeal to facts to argue that the rule in one case should not apply in a facially similar case. Methodologically speaking, in other words, the common law tradition resonates greatly with the type of theology advocated and practiced by Hauerwas himself. It provides, a better point of contact for Hauerwasian theology with the agora and the Areopagus of America's particular, historically conditioned liberal democracy than most work in liberal democratic theory. Let the systematic theologians talk to the systematic political theorists; theologians working in a Hauerwasian key will find a more congenial conversation partner in the common law.

Thus far, I have made a case for Hauerwas's engaging the common law tradition in general as part of Christian theology's engagement with the world. The next question pertains to the theological justification for such engagement: Why ought Hauerwas to consider it a legitimate endeavor, rather than a mere useless distraction from straightforward witnessing to the risen Christ? To address these questions, I think Hauerwas would do well to draw upon further resources from the thought of Karl Barth and Hans Frei, both of whom appear in his Gifford Lectures.

More specifically, I would like to suggest that Hauerwas might justify his theological engagement with the world by drawing upon the framework with which Karl Barth organizes the relationship of God and humanity, as well as relationships of human beings to one another: the framework of covenant theology, which is a key aspect of the Reformed tradition to which Barth belongs. Somewhat surprisingly, Hauerwas does not explicitly mention the covenantal aspect of Barth's thought in his Gifford Lectures, although I think many of his remarks are consistent with its insights.

In general terms, covenant theology understands the relationship of God and humanity in terms of the exchange of solemn promises, repeatedly enacted in the Old Testament in, for example, the covenants between God and Adam and Eve, between God and Noah (a renewed covenant for all humanity), and between God and Moses (the covenant between God and the Jewish people). God freely chooses to make human beings his covenant partners, and confers upon humanity the power freely to accept his offer. Furthermore, in Jesus Christ, whom Christians believe to be both fully human and divine, humanity's repeated breach of the covenant is decisively overcome by Christ's fidelity, and obedience, to God's call.

Barth sees the creation—the entire created world—as the *external basis* of the covenant between God and humanity that is sealed by the death and resurrection of Jesus Christ, and the covenant as being the *internal basis* of creation. Barth writes:

> Creation comes first in the series of works of the triune God, and is thus the beginning of all the things distinct from God Himself. Since it contains in itself the beginning of time, its historical reality eludes all historical observation and account, and can be expressed in the biblical creation narratives only in the form of pure saga. But according to this witness the purpose and therefore the meaning of creation is to make possible the history of God's covenant with man which has its beginning, its centre and its culmination in Jesus

> Christ. The history of this covenant is as much the goal of creation as creation itself is the beginning of this history.[43]

To put it another way, according to Barth, God created the world *for* covenant partnership with him, a covenant partnership that was first enacted fully with the Jewish people and then expanded to encompass all humanity through the message of the Gospel. Consequently, theologians do not need to construct a bridge between the Christian community and the broader world, as if they are two distant bodies. The two are intertwined, because they were divinely oriented toward one another from the beginning. Nonetheless, the two do not have equal status in interpreting the terms of the relationship. The true meaning of creation, and its orientation toward covenant relationship with God, can be only identified from the perspective of those who acknowledge the saving activity of Jesus Christ. The directionality of the interpretation has to remain one-way.

So a covenantal framework provides the theological basis for Hauerwas to allow the church to engage the world. What is the appropriate *method* of engagement? This is a difficult question. Christian theologians, according to both Barth and Hauerwas, cannot detach Christian claims from the biblical narrative in which their intelligibility rests; they therefore need to resist the futile endeavor to translate Christianity into other normative frameworks or systems. Both Hauerwas and Barth reject the project of natural theology as a comprehensive attempt to justify the belief in God on neutral philosophical or theological grounds. Relatedly, they also reject a full-blown project of apologetics, understood as attempting to provide reasons not rooted in faith that are themselves sufficient to justify belief in Christianity.

The fact that there are no well-paved, well-established highways between the church and the world does not mean there are no byways whatsoever. Theologians are free to make use of whatever intellectual or social material from the world—from the agora and the Areopagus—that helps them in their task of showing how the world is rightly known only from the perspective of the Christian story. As William Werpehowski argued, this task involves revealing how certain practices and patterns of activity engaged in by non-Christians are illuminated and assisted when set in the context of Christian claims. These efforts are not driven by intellectual system, but by context, need, and opportunity. They are, in Werpehowski's words, ad hoc apologetics:

> The attempt to describe some feature of Christian faith in order to make it sensible and credible (i.e., "reasonable") to a non-Christian

> must itself be expressive of the character of one who would stand faithfully in relationship with God in Christ. The substance, moreover, at least has to involve an appeal to the unbeliever that takes seriously his or her status as a creature of God, that is, as one whose own characteristic patterns of action and purpose bear some uneradicable relation to an origin in God. The Christian apologist thus seeks to establish common ground with the non-Christian as creature with reference to a particular context of action or a particular contested question or belief. That Christian identity is sustained thereby is what makes the apologetic *theological*. At the same time, the common ground sought and supportive of Christian identity also must be seen really to sustain and nurture the non-Christian in some particular area of belief or practice. The latter's projects and purposes would be advanced and would make more sense with the introduction of the theological factor securing the common ground. This is what makes the theological activity *apologetic*; reasonableness is displayed through conversation in a way that supports the non-Christian's identity.[44]

The project of ad hoc apologetics depends upon a broader, ad hoc account of theology's correlation to secular disciplines in its working out of the Christian story of redemption. What does this account entail? According to Hans Frei, this fourth type "argues that Christian theology is a non-systematic combination of normed Christian self-description and method founded on general theory. But . . . it does not propose a correlation between heterogeneous equals. . . . [T]he practical discipline of Christian self-description governs and limits the applicability of general criteria of meaning in theology, rather than vice versa."[45]

Although secular thought is frequently an aid to the task of Christian theology, theologians must guard against allowing the servant to become the master. Not surprisingly, Frei takes Barth as a prime example of the ad hoc correlationist approach. How does this approach relate to the Barthian account of the relationship between covenant and creation?[46] In my view, it tacitly presupposes that account. Since creation is the external basis of the covenant, theologians are free to make use of any intellectual tools they find in order to illuminate the Christian narrative, to make it more intelligible to persons within and outside the church. The history of Christianity is replete with fortuitous "borrowings" from secular thought in order to communicate truths rooted in the biblical narrative. The creeds themselves, for example, articulate the nature of God in the terms of Greek philosophy. One could argue that St. Paul himself engaged in ad hoc apologetics in his conversations on the Areopagus, showing the Athenians how his conception of their "unknown god" made more sense of their aspirations and purposes than their own religious beliefs did.

The Reformed tradition of Christianity, from Calvin to Barth, has expressed great skepticism about the capacity of human wisdom to understand the truth of the human condition, due to the enduring effects of sin on the intellect, as well as the will. Although correlation can ameliorate those effects, it cannot eradicate them. An ad hoc correlationist account is consistent with the heightened sense of epistemological limits in the Reformed tradition. Frei notes, "There can be no ultimate conflict between them [the truths of revelation and the truths of secular knowledge], but in finite existence and thought we cannot know how they fit together in principle."[47] The relationship of Christian doctrinal claims "to the broader or even universal linguistic or conceptual context within which they are generated remains only fragmentarily—perhaps at times negatively—specifiable; yet it is important to keep that relation open and constantly restate doctrinal statements in the light of cultural and conceptual change."[48]

How do we situate Hauerwas with respect to Barth, Frei, and Werpehowski on an ad hoc correlationist approach to the disciplines of the word? In my view, Hauerwas has on occasion so emphasized the distinctiveness of Christian theological claims that he has led some readers to think that he would not admit the legitimacy of even an ad hoc correlation with secular disciplines. If this were in fact his opinion, then Hauerwas would have no legitimate point of contact from which to engage the world; he could simply preach to it in distinctively Christian terms and pray for its conversion. Yet I do not believe that this is in fact Hauerwas's opinion. In his Gifford Lectures, Hauerwas has more fully integrated his approach with the Barthian approach of his teachers at Yale, particularly Hans Frei.[49] In so doing, he has also, in my view, placed his engagement with the secular world and its disciplines on a firmer theoretical basis.

The Natural Law and the Common Law

One more bridge needs to be crossed. Frei's focus is dogmatic theology; he says comparatively little about questions of ethics. How should Christian theologians interested in appropriating an ad hoc correlationist methodology address applied questions of ethics and political theology?

The Barthian notion of creation as the external basis of covenant would support the *existence* of a set of norms that is binding on all persons and communities simply by virtue of their basic human nature—which is created for redemption in Jesus Christ. Yet, at the same time, Barth's insistence upon the primacy of the Christian narrative would reject both the legitimacy and the effectiveness of any attempts to deduce these norms from universal first principles of morality. Both Barth and Frei would consider any attempt to formulate a neutral set of abstract moral principles that transcend Christianity and every other normative intellectual–moral system to be both theologically mistaken and intellectually false. Finally, a Barthian approach to generally applicable moral norms would need to take into account the Reformed tradition's insistence on pervasive effects of original sin, which not only impedes the human ability to conform to true moral norms but also, and more fundamentally, darkens our capacity to grasp those norms.

Here, of course, we are verging into the complicated question of the relationship of the Protestant branch of Christianity to the natural-law tradition. Some might ask, "What relationship?" To say categorically that all Protestants have always been opposed to natural-law methodology is a grave mistake. In the early modern period, Protestants did not reject "natural law" as providing a roughly workable basis for interactions in the secular world, although they denied that it could provide any kind of knowledge of morality sufficient for salvation. In fact, two of the fathers of international law, Hugo Grotius (d. 1645) and Samuel von Pufendorf (d. 1694), were Protestants.

In the twentieth century, however, the situation was very different. Seared by the experience of the First World War, and appalled by the rise of the Third Reich, Barth rejected "natural law" as a sufficient basis to formulate a sound morality that would prevent Christians from committing, endorsing, or passively accepting atrocities.[50] Moreover, in the United States in the first part of the twentieth century, many mainstream Protestant ethicists tended to associate natural law with the form it took in the Catholic neoscholastic tradition. In so doing, they assumed that natural law operated as a universally applicable and universally understandable set of moral norms that could be applied deductively and with certainty to an infinite range of factual circumstances. Protestant rejection of natural law became increasingly intertwined with its rejection of Catholic accounts of morality as too dependent upon unregenerate reason rather than Scripture.

That rejection, however, provided an opportunity for rediscovery. In the mid-twentieth century, the Protestant ethicist Paul Ramsey groped toward a reconceptualization of the natural-law tradition that would allow Protestants to appropriate the tradition's insights on their own terms. More specifically, as I discuss more fully in chapter 6, in *Nine Modern Moralists*, Ramsey resists attempts to interpret the natural law in too rationalistic and deductivist a way. Instead, he draws upon Jacques Maritain's understanding of the knowledge of natural law through inclination, through "connaturality," not through pure, disembodied reason. In this schema, "knowledge of the natural law no longer is a matter of reflecting upon essential human nature in abstraction from variable factual conditions and social relationships. Knowledge by connaturality, congeniality, inclination arises only vis-à-vis quite concrete conditions of fact. Judgments as to the fundamental law, quite as much as any other sort of law, are made only *in medias res*."[51]

It seems to me that Ramsey's account of natural law is congenial to the ad hoc correlationist approach suggested by the work of Barth and Frei. Moreover, I think it could furnish a platform for conversation between Hauerwas and the law, particularly the common law. In 1977, Hauerwas co-authored an article with David Burrell, which perceptively reflects on the relationships between norms, narrative, and character.[52] Hauerwas and Burrell argue that "quandary ethics," a genre of moral reasoning that applies abstract moral norms to stripped-down descriptions of controversial cases, are too abstract to reflect the richness and complexity of actual moral decisions. Although some might think the case-based reasoning in quandary ethics reflects the case-based approach in the common law tradition, in fact that is not so. Many key cases contain rich narratives, in which a legal norm is only understandable in light of the identity and character of the parties, as well as their broader social context. Very often, these narratives provide the basis not only for supporting the judgment of the court but also for calling it into question, as the work of John Noonan demonstrates.[53] In my view, Ramsey's retrieval and reformulation of a Protestant account of natural law is congenial to the insights of Hauerwas and Burrell, in part because it privileges the context-dependent, narrative-oriented approach of the common law as a locus for the articulation of moral norms.

Ramsey developed his account of natural law in conversation not only with Maritain, a revisionist Catholic philosopher, but also with Edmond Cahn, a secular Jewish law professor. Drawing upon their insights, he struggled to formulate a historically embedded, inductive account of natural moral norms that were inextricably intertwined with both the cultural norms instantiating them and the facts of the particular controversy.[54] There was, in Ramsey's view, no way to strain and purify the natural law of these elements; one engaged the natural law in and through engaging its operations in cases and contexts. Of necessity, this engagement was always tentative and partial; another case could come along that could force revision or even abandonment of the principle articulated to decide the case. Hauerwas and Burrell would doubtless agree.

Moreover, Ramsey does not want to separate inclination (which he identifies with natural law) from practical reason (which he identifies with human law, including the *jus gentium*). Nor does he want to separate inclination and natural law from their social embodiment. He sees "the straddle position" of *jus gentium*, containing "*both* characteristics which belong also to natural law (i.e., known not only as rationally inferred but also through inclination), and characteristics that go beyond the content of natural law (i.e., *only* rationally inferred, and not known through inclination)."[55] He asks rhetorically,

> Is the legislative decision against murder really strengthened or better understood when it is broken down as follows: "The prohibition of murder, insofar as this precept is *known by inclination*, belongs to natural law. The same prohibition of murder, if this precept is known as a conclusion inferred from a principle of natural law, pertains to *jus gentium*." The judgment here being made is indivisibly tendential, decisional, and conceptual; it is at once natural and positive law.[56]

Ramsey rejects the attempt to distill the natural law from its instantiations in the particularities of various societies and to separate it from the concrete, fallible decisions made by persons in those societies. This is precisely the reason he is open to the possibility that biblical morality has influenced the articulation of norms of justice that we now interpret as ecumenical or secular, rather than as specifically influenced by the biblical tradition. Here, Ramsey quotes Cahn:

> "The stubborn survival of some sort of faith in *natural* justice," [Cahn] wrote, "should point to a nucleus of truth." The sense of

> injustice, knowledge through inclination, is that nucleus. "Judges may speak of 'due process,' 'equal protection,' 'general welfare,' 'reasonableness'—all somehow cleansed of natural rights or higher law. But would the decision be the same if twenty-four centuries had not preached an indwelling justice?"[57]

Ramsey's account of natural law both validates and challenges Hauerwas's insistence that faithful commitment to the distinctive story of Christianity makes a difference to the identification and articulation of moral norms. For Ramsey, it has mattered that the basic norms of the Western legal tradition were formulated, implemented, and enforced by those committed to the salvific death and resurrection of Jesus Christ. It might have been otherwise, he concedes. But Ramsey would doubtless ask Hauerwas whether it would have been *better* otherwise, particularly for the weak and vulnerable.

Furthermore, Ramsey incorporates a characteristically Protestant distrust of postlapsarian moral reason by emphasizing the fundamentally negative nature of natural moral knowledge: after the fall, human beings tend to have a sense of *injustice*—of what is wrong to do in concrete circumstances, not a full, positive sense of justice that could fully outline in advance the requirements for morally correct action in all situations. Accordingly, he highlights Maritain's understanding of natural law as "knowledge through *dis*inclination," along with Cahn's insistence that moral analysis should "focus not only on an *act* but an act of *wrong*" identified by "the sense of *injustice*."[58]

In Ramsey's view, the common law tradition also reflects the provisionality about specific judgments that accords with the Protestant sensibilities about the limitations of moral reasoning. He writes that "a possible Protestant view of the fundamental nature of moral and legal decisions based on natural justice (or law) has a great deal in common with the jurisprudential understanding of judicial reasoning and moral decision in legal cases."[59] Key for Ramsey was the possibility of "unlimited discussion," by which he meant that the conversation about the right way to resolve a particular case was never in principle closed, although the judicial decision settled the matter practically.[60] His objection to the Catholic natural law tradition has to do with its propensity, in his view, to use church authority to shut down questions prematurely.[61]

It seems to me that Hauerwas, committed as he is to the kerygmatic function of Christianity, ought to find Ramsey's approach congenial.

Although Hauerwas may be opposed to "Christendom," he ought not to dismiss the efforts of Christians to discern, over the centuries, the concrete requirements of morality in particular cases and controversies, in light of the demands of justice—demands that are themselves shaped by the biblical narrative. It may or may not be true that the members of the contemporary bench, bar, and legal academy are irredeemably secularist. Nonetheless, in the Anglo-American common law tradition, today's legal minds must grapple with authoritative authors, sources, and subjects who were not secularists, but who were Christian believers—in fact, who were in the main Protestant Christians. The values and commitments of these earlier participants in the American legal tradition are embedded not only in the decisions but also in the framing of the narratives of the particular cases and controversies that occasioned those decisions.

Finally, I want to highlight the thoroughgoing narrativity of the common law, an idea toward which Ramsey is also groping, although he does not use the term. As I discuss in the next chapter, the common law tradition can provide a particularly rich conversation partner for any theologian who takes Alasdair MacIntyre's tradition theory seriously, because the cases intertwine norm and narrative context.

The realm of the common law, of course, is vast. Where in particular might Hauerwas begin his engagement? I would like to end this section by suggesting that the common law of contracts would be a particularly auspicious place for Hauerwas to begin engaging the American legal tradition, for at least two broad sets of reasons.

First, there is considerable historical and conceptual overlap in the development of the theological and legal ideas of covenant and contract. As I noted above, Karl Barth is a covenant theologian; he draws upon the repeated imagery of God's agreements with humanity in Scripture to provide his theological framework. He was not the first one to take this approach. Although Christian theologians had always paid due regard to the concept, it assumed a more central role in the thought of John Calvin (d. 1564) and grew to provide the organizing motif of some groups of his followers. Originating in Germany, covenant theology (sometimes called federal theology; the Latin word *foedus* is often translated as "pact") received fulsome development at the hands of the English and American Puritans in the sixteenth and seventeenth centuries. In developing their covenant theologies in sermons and religious tracts, the Puritans (who belonged to the emerging merchant class) tended to draw upon law knowledge of the nature of binding legal agreements in order to make their point. They tended, in fact, to use the terms "contract" and "covenant" interchangeably—as did many nontechnical legal discussions.[62]

Second, turning to the contemporary era, it seems to me that the norms embedded in and illustrated by the cases of contract law would bear fruitful consideration by Christian ethicists, particularly those of a narrative bent. Narrative theology, for example, would not limit its moral evaluation of promise-making and promise-keeping to the moment of commitment, but would instead view that obligation in a broad temporal frame that relates past, present, and future. So does contract law, especially through the concept of reliance. Promissory estoppel, for example, centrally enforces unbargained-for promises upon which the promisee has relied to his or her detriment, either by making further commitments (for example, going into debt upon the promise of a forthcoming payment) or by forgoing other opportunities (for example, relying on the promise of one job by declining another offer).

Reflecting upon the legal concept of reliance might also allow Christian ethicists more firmly to situate individual actions in a communal context for purposes of evaluating their moral import, particularly with respect to the potential for vulnerability they create. For example, promise-making is essentially a social act, as the institution of marriage suggests. Each spouse relies upon the other's promises in the joint expression of their positive freedom, creating a family together. Embarking upon that project, however, renders them far more vulnerable than they were before making or accepting the reciprocal promises of marriage. Women and men who are responsible for small children are not as free, flexible, and able to protect themselves financially as they were before those children came along. Reliance upon their mutual promises makes the two partners vulnerable; one purpose of treating those promises as legally binding is to protect them against the potential wounds.

I have argued, in short, that it is possible to articulate a theological basis for a Hauerwasian engagement with the law. That basis consists of three elements: (1) a Barthian understanding of the relationship of creation and covenant; (2) a general ad hoc correlationist methodology; and (3) a conviction that the moral norms of creation (natural law) appear through a glass darkly, inextricably entwined with cultural norms and particular facts and circumstances. Moreover, I think the common law can provide a particularly rich conversation partner not only for Hauerwas but also for any Christian theologian who takes Alasdair MacIntyre's tradition theory seriously—including Protestant theologians who do not make light of the effects of sin upon the reason and will.

In particular, I have proposed that the common law subject of contracts—the law surrounding enforceable promises—would be a good conversational starting point, for reasons both historical and normative. Historically, the tradition of covenant theology, in which Karl Barth participates, drew heavily upon images from widely known legal discourse pertaining to promise-keeping and debt in working out its understanding of the relationship between God and humanity. Normatively, Christians are centrally a people who have learned what it is to rely upon a promise—the divine promise that we are, and will always be, God's people. Relying on God's promise, Christians try to become reliable ourselves. A conversation about what communal and individual habits and practices are necessary to encourage us to be persons who can rely upon one another's promises is something about which both contract law and covenant theology have a great deal to say.

Some of the most important contributors to the discussion of contemporary Christian ethics and modern life, such as Jeffrey Stout, do not operate out of commitments to the theological traditions of Roman Catholicism or Protestantism. Instead, they find their intellectual centers of gravity in the history of critical reflection on the American political experiment, which includes persons of many different theistic and atheistic traditions. In the next chapter, taking Stout as my conversation partner, I will suggest that the tradition of Anglo-American case law is as fruitful a conversation partner for philosophers of democratic pluralism as it is for theologians living in pluralistic democratic societies.

3

Examples and Rules

Engaging Jeffrey Stout

IN *DEMOCRACY AND Tradition,* Jeffrey Stout makes a powerful case for the viability—and the virtue—of American constitutional democracy. Stout argues that the richness and complexity of the American democratic heritage is slighted both by secular liberals such as John Rawls and by religious "new traditionalists" such as Alasdair MacIntyre and Stanley Hauerwas.[1] Against the new traditionalists, Stout maintains that the American democratic heritage offers us an honorable and well-functioning moral and political tradition that "inculcates certain habits of reasoning, certain attitudes toward deference and authority in political discussion, and love for certain goods and virtues, as well as a disposition to respond to certain types of actions, events, or persons with admiration, pity, or horror."[2] Against Rawlsian liberals, he contends that respect for the American democratic heritage does not demand strict compliance with the requirements of a procedural conception of justice that gives absolute priority to fair terms of social cooperation over substantively rich conceptions of the good life, many of which have sources in religious traditions. "The notion of state neutrality and the reason-tradition dichotomy should not be seen as its [the American democratic tradition's] defining marks. Rawlsian liberalism should not be seen as its official mouthpiece."[3]

Where does Stout propose we look for the substance of the American democratic tradition? He contends that "[t]he ethical inheritance of American democracy consists, first of all, in a way of thinking and talking about ethical topics that is implicit in the behavior of ordinary people. Secondly, it also consists in the activity of intellectuals who attempt to make sense of that way of thinking and talking from a reflective, critical point of view."[4] Stout draws upon both sources in his rich and perceptive account of democratic virtues and practices. With respect to the first source, for example, he discusses the communal norms that developed in his own racially and economically mixed neighborhood of Community Park, in Princeton, New Jersey.[5] He also uses the game of soccer to develop the notion of what it means to be objectively excellent in a social practice.[6]

With respect to the second source, Stout encourages his readers to pay particular attention to the writings of independent American essayists such as Ralph Waldo Emerson, Walt Whitman, John Dewey, Meridel Le Sueur, James Baldwin, and Ralph Ellison.[7] The American essayist tradition occupies a particularly felicitous vantage point for moral reflection because it avoids two opposing and unhelpful approaches prominent in contemporary Anglo-American philosophical and theological ethics. The first approach gives priority to the formulation of moral principles and rules, which are then used neatly to subsume cases of moral quandaries. The neatness is artificial; it comes from the fact that the subsumed cases are inevitably described in abbreviated and abstract fashion, omitting any facts that would lead to an awkward fit between principle and case. Stout agrees with the critique of this approach mounted by Stanley Hauerwas and David Burrell forty years ago; they contended that it promotes an impoverished and distorted understanding of human persons and the particularities of their lives.[8] In contrast, Stout emphasizes that essayists offer thick, contextualized descriptions of character and situation, which more accurately reflect the complex situations of real people who confront moral decisions.

The more complicated the story gets, however, and the more multilayered the characters become, the harder it is to articulate a "moral" that is straightforwardly applicable to other situations. The particularities can become overwhelming. One might be tempted to react to this insight by adopting a radical narrative ethics that denies the usefulness of principles, rules, or even analogies in moral reflection, and that limits legitimate ethical reflection to the telling of stories. This stance is objectionable because it eclipses the fact that human persons have commonalities as well as differences, and because it ignores the possibility that human situations can be importantly similar, even if they are never identical. In so doing, it also undermines the possibility of philosophy, understood not narrowly as a technical analytic skill but more broadly, as Stout does, as disciplined moral reflection upon situations that can be of moral interest to persons other than those immediately involved in them.

The essayists, according to Stout, avoid both extremes; they stand *between* system and story. What does such a stance involve? Stout's description is worth quoting at length:

> [E]nriching descriptive detail in one's rendering of an example is a matter of adding assertions, and thus new commitments, to the ones already involved in the original rendering. But new commitments at the level of detailed description can have the effect of diminishing one's entitlement to the general conclusion licensed by the example in its original form. The reason for this is that the inferential license granted in practice by the original version of the example is defeasible. The license expires if new commitments undermine its authority. The general assertion that has been licensed by the old version of the example turns out to be incompatible with the new version. What, then, shall we do with the general assertion? Reject it? Qualify it? Restrict its scope? Or should we turn back to the example itself and modify the set of assertions that constitute its descriptive content? To ask these questions is to stand, as it were, between the commitments embodied in assertion of the example and the commitments embodied in the general assertion, reflecting on each. It is in [Robert] Musil's words, to stand "between example and doctrine."[9]

Stout goes on to claim that certain forms of moral discourse developed in the early modern era facilitate the pursuit of this set of questions, and are therefore highly valuable to citizens of modern democracies. Among such forms he includes the novel and the Shakespearean play, as well as the essay. In this chapter, I would like to make a case for serious consideration of another such form of moral discourse: the judicial opinion in the great common law subjects such as criminal law, torts, or contracts. In making this case, I will be delving more deeply into ideas that I have lightly touched upon in the first two chapters.

The description Stout gives of what it means to negotiate the space between example and doctrine, between system and story, perfectly captures the practice of the Anglo-American common law tradition. In making my case, my focus will be the common law subject of contracts, as it is taught to first-year students in law schools across the United States. As

I indicated in chapter 2, I think that both the teaching method and the material taught in a first-year contracts class demonstrate that the Anglo-American common law constitutes a complex and well-functioning tradition of moral inquiry. Consequently, it provides another reason to think that MacIntyre and Hauerwas are overly pessimistic in their assessment of the moral resources of the American democratic tradition.

The cases commonly included in the textbooks for first-year contracts courses are a source of moral reflection that is substantively rich and detailed, without being rooted in a specific religious tradition. But these judgments are not hostile to religion, either. They exemplify Stout's claim that "[e]thical discourse in religiously plural modern democracies is secularized . . . only in the sense that it does not take for granted a set of agreed-upon assumptions about the nature and existence of God."[10] The opinions in common law cases concretely demonstrate that it is not necessary to sacrifice substantive moral richness to preserve the healthy secularity appropriate to a pluralistic society. For this reason, they ought to be of interest to both Rawlsian political theorists and their religious critics.

Contract law nicely combines the two sources of moral reflection that Stout has identified as particularly appropriate to a democratic tradition: the ways of thinking and talking about ethical matters embedded in the lives of ordinary people, and the reflections of intellectuals who attempt to make sense of such thinking and talking from a critical point of view. Contract law is private law, not public law. More specifically, binding contracts are not imposed by governmental officials from on high; they can be created by only the agreement of the parties whom they bind. Moreover, entering into a contract is not an extraordinary opportunity reserved only for the rich and the powerful. Ordinary people enter into contracts every day. For example, a man who walks into a barber shop and sits down in the chair enters into a contract with the barber who picks up his scissors, even though the two never exchange a word: the barber will cut the customer's hair in exchange for the price posted on the wall.

Courts get involved only when contractual relationships turn sour; their job is to interpret and apply the private law enacted by the disputed contract in light of broader social and legal norms concerning the nature and scope of promissory obligations. Consequently, the most widely admired common law judges established their reputations not by dealing with esoterica but by wisely settling countless ordinary disputes between ordinary people; their brilliance is defined in part by the innovative way in which they develop legal doctrine to address the specific contours of a factual situation. These developments are recognizable both for their fidelity to the legal tradition in which they operate and for their creative responsiveness to the situation of the parties before them. One might say that great common law judges practice interstitial creativity.[11]

In the remainder of this chapter, I would like to accomplish three tasks. First, drawing upon my experience teaching contracts to first-year law students, I will make a case for why we should consider Anglo-American common law a well-functioning Maclntyrean tradition, which operates in ways that confirm Stout's general thesis in *Democracy and Tradition*. Second, I will examine the relationship of tradition and authority, which raises neuralgic questions for both secular and religious traditions. Third, I will focus in more detail on one particular case, showing how it grapples with moral issues of enduring interest to all members of our democratic polity, whether they are religious believers or not. All the cases I will discuss are included (in abridged form) in the book from which I teach, *Problems in Contract Law: Cases and Materials*.[12]

Contract Law and MacIntyrean Tradition Theory

What is a tradition? According to Maclntyre, it is "an historically extended, socially embodied argument, and an argument precisely in part about the goods which constitute that tradition."[13] The goods of a tradition are embedded in its constitutive social practices, which are sustained through time by institutions created for that purpose. Virtues, in his view, are those dispositions of character that enable us to identify and realize the goods internal to those practices.

The American judicial system, in my opinion should be viewed as an institution that sustains a uniquely important social practice having to do with the systematic identification, promotion, and protection of the goods internal to the American democratic tradition. Its importance, and its uniqueness, lies in the fact that a key task of judges in common law systems is precisely to give explicit articulation to those goods and to prioritize them in situations of conflict. Maclntyre writes that among the virtues "whose importance is perhaps most obvious when it is least present" is "the virtue of having an adequate sense of the traditions to which one belongs or which confront one."[14] This observation is most useful with respect to the development of the tradition of Anglo-American common law.

In *Whose Justice? Which Rationality?*, MacIntyre argues that the notion of rationality promulgated by the Enlightenment, which requires the subsumption of cases under universally applicable principles, "made us for the most part blind to . . . a conception of rational enquiry as embodied in a tradition."[15] In my judgment, one of the tasks of law professors is to initiate first-year students into precisely such a concept of rational inquiry. More specifically, I believe common law reasoning exemplifies four features of tradition-constituted inquiry that MacIntyre believes to be largely absent from moral discourse in liberal societies.

First, the common law tradition employs an essentially historical understanding of rational inquiry and justification. "To justify is to narrate how the argument has gone so far,"[16]—so does an understanding of judicial decision making rooted in the common law, which requires the judge to situate his or her opinion in the context of relevant precedent.

Second, MacIntyre emphasizes that "from the standpoint of tradition-constituted and tradition-constitutive inquiry, what a particular doctrine claims is always a matter of how precisely it was in fact advanced, of the linguistic particularities of its formulation, of what in that time and place had to be denied, if it was to be asserted, of what was at that time and place presupposed by its assertion, and so on."[17] What common law judges do in considering whether and how to extend a legal doctrine to a new set of facts is to consider precisely the set of factors that MacIntyre identifies. Consequently, to be able to argue that a particular decision rendered in the past should serve (or not serve) as precedent for the case to be decided here and now, law students must learn to parse judicial formulations of legal doctrines, to make explicit the background assumptions tacitly held by those who first articulated those doctrines, and to articulate in a nuanced way how those assumptions hold or do not hold with respect to the case at hand.

Third, MacIntyre notes that "rationality itself, whether theoretical or practical, is a concept with a history: indeed, since there are a diversity of traditions of enquiry, with histories, there are, so it will turn out, rationalities rather than rationality, just as it will also turn out that there are justices rather than justice."[18] In my view, this recognition is at the core of the Anglo-American common law system. In deciding cases in contract law, for example, most judges are aware that they are developing a rich and nuanced understanding of commutative justice that is embedded in *our* culture, *our* tradition, which may not reflect the tradition and culture of others on every point. For example, the Anglo-American legal tradition has always treated land—and property interests in land—with particular care and concern. Each piece of real estate is presumed to be unique and irreplaceable, even if it is but a tiny lot in an unimaginative, anonymous suburban development. Consequently, courts generally and routinely award specific performance in breach-of-contract cases involving sales of real estate (for example, by ordering the actual transfer of the land), despite the fact that in most other cases, nonbreaching parties can get only monetary damages.[19] Other legal traditions are more inclined to award specific performance in other types of cases, even as they are less inclined to see land as uniquely special.

Moreover, the study of Anglo-American common law concretely demonstrates a key aspect of MacIntyre's thesis that is hard to grasp in the abstract: the way in which conceptions of justice and conceptions of practical rationality are intimately intertwined in the context of the development of a moral tradition. The common law of contracts deals with three central issues: (1) which of the many implicit and explicit promises that people make to one another in the course of their lives merit legal enforcement?; (2) what counts as the breach of enforceable promises and what counts as excusable nonperformance?; and (3) how should courts respond to breached promises in order to ameliorate the injury to the nonbreaching party? Broadly speaking, these are questions of commutative justice, although questions of distributive justice also enter into the picture, given the use of common financial resources to maintain the judicial system. The standard of "reasonableness" shapes judicial responses to all three questions.

For example, consider the doctrine of promissory estoppel. As I noted briefly in the last chapter, its focus is the concept of reliance. According to Section 90 of the Restatement (Second) of Contracts, this doctrine specifies that "a promise which the promisor should *reasonably* expect to induce action or forbearance on the part of the promisee or a third person and which does induce such action or forbearance is binding if *injustice* can be avoided only by enforcement of the promise. The remedy granted for breach may be limited as *justice* requires."[20] The Restatement is not itself law; it is a distillation of the flesh-and-blood body of case law into skeletal principles by the American Law Institute—an advisory body comprised of eminent legal academics, practicing lawyers, and judges.[21] The meanings of "reasonably," "justice," and "injustice" are normatively determined by judges and juries, who draw upon a wide range of social norms in making their determinations in countless particular cases. Moreover, the meanings of these terms are ineluctably connected. It is not a violation of commutative justice to deny recovery to someone who unreasonably relies on a promise. What counts as *unreasonable* reliance on a promise? A contemporary example would be someone who relied upon the "puffery" in a late-night television infomercial—its more or less explicit assurances of a totally transformed life—in making a decision to purchase a weight-loss system or an exercise machine. Competent adults in our capitalistic society are expected to recognize puffery for what it is and make their decisions accordingly.[22]

The foregoing observation leads naturally to MacIntyre's fourth and final claim about the concept of tradition-constituted inquiry: it "cannot be elucidated apart from its exemplifications."[23] By this claim, MacIntyre clearly means to say that the broad idea of tradition-constituted inquiry as such cannot be understood without taking specific traditions as examples. But the claim could also be understood more narrowly to mean that what counts as rational inquiry *within* a particular tradition cannot be understood without looking at the particular questions and issues that its adherents have pondered within the course of its development. The narrow claim, in my view, is equally true; in order to honor that truth, I will closely examine a well-known contracts case later in this chapter.

Now, however, I will turn to four particular features of tradition-constituted inquiry that the first-year law students must master to become successful in their chosen profession. These features are (1) the relationship of rules and facts in common law cases; (2) the importance of understanding the foundational narratives of contract law; (3) the need to move beyond both skepticism about legal reasoning and the quest for an unattainable certainty about the law; and (4) the role of authority in the development of the law. Neither MacIntyre nor Stout would be surprised that introducing today's students to the operation of tradition-constituted inquiry is not an easy task; it requires disabusing them of a number of preconceptions about what the law is and what the law should be.

Students typically enroll in law school with serious misconceptions about the habits of reasoning characteristically associated with being a lawyer. As someone who teaches the common law of contracts to first-year students, it is part of my job to dispel these ideas. The first misconception concerns the process of legal reasoning. What new law students expect that they will be doing is accurately captured in Stout's discussion of quandary ethics in chapter 7 of *Democracy and Tradition:* they want to learn general principles and rules under which they can subsume cases.

Stout notes, "[w]hen ethical judgment is conceived simply as an attempt to subsume cases under principles, human beings can appear in ethical discourse only in relatively abstract and generalized terms. The project of subsumption requires thin description of selves and cases."[24]

The same holds true for legal judgment. Students can maintain their illusory conception of legal judgment as the subsumption of cases only if they ignore or minimize the wealth of facts that shape and contextualize the articulation of principles and rules in the common law. Not surprisingly, however, there is a highly profitable industry that markets study guides to first-year students by playing to their disastrous preconceptions in this regard. Companies such as Emmanuel's and Gilbert's sell outlines of first-year courses that present legal doctrine in bare-bones form (sometimes called the "black-letter law"), containing only thin descriptions of the facts of the cases they discuss. Seduced by the apparent simplicity of the outlines, some first-year students think they can streamline the process of becoming a lawyer by memorizing the rules those outlines contain, to construct for themselves a legal "toolkit" that then can be applied to "fix" any legal problem with which they are presented.

As they usually discover when they receive their grades on the first set of exams, such students are sadly mistaken. A major reason why contracts professors require their students to read cases is to teach them how facts and rules are not only inseparable but also mutually interpreting. The process of legal reasoning is complicated; it is not completely captured either by the linear process of applying rules to facts or by the analogical process of drawing comparisons between factual circumstances. The black-letter laws (the rules) matter, but the facts shape the way a rule is understood, not merely by justifying an exception at the margins but also more integrally by affecting the breadth, depth, reach, and strength of a rule.

Facts make a rule multidimensional. Because legal reasoning is multidimensional, it cannot be graphed linearly, or even on a two-dimensional x/y axis. One cannot realistically expect to formulate a completely exhaustive series of legal rules with well-defined exceptions. Different aspects of a superficially similar situation—including character, place, and circumstance—can combine with one another in different ways to yield different legal judgments. Sometimes, the most important question is not how to apply the rule but which rule to apply, which in turn depends upon how one frames the legal question, which in turn depends upon how one perceives the total constellation of facts in light of the total constellation of the law, both statutory law and common law. Ultimately, the successful resolution of hard cases requires judgment—the judgment of one who is *phronimos tō nomō*—one who is wise with respect to the law.

So how does one prepare students to enter this tradition in a way that will allow them both to apply it and to extend it as necessary? First, it is important to note that there is an informal canon of cases taught to first-year students of contracts across the country. The cases are narratives. They function in the system of legal education in much the same way that Bible stories function in religious education or fairy tales function in the more general process of socializing a child. Through these stories, these paradigmatic cases, law students learn not just what the rules are but also who the characteristic characters are and what the characteristic plot lines are in the moral universe instantiated by contract law.[25] By reading these cases, law students learn to know the characteristic narratives well enough to "absorb the world into the text," to borrow the description of a pre- and postcritical way of making use of the biblical narrative proposed by postliberal theologians such as Hans Frei and George Lindbeck.[26] They can, in other words, begin trying to fit new scenarios into the normative worldview intricately woven by the legal cases.

Who, for example, are some of the paradigmatic characters in contract law? Sympathetic characters, characters whom courts take special pains to support and protect, include little old ladies,[27] charities of all stripes,[28] and homeowners struggling to maintain the family home.[29] Less sympathetic characters, whose actions or effects courts tend to scrutinize with particular suspicion, include insurance companies,[30] banks (particularly in transactions with clients who are individuals and not corporations),[31] and bugs (particularly when they infest a family homestead).[32]

How can one begin to describe the moral universe instantiated by contract law? In part, by paying attention to the ways in which basic principles of contract law reflect and reinforce societal understandings of how Americans ought to behave, particularly in adverse circumstances. To take but one example, in the United States contract law generally makes the breaching party pay *expectation damages* to the nonbreaching party, which are designed to put the latter in the same position it would have been in had the former fulfilled its contractual obligations.[33] At the same time, the law generally expects that the nonbreaching party will not simply curl up in a corner, defeated, after learning of the breach. Instead, the nonbreaching party is expected to take steps to *mitigate* the damages by actively pursuing alternative arrangements that will allow its original plan to be fulfilled to the extent possible.[34] Among the presuppositions of this expectation are characteristically American assumptions about how one should face adversity. As the almost mythical stories of the pioneers who settled the West demonstrate, we Americans expect to see independence, ingenuity, and determination in the face of unexpected hardship, not fatalistic defeatism.

Another way to discern the moral universe instantiated by contract law is by paying attention to the factual details that judges include in their opinions—details that are irrelevant from a narrowly doctrinal point of view, but entirely relevant from the perspective of someone who is trying to resolve a dispute between two parties in a substantively just way. For example, in *Katz v. Danny Dare, Inc.* (1980),[35] students encounter a situation in which the president of a company promised an employee a pension, in an attempt to induce him to retire; relying on that promise, the employee relinquished his position. When the employee started working part time for another company, the president of the first company tried to reduce the pension. The employee sued. In the opinion, which found for the employee, the judge mentioned that (1) the employee's need to retire was precipitated by an injury he received by trying to prevent a robbery at work; and (2) the employee was the brother-in-law of the president of the company. Neither of these facts is strictly relevant to the outcome of the case. Nonetheless, the first fact affects our sense of the underlying moral value of the promise, and the second fact answers the question why it might have been in the interest of the president of the company to convince the employee to retire voluntarily rather than firing him outright, which the president would have been legally permitted to do. Taken together, these facts indicate that the promise of the pension was not an entirely altruistic act; rather, it was motivated by professional gratitude and reinforced by a desire for familial peace. In short, these facts situate the legal decision within a richer, nonlegal sense of commutative justice.

Calling these superficially irrelevant details in the opinion to the attention of my students is part of my role as a law professor. To become competent lawyers, first-year students need to learn how to suspend legal norms within a broader and more diffuse set of cultural norms. All things being equal, judges and juries want to render verdicts that accord with a widely held sense of justice.

At the beginning of the year, many first-year students are convinced that attending law school will confer upon them a key that decodes an esoteric Book of Law, in which they will be able to find the single, unambiguously correct answer to every conceivable legal problem. As I briefly observed in the first chapter, a major function of the first semester of law school is to dispel not only the expectation of such certainty but also the desire for it. First, students learn that common law judges do not only interpret the law; they also make it. They see that "the law of the case" is not delivered from on high, but is simply one judge's account of the obligations of commutative justice as they apply to the contesting parties before the bench, in light of the parties' own agreement and the background legal and moral norms of the society. Second, students learn that in many cases, these judgments are neither uncontestable nor uncontested by people of good will. There may be a number of legal arguments to be made on behalf of the plaintiff and on behalf of the defendant, some of which are adequately treated in the opinion, and others of which are not. Third, many cases are not clear. No one legal theory of obligation may fit perfectly; three or four theories may fit more or less well. Fourth, some cases turn on legal doctrines whose scope and reach can seem so uncertain as to be almost arbitrary.[36]

At the end of the first semester, most students have given up their expectation that the law offers them certainty. In fact, many have swung to the opposite extreme, adopting a deep cynicism toward legal reasoning that holds there is no way of rationally evaluating the competing arguments that may be raised in connection with a legal case. What they go on to learn in the second semester is that even if there is rarely an unarguably correct response to a legal problem worth its salt, there are always clearly incorrect responses. Moreover, there frequently are responses that can be identified as relatively better or worse, according to (1) the response's ability to identify and account for the relevant facts; (2) its coherence with the broader patterns of characters, plots, norms, and values developed in the case law; and (3) its practical workability, both for the parties directly involved and as precedent for future parties and courts.

In my view, the process of disabusing first-year law students of their initial, illusory desire for certainty about legal judgments, as well as the cynicism about legal reasoning that frequently arises after they lose their illusions, bears a striking resemblance to Stout's attempts to disabuse his readers of both moral foundationalism and moral skepticism, which also feed off each other, as he shows us. When students enter law school, they fantasize about making legal arguments on behalf of their clients that are akin to the "superpower view of defense" described so memorably in Stout's "Lexicon of Postmodern Philosophy" at the end of *Ethics after Babel*. They believe that you "have adequately defended a position 'only if you can annihilate the other side' "; they hope to make ' "arguments so powerful they set up reverberations in the brain: if the person refuses to accept the conclusion, he dies.' "[37] When they realize that such arguments are not available, they fall into despair, utterly skeptical about the possibility of ever making a true legal argument. Law, they now conclude, is not "objective"; it is purely "subjective." It is completely malleable to the purposes of the lawyers and judges who use it to achieve their own ends.

What is required of a law professor at this point is to offer a type of Wittgensteinian therapy of the sort advocated and practiced by Stout; my task, in other words, is to help them see that their despair has been precipitated by a desire for a type of certainty regarding the law's requirements that is both illusory and unnecessary. Instead, like soccer, the common law requires of its practitioners "objectivity in the context of a social practice."[38] With hard work and a little luck, law students will end up adopting an approach to truth and justification in legal reasoning that looks a great deal like the modest, pragmatic approach to truth and justification in ethical reasoning that Stout defends in *Democracy and Tradition*. "What I am calling pragmatism here is not to be interpreted as a form of subjectivism.... It offers a *social* theory of moral objectivity—according to which both objective ethical norms and the subjectivity of those who apply them are made possible in part by social interactions among individuals."[39]

As Stout notes, this approach requires students to pay due attention to the role of both subjectivity and objectivity in creating the norms embedded in social practices. The practices are subjective in that they are not delivered from on high, but are created and maintained by human beings. Judges, and the lawyers who argue before them, must take responsibility for their contribution to the social practices of the law. It is important, in my view, for law students to study cases in which there has been a conspicuous failure to take such responsibility, with the result that the practice of the legal system is corrupted by political expediency. A timely example is *Korematsu v. United States* (1944),[40] in which the U.S. Supreme Court upheld the constitutionality of the federal government's practice of severely restricting the freedom of citizens of Japanese descent during the Second World War. The restrictions were justified, according to the Court, because of the exigencies of war and the threat to national security.

At the same time, like score-keeping in soccer or baseball, "score-keeping" in law requires compliance with a number of objective constraints—that is, constraints directing one's attention to the question at hand, and not to one's own feelings about it. As Stout notes, these "constraints are object-directed in the sense that they involve attentiveness to something being investigated as well as disciplined avoidance of wishful thinking, rationalization, and related intrusion of 'merely subjective' factors."[41] If the legal system is to function well, it is crucial that judges (and lawyers) demonstrate precisely this sort of objectivity about the law. In fact, a commitment to precisely this sort of objectivity is necessary to achieve the goods internal to the practice of legal adjudication in highly politically, financially, or emotionally charged situations.

Furthermore, if it succeeds, the Wittgensteinian therapy practiced by law professors upon first-year students will give them a different way of understanding the task of judges in hard cases. As Stout notes, it is the hard cases, the controversial cases, that engender the nagging suspicion that "the decision of whether or not to revise a norm is a matter of subjective choice," and that "the entire practice is, at bottom, a reflection of arbitrary will, a subjective affair."[42] By carefully working through the cases, both the facts and the law, students come to see that "in such cases what we are actually faced with is a conflict or balance of rational considerations, not an absence of such considerations."[43] To put it another way, the hard cases are hard for a reason. Furthermore,

> "[t]he endeavor of weighing those considerations can be an objective affair (in the only sense worth bothering with in this context), even if it does not lead to an unambiguous result. Why? Because the considerations we are weighing direct our attention away from our subjective states to how things and persons are in the world and how things and persons would be if we revised our norms."[44]

Good common law judges would recognize their life's work in Stout's description.

Tradition and Authority

What is the role of authority in a modern democratic culture? This is a question that has preoccupied Jeffrey Stout; his first book argues that "modern thought was born in a crisis of authority, took shape in flight from authority, and aspired from the start to autonomy from all traditional influence whatsoever."[45] Can authority have any role in shaping ethical judgments in a modern democracy? In *Democracy and Tradition*, Stout contends that "[t]he only defensible form of democratic community is one in which ethical authority is treated as an entitlement (to deference) that one must earn by repeatedly demonstrating one's reliability as an ethical judge."[46]

In my view, the central question here is the relationship between what I will call extrinsic authority and intrinsic authority. By "extrinsic authority" I mean that from which, according to Stout, modern thought has fled; it is the authority that is based on position or power. Stout describes it in the following way: "Where the default position in a given community is that the ethical judgments of those in ecclesial or political office are correct, we have a pattern of deference to one kind of authority. The authoritarian extreme is reached whenever such a default position is treated as indefeasible and the authority is treated as self-interpreting."[47]

"Intrinsic authority," in contrast, is the name I give to the authority that one earns by demonstrating one's capacity for making judgments about the relevant social practice—in particular, about the goods internal to the practice. Competent judges in music, soccer, or ethics are able to appreciate excellent instantiations of the goods internal to their respective practices. A competent judge, in Stout's terms, is "someone who has become adept at the patterns of approval and disapproval essential to a social practice involving kinds of things taken to be worthy of love or admiration."[48] The process of developing into a competent judge about a relevant practice takes training, time, and experience. One becomes a competent judge by demonstrating one's ability to make assessments in cases that are increasingly difficult, but that have a clear resolution according to the standards of the practice. After reliable success in making many judgments about cases commonly recognized to be susceptible to more or less clear resolution, other people start asking one's opinion about the truly difficult cases—cases that do not have a clear answer on any account. One becomes a *phronimos*, someone who, as Aristotle acknowledged, is the best guide to the proper resolution of perplexing cases.

Stout is emphatic that intrinsic authority has a prominent place within the American democratic tradition. He is clearly worried, however, about giving too prominent a role to extrinsic authority—he believes it to be the hallmark of an undemocratic and authoritarian tradition. At some points, Stout seems to suggest that the two types of authority may not be compatible, even if they are not mutually exclusive. For example, Stout cites approvingly Susan Moller Okin's critique of Alasdair MacIntyre: "[H]e gives conflicting accounts of what a tradition *is*. At times he describes it as a defining context, stressing the authoritative nature of its 'texts'; at times he talks of a tradition as 'living,' as a 'not-yet-completed narrative,' as an argument about the goods that constitute the tradition."[49]

But no tradition, even a democratic tradition, can long survive without some form of extrinsic authority. Why not? Here it is important to attend to what MacIntyre has to say about the relationship between practices and institutions in the life of a tradition:

> Institutions are characteristically and necessarily concerned with what I have called external goods. They are involved in acquiring money and other material goods; they are structured in terms of power and status, and they distribute money, power and status as rewards. Nor could they do otherwise if they are to sustain not only themselves, but also the practices of which they are the bearers. For no practices can survive for any length of time unsustained by institutions.[50]

Extrinsic authority—the authority to settle a disputed question arising within a practice that is based solely or primarily upon one's position or status—is in fact the authority associated with institutions. As MacIntyre would predict, extrinsic authority is essential if we are to sustain a practice through time. More specifically, such authority is practically necessary to settle disputes that can seriously interrupt, if not completely impede, the orderly conduct of the practice. In sports, for example, we need an umpire to make an authoritative decision about whether a goal was scored in a relatively short time if we want to be sure that we will be able to continue with the game. At the same time, as MacIntyre recognizes, extrinsic authority can threaten the integrity of the practices whose life it purportedly sustains, particularly if those who exercise that authority are not competent judges of the goods internal to those practices, or if they are moved less by love of those internal goods than by desire for external goods such as money, power, and prestige.

Any tradition, therefore, must negotiate the tensions between the practices that constitute it and the institutions that sustain it over time. How do we go about doing so? First, we need to rule out ways of identifying and enabling extrinsic authority that corrodes the practices of nearly any worthwhile intellectual and moral tradition. We would not want, for example, to institutionalize a system in which extrinsic authority is for sale to the highest bidder. Second, we need to consider what forms of extrinsic authority are more likely to reflect, confirm, and preserve the understanding of intrinsic authority that has developed in our particular tradition, given its practices and understanding of the goods internal to those practices.

Where should we look if we want to examine how to structure extrinsic authority in a way consistent with democratic values? In my view, the patterns that have developed around the adjudication of disputes at common law provide a helpful example. A cursory examination of a state trial court's civil docket demonstrates the necessity of extrinsic authority in a democratic society. Disputes need to be settled in matters other than sports. For people to get on with their lives, for example, we need someone to decide authoritatively which of two innocent buyers should be awarded the house sold to both of them by an unscrupulous seller, and which should get monetary damages to compensate for the loss. At some point, and in some way, the argument must come to an end; a decision must be made and implemented. In our legal system, this is the task of judges and juries, a task that they fulfill by virtue of their position, by virtue of their extrinsic authority.

How, then, can putting an authoritative end to an argument about justice be compatible with democratic values, which Stout rightly notes give priority to intrinsic authority rather than extrinsic authority? A close examination of the practices of the judicial system provides helpful clues to the answer. First, in our legal system, judges are lawyers, which means they have received significant socialization in the practices of the law, as I have described. Ideally, lawyers who become judges are chosen because they exhibit the virtues that enable them to appreciate and identify the goods internal to the practices of law.

Second, when one examines the legal system in some detail, one finds not an undifferentiated "deference to higher authority" but, rather, intricate patterns of deference to different types of authority about different matters. For example, consider how an appellate court reviews the decision of a trial court in a civil case. It is not a complete "do-over." The appellate court reviews findings of fact made by the jury (or the judge in cases of a bench trial) for "clear error," recognizing that these findings frequently involve judgments of the credibility of witnesses that the appellate court is not in a position to question.[51] Judgments of law are, however, reviewed *de novo*.[52] Why? In my view, for two very good reasons. Trial court judges are extremely busy keeping numerous disputes moving through the legal system; they generally do not have the time to devote themselves to the extensive study and deliberation necessary to resolve hard questions of law. Moreover, while not mutually exclusive, the central virtues of a good trial court judge are different from those of a good appellate court judge; roughly speaking, one set of virtues focuses on "street smarts," while the other concentrates more on "book smarts."

Third, the culture of our judicial system incorporates high regard for the mutual reason-giving that Stout believes to be characteristic of democratic ethical practice; in fact, it would be an understatement to say that judges are "disposed to hold one another responsible in the exchange of reasons."[53] Furthermore, our judicial system's structure also incorporates a clear recognition that any legal judgment—rendered by any extrinsic legal authority—might be mistaken. Cases on appeal are generally decided by majority vote of a panel of judges sitting as the appellate court. A judge in the majority writes the opinion of the court, in which reasons are given for the judgment rendered. Yet a judge who does not agree with the majority is free to write a dissenting opinion rejecting the majority's decision, or a concurring opinion that proposes an alternate legal rationale for reaching the same result. These dissenting and concurring opinions are published together with the majority opinion, a practice that not only allows but also facilitates reconsideration of the relevant legal issue at a later date by a higher court (if one exists) or by the same court at a later point in time. In my view, this habit of publishing all opinions rendered in significant appellate cases is a practical instantiation of the commonsense view of the difference between truth and justification that Stout defends.[54] It also helps inculcate the epistemic humility that Stout recognizes is the appropriate response to this distinction.[55]

Syester v. Banta: *A Case Study*

The thesis of this chapter is that the Anglo-American common law, particularly the law of contracts, instantiates a substantively rich MacIntyrean tradition that is neither dependent upon nor hostile to highly particular claims about the existence or nature of God. In the first part of this chapter I made the case for considering the common law a MacIntyrean tradition. In this part, I want to illustrate its moral richness by considering *Syester v. Banta,* a case decided by the Iowa Supreme Court in 1965. A slightly abridged version of the case is included in the case book from which I teach; I offer it here in order to illustrate how fraud or misrepresentation on the part of one party to a contract can affect its enforceability.[56]

The Iowa Supreme Court begins its account of the facts underlying this 1965 case, which involves a suit for fraud and misrepresentation against an Arthur Murray Dance Studio in Des Moines, in the following way: "Plaintiff is a widow living alone. She has no family. Her exact age does not appear but a former employee of defendants and a favorite dancing instructor of plaintiff testified "that during the period from 1957 through the fall of 1960 she was 68 years old."[57] She is also, we are told, a "coffee girl" at a local cafeteria. From 1954 to 1960, Mrs. Syester's local Arthur Murray Dance Studio sold her over 4,000 hours of dance lessons, at a price of a little over $29,000. That is a lot of dance lessons; taking them for 40 hours a week, it would require about two years to use them all up. Furthermore, that is a lot of money; in 2015 dollars, it is about $232,000.[58]

How did this situation transpire? As the court describes, the dance studio required its instructors to engage in high-pressure sales techniques— to use a combination of flattery and pressure to convince clients to purchase expensive contracts for dance lessons. The court wryly notes:

> Theoretically, for advancing proficiency in dancing (the jury must have thought that $29,000 had something to do with it), plaintiff was awarded a Bronze Medal, then a Silver Medal and then a Gold Medal. These awards were given plaintiff all in the same year although defendants' manager testified that it takes approximately two to four years to qualify for a Bronze Medal, five to seven years for a Silver Medal and anytime after 1200 hours a student could qualify for the Gold Medal.[59]

Finally, the studio tried to sell her a package of Gold Star dancing lessons, which, as her instructor testified, purported to teach "English quick step and is the type of dancing done by Ginger Rogers and Fred Astaire only about twice as difficult." The lessons were started, despite the fact that the instructor was "faking it," as he later admitted in court.[60]

What prompted Mrs. Syester to spend so much money on dance lessons? The court implies that she had quite a crush on Mr. Carey, her dance instructor. "He was about twenty-five years old and apparently quite charming and fascinating to plaintiff. She gave him a diamond ring for his birthday in 1960."[61] The court also suggests that it was the studio's decision to fire Mr. Carey in the fall of 1960 that precipitated Mrs. Syester's increasing dissatisfaction with her arrangement with it. This dissatisfaction culminated in her own decision to hire a lawyer to sue the studio in January 1961. The court's hypothesis seems correct, especially in light of the fact that the studio rehired Mr. Carey with the sole purpose of convincing her to drop the suit. It took some doing, but he was ultimately successful. The court quotes extensively from Mr. Carey's testimony at the trial:

> I told her that I was going to the party [at the studio] and I would save her some waltzes. I knew this was her favorite dance. And I felt that if she would pass up this waltz, she was not interested in dancing. She did not come to the studio so the next day I went down to Bishop's [the cafeteria where Mrs. Syester worked] and told her she disappointed me very much. Then I started talking about all of the lessons she and I had had and all of the months we had danced and the fun we had together. I told her how wonderful she had done. I painted word pictures and things so she could see this.[62]

The word pictures worked. Mrs. Syester discharged her lawyer, dropped her lawsuit, and resumed her waltzes with Mr. Carey. She signed two contractual documents broadly releasing the studio from liability, one in March 1960 in exchange for $6,090 (which she received) and the other in January 1963 for $4,000 (which she did not). But in March 1963, the situation soured again. Mrs. Syester filed a new claim for monetary damages against the studio. The opinon does not say what went precipitated this new lawsuit.

To be successful in her claim against the studio, Mrs. Syester had to clear two legal hurdles. First, she had to find a way to invalidate the two releases that she had signed, which legally absolved the studio of all wrongdoing against her in exchange for a specified monetary compensation. Second, she had to devise a strategy for invalidating the underlying contracts for the sale of dance lessons. Despite the outrageousness of the facts, neither hurdle was particularly easy to surmount.

With respect to the first hurdle, the court says:

> The issue involving the releases was essentially factual. That plaintiff was easily influenced appears without question. The consideration for the first release was wholly inadequate. It was only a partial return of an unconscionable overcharge. The consideration for the second release was not paid. The evidence was such that the jury could find that there was such a concerted effort, lacking in propriety, to obtain the releases as to constitute fraudulent overreaching. The jury obviously concluded that there was a predatory play on the vanity and the credulity of an old lady.[63]

There are, however, several difficulties with this analysis. First, courts tend to look favorably on the execution of valid releases, not only because they are settlement agreements worked out by the parties themselves but also because they conserve the resources of the judicial system. Second, courts do not normally look at the sufficiency of consideration in evaluating the validity of a contract. Provided the terms of the contract are bargained for by parties who are competent to contract, so that each party receives from the exchange something it believes to be of value, the requirement for consideration is satisfied.[64] Third, Mrs. Syester was not only legally competent at the time she signed the releases but she was also originally represented by counsel in her dealings with the studio.[65] Fourth, it is doubtful that most of Mr. Carey's blandishments rise to the level of legally cognizable fraud.

Legally speaking, fraud is at the heart of the case, as becomes clear when we turn to Mrs. Syester's second hurdle to recovery, which is making a successful challenge to the validity of the underlying dance contracts. In a nutshell, a plaintiff must prove four elements in order to sustain a claim of fraud sufficient to invalidate a contract. A successful claim requires proof that the defendant made (1) a false statement about a material aspect of the transaction, (2) with intent to deceive, (3) which was reasonably relied upon by the plaintiff, (4) to the effect that if she had not believed the statement, she would not have entered into the contract.[66]

Mrs. Syester's first problem is that it would not have been reasonable for her to rely upon the vast majority of fraudulent statements made to her by the studio's owners or employees, either in the context of the initial sale of the lessons or in the context of deliberating whether to sign the release. As an example of a fraudulent statement, the court points to the fact that Mrs. Syester was repeatedly told that she could become a professional dancer.[67] But clearly, no sixty-eight-year-old woman who has never danced before—in fact, no eighteen-year-old woman who has never danced before—could reasonably rely on that statement.[68]

Mrs. Syester's second problem is that it is not clear she actually relied on the fraudulent statement in committing herself to the dance contracts. Did she really take dance lessons in order to become a professional dancer? Did she really believe she was going to become a professional dancer? Very likely not. As the court's own narrative suggests, she took the dance lessons because she was lonely. In fact, the one statement that probably convinced her to drop the first lawsuit was probably the stone-cold truth. Mr. Carey, the young object of her affection, testified: "I told her that she did not need an attorney; after all Mrs. Theiss [the wife of the studio's owner] and myself were her only friends and we wanted her back at the studio to continue with her Gold Star and reminded her of all the waltzes we would do together."[69]

So, was Agnes Syester successful in her claim against the Arthur Murray Dance Studio in Des Moines, Iowa? Astonishingly so. The Iowa Supreme Court upheld the jury's verdict for $14,300 in actual damages and $40,000 in punitive damages; the latter are awarded only when the defendant's acts constitute "malicious or willful and wanton conduct."[70]

Softening the standard, the Iowa Supreme Court states that "malice may be inferred where defendant's act is illegal or improper; where the nature of the illegal act is such as to negative [*sic.*] any inference of feeling toward the person injured, and is in fact consistent with a complete indifference on the part of defendant."[71] The punitive damage award is startling; punitive damages are not normally given in connection with a contracts case, no matter how outrageous the breach. It is especially startling because the outrageous behavior of the defendant was arguably not the tort itself; as I have argued, the claim of fraud is highly questionable. And indeed, the court indicated that it was upholding the award of punitive damage award because "the evidence of greed and avariciousness on the part of defendants is shocking to our sense of justice as it obviously was to the jury."[72]

Mrs. Syester's claims of fraud are undeniably shaky with respect to most of the assertions made to her by the dance studio. Arguably, the jury was incorrect in crediting those claims. Why, then, did the Iowa Supreme Court uphold the jury's awards of actual and (large) punitive damages? Here, it is important to remember that because the court was sitting as an appellate court, it was not permitted to overturn a jury verdict unless it judged that no reasonable fact-finder could have reached the jury's conclusion.[73]

What allowed the court to judge that a reasonable jury might (just barely) have found that the contractual arrangements to provide dance lessons to Mrs. Syester were procured by fraud? The key, in my view, is the fact that one transaction—the sale of a course of Gold Star dance lessons in English tap dancing—was clearly based on a fraudulent assertion about what was being supplied. For, the instructor admitted to the trial court that he had been "faking it." So the studio's assertion (express or implied) that it could and would teach her to tap dance like the English was undeniably both false and intended to deceive her. This fraud could reasonably be seen by the jury as tainting the studio's other dealings with her, whether by making it far more likely that the studio had intentionally made other misrepresentations or by deepening other evidence of its avarice.

So, *Syester v. Banta* shows not only the intimate relationship between law and facts but also the intimate relationship between and among facts themselves. The fact that one transaction was undeniably fraudulent can significantly influence a reasonable view of the other transactions, and could even make a not unreasonable impact on the appellate court's interpretation of its duty of deference to jury verdicts.

As I hope to have illustrated by a close reading of the case, the saga of Agnes Syester offers us a rich moral narrative of the sort that would satisfy Maclntyre, Hauerwas, and Stout. Character, plot, and circumstance are all developed in detail. In fact, the ultimate decision of the Iowa Supreme Court to uphold the jury verdict is only intelligible in the context of such detail. Moreover, the opinion broadens the possibility for moral discussion in a liberal democratic society in a fashion that Stout would find highly congenial.

What, then, does this case teach us about the moral norms embedded in Anglo-American contract law? As I tell my students, the short lesson is that the little old lady always wins. Why? Perhaps because in our culture, influenced as it is by Jewish and Christian scriptures, the widow is a paradigmatic personification of the vulnerable, along with the orphan and the stranger.[74] This is not always the case, of course. But the fact that a party to a dispute is a little old lady will strongly affect perceptions of both the judge and the jury—something a good attorney must take into account in framing the client's case.

The lesson of intermediate length is that specific facts always exert moral pressure on abstract rules and categories in the context of practical, legal–moral decision making. This opinion involves the rule that a successful case for fraud requires the victim to demonstrate reasonable reliance upon the fraudulent claim; it also implicates the law's categorical division of human beings into two clear categories—those who are competent to contract and those who are incompetent. Yet the relevant rule and the relevant category were reshaped under the pressure of the facts. The case makes clear that our common morality does not easily acquiesce to the acts of "greed and avariciousness," at least when such acts involve taking advantage of the vulnerabilities of other persons owing to age, circumstances, or physical condition. The court's opinion tacitly recognizes that we are not disembodied choosers, contracting from a position of equal strength. Instead, we are embodied choosers, and the vulnerabilities of our embodiment can bring weaknesses that should not be exploited. MacIntyre's work is relevant here, not *After Virtue*, but *Dependent Rational Animals*.[75]

But *Syester v. Banta* also invites us to consider a long lesson, which reinforces the difference between truth and justification, and it calls for both moral and epistemological humility. Full consideration of the case requires us to consider how well our categorizations of vulnerable and invulnerable parties hold up under scrutiny. Are those categories too broad or too narrow? Are they based in objective observations (objective, that is, in Stout's sense), or are they simply stereotypes or projections of our unexamined assumptions and feelings? Suppose, for example, that this case had involved a sixty-eight-year-old man, who had a crush on a twenty-five-year-old female dance instructor. Would our moral reactions be the same? Or would we simply say that he is a "dirty old man" able and willing to pay for the companionship of a young, attractive woman? One might be tempted to say that we should always err on the side of categorizing someone as vulnerable. But as feminist legal theorists and scholars of critical race theory have reminded us, many laws that have restricted the ability of women and racial minorities to flourish have been enacted under the guise of protecting them against their own vulnerabilities and defective judgment. Thinking about this case at its deepest level requires us to ponder our fundamental societal commitments to equality and well-being, as well as the tensions that can arise between the two values. There are no easy answers.

Generally speaking, when theologians and philosophers reflect on the relationship of law and morality, they focus on the question "How, if at all, should we use the law to impose moral norms?" or its close variant "If a particular activity is immoral, should it be illegal?" In many cases, these questions unreflectively presuppose that the law's function is not to articulate morals but simply to enforce them. I hope that my reflections in this chapter have suggested that such a picture of the law's role with respect to morality is too simplistic. Courts, particularly those hearing cases in the great common law subjects, do in fact discern and articulate the requirements of our common morality as they bear upon particular cases. Furthermore, close analysis of the judicial opinions in tort and contract law frequently reveals a rich and subtle sensibility on the part of the judges writing those opinions—a sensibility that takes account of not only the relevant rules and principles but also the relevant virtues and vices, as well as the relevant strengths and vulnerabilities, of the contested parties. In my judgment, these opinions deserve more attention as a source of moral wisdom from secular and religious ethicists alike, in large part because they focus our attention on the convergences in our moral judgments rather than merely accentuating our differences.

IN THE NEXT section of the book, I will continue to draw upon specific cases to illuminate different facets of an enduring problematic in theological ethics: the relationship between love and justice. As John Noonan has indicated so eloquently, one pressing form of the problematic is the tension between attending to the needs and experiences of particular persons, on the one hand, and formulating impersonal rules that will apply to a wide variety of persons, both seen and unseen. Engaging Gene Outka, Margaret Farley, and Paul Ramsey will clarify the tension, although not resolve it.

PART II

Love, Justice, and Law

4

Neighbor Love and Legal Precedent

Engaging Gene Outka

WE ALL KNOW the parable of the Good Samaritan.[1] A man was beaten by robbers and left for dead on his way to Jericho. Two passers-by, a priest and a Levite, crossed to the other side of the road rather than help him. But a Samaritan man who saw him was moved to pity. After bandaging the injured man's wounds, the Samaritan contributed his own funds to pay an innkeeper to nurse the man back to health.

As Robert Wuthnow has shown, despite its social and cultural familiarity, many Americans are fuzzy not only about the details of the parable but also about its framing narrative.[2] Rereading that narrative again in the Gospel of Luke, it reminded me of the contest of wits and wills between teachers and students familiar to anyone who has spent time in law school. The parable, we are told, is elicited by the question of a *lawyer*; we are told he "stood up to test Jesus." He strikes me as young, earnest, and ambitious—someone whom those of us who teach first-year law students might call a "gunner."

"Teacher," he says, "what must I do to inherit eternal life?" Jesus, evidently a natural expert in the Socratic method, immediately throws the question back to the lawyer. "What is written in the law? What do you read there?" The lawyer answers, "You shall love the Lord your God with all your heart, and with all your soul, and with all your strength, and with all your mind; and your neighbor as yourself." After acknowledging the answer to be correct, Jesus tries to exit the conversation and move on. He responds, "You have given the right answer; do this, and you will live." But the lawyer is not ready to let the matter go. "Wanting to justify himself," we are told by Luke, and evidently wanting to impress Jesus, he asks a follow-up question: "And who is my neighbor?" It is in response to that second question that Jesus gives us the parable of the Good Samaritan.

Three observations come to mind. First, Jesus reframes the question in responding to it: After finishing the parable, Jesus asks the lawyer which of the three passers-by "was a neighbor to the man who fell into the hands of the robbers." As his acceptance of the lawyer's response, "the one who showed him mercy," indicates, the question Jesus actually addressed in the parable is "What does being a neighbor require of us?"

Second, the lawyer's actual question—"Who is my neighbor?"—is never directly answered by Jesus. Nor, for that matter, are more advanced conundrums flowing from that question, such as "What should I do if there is a conflict between myself and a neighbor?" or "How do I handle a dispute between two or more neighbors?"

Third, it is difficult to avoid the suspicion that Jesus—the consummate law teacher or rabbi—saved these harder questions for the test—the life decisions made by those who claim to be his followers. These questions become even more confusing if they are asked not only with reference to individual selves and neighbors but also with reference to the communities that shape and are shaped by selves and neighbors. These communities, of course, are also shaped by law, which is one of the most important social tools for regulating relations between self and neighbors. Thus the concept of neighbor love is not irrelevant to law. Nor, for that matter, is the idea of conflict among neighbors. It is through our legal system that many of the most serious disputes between and among our neighbors, and between and among our neighbors and ourselves, are articulated, addressed, and resolved.

The first three chapters of this book examined the insights that can be gleaned by viewing both law and theological ethics as historically constituted moral traditions that operate in the manner contemplated by Alasdair MacIntyre. In chapters 4, 5, and 6, I would like to sharpen my focus, examining the fruitfulness of interdisciplinary work on matters pertaining to the relationship of love and justice. The extensive normative reflections of religious ethics on the overarching nature and purpose of human society can provide vantage points from which to critique the quotidian decisions of legislatures and courts. Conversely, the manner in which the legal system settles specific cases offers rich material with which to test and to hone more abstract theological and philosophical reflections about personal and social obligations. The fields of law and religious ethics are mutually illuminating in a number of ways.

In this chapter, my aim is to explore some of the tensions between love and justice by bringing two seemingly different perspectives into conversation: that of the distinguished Protestant ethicist Gene Outka and that of the contemporary American common law tradition, as crystallized in the strange Wisconsin case of *Watts v. Watts*.[3] No contemporary religious ethicist has thought more deeply about Christian love than has Gene Outka, first in his book *Agape*,[4] and more recently in his extended essay "Universal Love and Impartiality."[5] In that essay, which is really a small book, he makes a theocentric case for love of neighbor: Outka argues that "Love for God—as the most basic and comprehensive human love of all—includes fidelity to God in loving whom God loves."[6] In addition, he emphasizes the correspondence between the scope of divine love and the scope of our own duty to love: "[A]ll people are created, sustained, and redeemed by God. Thus, our love should correspond as far as possible to this universal scope."[7] He then goes on to analyze the extent to which the Christian call to universal love accurately can be understood as a call to impartiality. Outka devotes the bulk of his attention to examining whether universal love can be construed as impartiality between our regard for ourselves, on the one hand, and our regard for our neighbor, on the other. Yet he also addresses the question of what it would mean for universal love to be impartial vis-à-vis the conflicting claims of two or more neighbors.

The common law is a fruitful conversation partner for Outka because both employ some of the same presuppositions in order to grapple with some of the same issues. A Christian ethicist can find in it many echoes of key Christian commitments with respect to moral anthropology, such as the fundamental equality of all human beings. Moreover, the common law is regularly forced to grapple with the question of what protecting the equal dignity of human beings means in concrete and difficult circumstances. One reason these circumstances are difficult, of course, has to do with what Christian ethicists call sin. For example, the realm of contracts is the realm of promises. People do not always keep their promises. They betray and disappoint one another. In these cases, the legal system frequently has the responsibility to pick up the pieces—and to decide who gets which piece. Not only does contract law force us to deal with conflicts between two or more neighbors, it also forces us to grapple with the fact that many conflicts occur between neighbors who cannot each be assigned a halo or a pitchfork, but who are all a mixture of good and bad.

Finally, while Outka does not explicitly address the broader relationship between love and justice, the issue permeates the essay. That relationship, of course, has received a great deal of attention from Christian ethicists on other occasions, including Outka himself. The precise way in which an ethicist relates love and justice depends, of course, upon his or her definition of the terms. For example, an ethicist who endorses Anders Nygren's view of Christian love (agape) as selfless *kenosis* will likely want to stress that it operates in a very different sphere from that of justice, which operates to give each person his or her due.[8] Even an advocate of such a view of agape, however, may find it helpful to pay some attention to the requirements of justice, if only because it provides the baseline from which the self-emptying acts of agape are assessed.

Other theological accounts of the relationship between love and justice are more positive. Paul Ramsey accepted Nygren's account that agape requires self-sacrificial behavior in the case of a Christian confronted with the demands of a single neighbor. Following Augustine, however, he argued that an articulation of the demands of justice was the response of love to a conflict between two or more neighbors. Justice, on this view, is the form that love takes in social contexts and social controversies.[9]

Outka's own analytical framework offers the possibility of a richly textured relationship between love and justice. Like Ramsey, he is sympathetic to the claim that Christian love demands the pursuit of social justice, and the steadfast determination to overcome patterns of injustice that have oppressed both near and distant neighbors. Moreover, Outka's definition of love as universal regard for all those whom God loves provides additional possibilities for considering the relationship of love and justice. In the essay at hand, for example, he considers the ways in which impartiality reflects the demands of universal love of neighbor. Impartiality, of course, is an aspect of justice as well as love. One might extend Outka's questions, asking what love requires in the context of administering justice. How do the requirements of universal love shape the way we understand the demands of impartiality in specific cases?

The Wattses' Private Marriage

In my view, the common law can help us illuminate these questions, not least because general rules are developed in the context of the actual disputes of particular neighbors, whose particular names and situations remain forever tied to the rule. In order to focus upon these questions as sharply as I can, I will sacrifice breadth for depth, focusing my discussion on one case, *Watts v. Watts*.[10] Decided by the Wisconsin Supreme Court in 1987, it is included in many first-year textbooks in contract law. It is, however, equally relevant to courses on family law and statutory interpretation, since the case requires the court to determine what sort of private agreements between unmarried heterosexual couples are consistent with the legislative commitment to legal marriage as socially beneficial to the common good.[11]

Sue Ann and James Watts met in 1967, as the cultural and social revolution of the sixties moved from the coasts to the heartland. She was nineteen years old, living with her parents and working full time as a nurse's aide. Shortly after they met, James persuaded her to give up her job and her dream of becoming a nurse one day and move into an apartment that he rented. According to the court, he "indicated" that he would provide for her. Early in 1969, the couple began living together in a "marriage-like" relationship. They held themselves out to the public as husband and wife. Sue Ann took James's last name. They filed joint income tax returns and maintained joint bank accounts as husband and wife. James listed Sue Ann as his wife on medical and life insurance policies. They purchased property and took out loans as husband and wife. Moreover, they had two children together, both of whom were given James's last name.

For over a decade, Sue Ann was a good "wife" to James. She took care of the children, cleaned, cooked, washed the laundry, did the shopping, ran errands, and even maintained the lawn. She acted as his hostess at both social and business-related events. Sue Ann's commitment to his projects, it seems, was both energetic and generous. She fed and cleaned up after James and his employees while his landscaping business built a golf course. Moreover, Sue Ann performed office work at his place of business, and even started an enterprise of her own with James's sister-in-law. All these common purposes, however, were not enough to cement their loyalty to one another. By 1981, their relationship had broken down irretrievably. Sue Ann claimed that James had made the situation so intolerable that she was forced to move from her home. In addition, she asserted that he also barred her from her own place of business.

After a relationship breaks down, the sad matter of dividing the property comes up. Sue Ann claimed that since James and she had functioned like a married couple while they were together, they should function like a divorcing couple now that they were permanently separating. Because Wisconsin is a community property state, she wanted James to transfer to her half the assets they had accumulated in the course of their twelve-year relationship, including the assets of his landscaping business.

The difficulty, of course, is that they never actually *were* legally married. They did not comply with the conditions necessary to achieve legal marriage specified under Wisconsin law. What about common law marriage? Unfortunately for Sue Ann, Wisconsin had abolished common law marriage many years prior to her controversy with James. Under the applicable law, marriages contracted in violation of the specified legal requirements were void.

What about James's position? The man who had enticed nineteen-year-old Sue Ann to leave her parents' home and move in with him without so much as a dime store promise ring on her finger suddenly became a charter member of the "Family Values Club." He argued that their relationship undermined Wisconsin public policy stressing the importance of the marital relationship; consequently, the court should not only refuse to divide the property according to the provisions for divorce in the Wisconsin Family Act, it should also refuse to involve itself in such a sordid and immoral situation at all. Instead, the court should leave the money where it was—as it just so happened, entirely with him.

Where do these facts come from? Whose perspective controls their presentation? Who determines the narrative? The answers to these important questions are determined in large part by the procedure of the case: Sue Ann Watts is the plaintiff in *Watts v. Watts,* James is the defendant. Sue Ann filed a complaint setting forth these facts and seeking relief based upon a number of legal theories in the trial court. The judge dismissed the complaint for failure to state a claim upon which relief could be granted. Sue Ann then appealed the dismissal of her case to the Wisconsin Supreme Court. For purposes of considering her appeal, the higher court relied upon the version of the facts set forth in her complaint, and asked whether they constitute a valid claim for relief under any legitimate legal theory.

So, the facts presented in the opinion reflect Sue Ann's account of the situation. The narrative, however, is the Supreme Court's—the controlling majority selects, orders, and emphasizes certain facts in the course of developing the analysis of the case. We do not, therefore, have access to the essences of Sue Ann or James Watts. In the case of Sue Ann, what we have is a third-hand account. Sue Ann told her story to her lawyer, who shaped it for presentation to the court. The court, in turn, reshaped it for presentation to us. James, alas, appears to us through a lens that is even more distant and distorted. We see his character and actions entirely through Sue Ann's eyes. In essence, his lawyer's argument is that even if he had acted in precisely the beastly manner she said he did, Sue Ann would not be entitled to a penny.

Confronted with the battling Wattses, we can ask how the requirements of the command to universal love, as understood by Outka, bear upon the common law, as crystallized in the case of *Watts v. Watts*? This question, too, is very general. I think, however, we can begin to tackle it by addressing three more specific issues, each of which engages a different aspect of Outka's essay on impartiality. First, we can ask about the focus of neighbor love: Upon what aspect of the neighbor does universal love focus its regard—aspects that are unique to him or her, or aspects that are held in common with other human beings? Second, we can consider the relationship among persons, rules, and circumstances. In addressing conflicts between neighbors, to what degree should we rely upon rules and to what degree should we take into account distinguishing facts and circumstances of particular cases and people? Needless to say, this question presses important themes raised by John Noonan and discussed in the first chapter. Third, we can evaluate the consequences of an inelimnable asymmetry of agency in human social life: there are some things that agents can do voluntarily—for themselves and for their neighbors—that third-party bystanders simply cannot make them do.

Outka touches upon all three issues in his long essay, albeit in varying degrees of detail. The common law, as crystallized in *Watts*, furthers our consideration of them. It also engenders questions of its own, questions that advance our understanding of universal love and impartiality. Before going any further, however, it is necessary for me to say something about the stance or vantage point that will organize my consideration of the *Watts* case. In probing the requirements of love, justice, and impartiality, my perspective will largely be that of a judge in the case. It is the judge, after all, who is confronted with the conflicting demands of two or more neighbors: Sue Ann and James Watts. It is the judge who needs to decide their case, considering not only unique aspects of their situation, but also aspects they share in common with other similarly situated men and women. It is the judge who must formulate a rule that will affect not only the litigants before him but also other persons in roughly the same circumstances. It is the judge who must recognize the limits of the judicial ability to remedy situations of human sin, failure, and brokenness.

The Focus of Neighbor Love

According to Outka, all human beings possess "a common status as distinctive creatures of God," along with "a common plight as creatures who sin against God" and who are redeemed by Jesus Christ, and a common dignity as creatures whose value is not earned, but conferred upon each of us by God.[12] In his view, the task of love is to promote the dignity of every human being.

Outka does not go into detail about what promoting human dignity entails. Clearly, however, it includes nurturing respect for the autonomy of each human being. At the same time, he strongly warns against the "tacit equation of dignity and autonomy." As he recognizes, "[a]utonomy is integral to the neighbor's dignity, but not exhaustive of it."[13] Earlier in the essay, in fact, he talks more broadly of promoting the neighbor's well-being, which clearly encompasses other elements of human flourishing. He also approvingly quotes Basil Mitchell: "The love of others, which the Christian ethic demands, involves an active concern for their well-being, and that in turn implies a clear conception of what is best for them, which must, in consistency, be also in essentials what is best for ourselves."[14] Respect for a neighbor's dignity, therefore, means respect for their autonomous self-determination; at the same time, it also requires concern for other aspects of their well-being whose value is not purely subjective.

Outka does not, however, address two key questions that I want to consider here: What does it mean to respect an agent's autonomy? What is the relationship between respect for autonomy and respect for other aspects of well-being, both with regard to a single agent, and with respect to multiple agents? These questions, alas, are the bread and butter of contract law.

Contract law's basic premise is that the widespread practice of making and keeping promises of exchange allows all involved to bring into being a future that they conceive to be better for themselves and those with whom they are associated.[15] Individual autonomy is honored within the framework of contract law. It is not, however, honored in isolation. Rather, one agent's autonomy is always situated within a broader context that includes the autonomous decision making of other agents, particularly that individual's contracting partner. Furthermore, autonomy is seen not as an abstract value. Even a cursory examination of the case law reveals its status as a crucial instrument of pursuing individual and social well-being. The law of contracts is practical; it presupposes that the point of autonomy is to exercise it in order to bring about a better future, not to save it in pristine form as a pure capacity.

Moreover, contract law is based upon the public recognition of private promises. This society has decided that the exchange of reliable promises by private persons is so important to the well-being of the whole community that the government, in the form of its judicial branch, regularly devotes public resources to managing private disputes. Not only will courts decide if a legally enforceable agreement exists, they will also interpret its terms, determine if it was breached, and provide a remedy (usually monetary damages) ideally designed to put the nonbreaching party into the position he or she would have been in had the breach not occurred.

In this setting, then, what does it mean to respect autonomy? The case law reveals that respecting autonomy is a multifaceted task. First, we need to distinguish autonomy as a capacity—a capacity, as the legal philosopher Joseph Raz writes, to be "part author" of one's own life.[16] Generally speaking, classical contract law *presumes* that an adult individual is autonomous—and therefore has the capacity to contract. Respect for autonomy—and for equal dignity—comes in that rough-and-ready presumption that another adult is capable of making a legally effective promise. So, Sue Ann Watts is presumed to have the capacity to make autonomous choices. It does not matter that she is young, provided she is over the age of majority. While the court presents her as naive—and, dare I say, ditzy—those qualities do not prevent her from making decisions about how to live her life that will be taken seriously by others, and given binding effect by the representatives of society.

Second, we need to think about the external conditions that allow the capacity for autonomy to be exercised. Traditionally, the common law has allowed contracts to be avoided on account of improper pressure exerted by one of the parties at the time the contract was made. The qualifying conditions, however, have been interpreted fairly narrowly. To avoid a contract for duress, for example, requires a party to prove that the other party made an improper (illegal or immoral) threat; it is generally not enough to show that the other party took advantage of circumstances to charge an outrageous price. More recently, defenses such as undue influence (improper pressure placed upon a susceptible party) and unconscionability ("iffy" bargaining conditions conjoined with an "iffy" substantive deal) have given parties more options to avoid the promises they made under difficult circumstances. Even these categories, however, are interpreted fairly narrowly by the courts.

Third, respecting someone's autonomy in the context of contract law frequently means holding that person to the promise that he or she made at the "magic moment" in which a contract came into being, in which the promise was exchanged for a corresponding promise, or for some other form of consideration. As I have noted, the system creates a heavy presumption in favor of every adult's effective exercise of autonomy. Consequently, respecting autonomy very often means holding agents accountable to a decision to limit their autonomy in order to further another aspect of their well-being, perhaps even to facilitate the exercise of autonomy at a later point in time. For example, if I promise to landscape your yard on Saturday in exchange for your promise to pay me $500, I am no longer free to do what I want on Saturday from that moment forward. But I may take the money to pay my rent, buy my food, or commit to purchase something else that I desire more than my freedom on one Saturday.

What, then, is the relationship between autonomy and well-being? As the foregoing example shows, that relationship is complicated. We need to distinguish between the situation of the *promisor*—the one who autonomously made a commitment to do something in exchange for something else in return—and the *promisee*, the one who received that commitment.

In some cases, a promisor will seek legally to avoid a promise made in somewhat compromised circumstances, perhaps by arguing that the stress or financial pressure or lack of options fatally wounded his or her autonomy to promise. A good example is the phenomenon of rent-to-own contracts, which offer televisions and furniture to people with bad financial histories at exorbitant rates, and sometimes with distasteful penalty clauses.[17] It is understandable that someone might try to avoid such a contract on the grounds of duress or unconscionability. But such an attempt always comes at a price. If such contracts are not enforced, the rent-to-own company may take its business elsewhere. It would be nice if it did not do so. But it can and it will. And if it does, both the range of my exercise of autonomy and my well-being may be limited. If the promises I make are not enforceable, no one will do business with me. If no one will do business with me, my options inevitably diminish. My options in this less than perfect world, alas, do not include a loan at the prime interest rate or a free television. My options are two: either no television at all or a very expensive television whose price to me exceeds its actual value in most markets by a considerable amount.[18]

Relatedly, it can be tempting to allow some persons or group of persons to avoid disadvantageous contracts by deeming them incapable of forming a valid contract. As feminist legal scholars and critical race theorists have shown, however,[19] the well-being of a person or a socially defined class of people is connected to the power to have one's promises taken as seriously as anyone else's promises—and taking them seriously means enforcing them if necessary. At this point, their insights converge with Gene Outka's. Although he ultimately rejects impartiality as a full articulation of universal love, he recognizes that it creates a default presumption that we extend the same rights, privileges, and duties to all adult human beings.

More generally, to say of someone that he or she is unable to contract—to promise and to be relied upon in promising—is to cut the person out of a major human activity: exchanging one's own strengths for those of another. I do not mean for a moment to deny the importance of questions concerning the capacity of demonstrably physically or mentally impaired persons to make legally effective autonomous choices. At the same time, I think we need to recognize that it threatens our commitment to the equal dignity of all human beings to be too quick to deprive even vulnerable members of the community of the legal power to exercise their autonomy.

What about the promisee? In deciding whether and how to enforce a promise, it is important to remember that both parties to a contract exercise their autonomy to pursue their own conceptions of well-being. Very often, each party pursues that conception by *relying* on the other party's promise in making further autonomous decisions, including decisions to make more promises to other people. You rely on my promise to landscape your yard on Saturday; perhaps you plan to host a career-enhancing corporate picnic on Sunday. You hire caterers and book entertainment. You make other promises and exact other commitments, weaving them together with my promise in order to build your future, in order to promote the cause of your well-being. The concept of *reliance* is crucial in contract law; it is, I think, underutilized in theological ethics. A richer understanding of the relationship of autonomy and reliance in contract law may help us move beyond a truncated view of autonomy as exclusively associated with and contributing to a radical individualism.

In the American legal system, therefore, the general rule is that from the moment the parties exchange promises, those promises are enforceable. Yet this rule goes beyond reliance in two senses. First, one party does not have to rely upon the other party's promise before it becomes enforceable. Second, enforcing a promise characteristically means giving the nonbreaching party its full value, not merely compensating for out-of-pocket expenses incurred by the time of the breach. Ordinarily, the courts attempt to give what is called expectation damages; that is, they attempt to put the non-breaching parties in the position they would have been in had the promises to them been fulfilled, not merely to put them back in the position they were in before they relied upon the broken promise. An example may help: If you and I agree on a cold day in February that I will rent you my fabulous waterfront beach house on Cape Cod for $1,000 for the entire summer, my promise is enforceable as soon as it is made, even *before* you rely on it by purchasing your plane tickets in March. And if I change my mind in April, you are entitled to the full value of that summer rental for $1,000, not merely compensation for the cost of your tickets.

As this example shows, contract law generally protects the promisee's expectation interest, not merely the reliance interest. Why? While this question is disputed among legal theorists, in my view the most persuasive answer recognizes not only the role of the *promisor's* autonomy in making the promise but also the relationship of the *promisee's* autonomy and reliance in accepting it. More specifically, we want to encourage promisees to rely upon the promises they receive, to build on them, to count on them in pursuing, confidently, their own notion of well-being. As Lon Fuller said, "to encourage reliance we must therefore dispense with its proof."[20]

Reliance is the relational counterpart of a promisor's autonomous commitment; it is incorporated as one plank of the promisee's practical reasoning about the future. As Gene Outka repeatedly cautions, human beings are not isolated monads, but are social beings. That means, of course, that their autonomy is not the exercise of will of an autonomous monad. Outka recognizes the fact that sociality can result in undue pressure on the individual exercising autonomy.[21] As I noted earlier, contract law does as well. But what he might want to explore, in my view, is how in the best of cases, one individual's autonomy and well-being rely upon the autonomous commitments of others. Our autonomous choices are not of interest merely to ourselves, but also to our neighbors. They not only predict them from afar but they also attempt to secure them by folding them into binding agreements. And they do so because they want to build upon them in the course of exercising their own autonomy and pursuing their own well-being.

Where could there or should there be a point of contact between Outka's understanding of neighbor love and the contract law's account of reliance? I myself think that drawing in an element from Paul Ramsey's account of love might be helpful. Modeling Christian obligations on God's covenant fidelity to humanity, Ramsey defines agape as steadfast love; one might say *reliable* love.[22] A covenant is another word for a contract.[23] It accounts, in his view, for the capacity of love to bind itself in service to the neighbor, and for the neighbor to rely upon that expression of being bound, even in difficult circumstances.

Reliance, in the context of universal love, can be seen as a response of human sociality, finitude, and contingency to the loving exercise of autonomy. Human beings need to trust and to depend upon one another in order to address problems of finitude and contingency. There is a resultant vulnerability that comes from dependency created by trust. Given human finitude and sin, there is the possibility of that vulnerability and dependency being betrayed. It is no accident that Ramsey's account of steadfast love did the most work in his groundbreaking book on medical ethics, *The Patient as Person*. Ramsey attempts to enfold the most vulnerable members of the population with a secure promise to care for them. As I noted earlier, in his theocentric account of love, Outka claims that love for God "includes fidelity to God in loving whom God loves."[24] I would suggest that Outka's notion of fidelity or steadfastness applies not only to *whom* God loves but also *how* God loves them, in the manner specified by Ramsey.

How does the foregoing analysis further our insight into our neighbors, the battling Wattses? The fundamental problem that the court is grappling with in *Watts v. Watts* is that there is clearly reliance, but possibly no promise. More precisely, there is no legally sanctioned promise, made in the context of the exchange of wedding vows. To put it another way, there is reliance, but no solemn covenant upon which to rely.

Can we infer private promises to treat each other as spouses back from the parties' mutual reliance: the tax returns, the kids, the business entertaining? It seems to me that this is not difficult. Contract law frequently infers promises from the activities of the parties, holding that their reality and legal effectiveness are no less real because they are tacit rather than explicit. One could certainly infer that by holding themselves out to third parties as married, the Wattses held themselves out to each other to be married.[25]

What kind of a contract does being married involve? It is, in my view, at the far end of a spectrum. At the near end, we can envisage a one-time exchange in which each party's duties are clear: I hire a person to walk my dog. In the middle, we can imagine an ongoing exchange in which one party's duties are subject to a great deal of self-definition: suppose a college hires a new president, who will have a great deal of discretion in defining the actual content of his or her day-to-day duties. At the far end, we can contemplate an ongoing exchange in which each party's contributions build upon the contributions of the other party: a partnership, in which each shares equally in the costs, risks, benefits, and rewards of the enterprise. The success or failure of one party depends not only on his efforts, but also upon hers.

Marriage, after all, is the quintessential open-ended partnership. Autonomy, reliance, and well-being are intertwined as closely as they could be in this case. It seems clear from the facts set forth in the opinion that Sue Ann and James repeatedly made possibly explicit and clearly tacit promises to each other to engage in the kind of open-ended partnership that is marriage. It is also clear that Sue Ann relied upon these promises in numerous ways. We can see the positive reliance in all the things she did, in all her efforts expended on behalf of the landscaping business.

At the same time, and crucially, we can also see it in what she failed to do, in "negative reliance." She did not retain her birth name, make an independent life for herself, or even obtain the training she needed to be financially secure, since she counted on her relationship with James. Moreover, she did not formalize their relationship by pressing to marry him in accordance with Wisconsin law.

Why not make it legal? We could look at this question in two ways—in terms of larger social context and in terms of personal incentives. Viewed in terms of broader cultural currents, it is understandable that they didn't get married right away; it was, after all, the 1960s. But they soon moved into the middle class, tax-paying respectability that was and continues to be so intimately connected with legal marriage.[26]

The situation with respect to individual incentives, however, is a bit more complicated—one might even say paradoxical. If a couple is living together peaceably, there may be no perceived need for the piece of paper that formalizes their relationship. Moreover, as time goes on, legalizing the situation could be embarrassing, particularly for the Wattses, since they had held themselves out as legally married for so long. What would they tell the children? Finally, regularizing their situation could be financially costly and even legally dangerous, since doing so would likely reveal that they had lied to the IRS and other public and private bodies about their marital status. If, on the other hand, the relationship is under threat of dissolving, there is no incentive (especially on his part) to cement the partnership.

In short, for the Wattses, as for many couples, there was a "magic moment," a time at which social forces and personal incentives aligned to encourage them to formalize their relationship and the patterns of reliance that relationship engendered. But they missed that moment. Crucially, however, their life together proceeded in virtually every respect as if they had captured it. Until it didn't.

Persons, Rules, and Circumstances

While he does not belabor the point, Outka assumes that one form appropriate for universal love to take is to develop rules of general applicability. He emphasizes, for instance that "moral principles not only tell agents what they may and should do and not do, but also what they may and should resist, object to, and demand."[27] I want to suggest that the common law will force us to face head-on a question that Outka acknowledges but does not fully grapple with in his extended essay: the relationship between universal love and the use of normative rules.

The debate in the 1960s between Paul Ramsey and Joseph Fletcher revealed the complicated nature of the relationship between rules and love.[28] While a full analysis is beyond my scope here, I note that one aspect of their debate is not about whether universal love can be applied in and through rules, but *which* rules should govern: an overarching utilitarian rule that invites us to maximize good consequences across persons, or other rules that place other limits on action that are not consequence based.

I would like to focus on a different, and perhaps prior, issue. In thinking about what it means to respect or regard the dignity of our fellow human beings, how do we balance regard for their uniqueness as a child of God, and the unique course that their lives take, with regard for the characteristics, needs, and temptations that they have in common with other human beings? This question, it seems to me, is inevitably involved in rule-making.

A good legal or moral rule picks out certain features of a situation as decisive for analysis and places others in the shadows. The substantive justice of a rule depends upon the wisdom and validity of the features selected to count and those dismissed as irrelevant to moral and legal analysis. A substantively unjust rule—say, "All people over six feet tall get a $2,000 income tax credit"—can be applied in a procedurally fair way. Its fair procedural application does not obviate its substantive injustice.

In my judgment, the Anglo-American common law tradition acutely raises the question about the relationship of unique persons and situations and general rules in a way worthy of reflection by theological and philosophical ethicists. In fact, the distinguishing feature of that tradition is that judges articulate legal rules and principles not in the abstract, but, rather, in the course of deciding a specific case or controversy. As I argued in chapter 1, John Noonan captures the situation in his classic book, *Persons and Masks of the Law*:

> No person itself, the law lives in persons. Rules of law are formed by human beings to shape the attitude and conduct of human beings and applied by human beings to human beings. The human beings are persons. The rules are communications uttered, comprehended, and responded to by persons. They affect attitude and conduct as communications from persons to persons. They exist as rules—not as words on paper—in the mind of persons.[29]

As Noonan's book shows, the common law is constructed around the hopes, disappointments, and controversies of specific persons whose names give title to each case in the law books. It is *their* case or controversy that the judge and jury are charged with deciding. That case is irreducibly particular, because it involves the background, training, and social roles, as well as the character strengths and flaws, of the parties to the case. It is set in a particular time and place, which shapes the decision-making process of the plaintiff, defendant, and other agents involved. From God's point of view, the list of facts and circumstances potentially relevant to a full moral analysis of the actions of the parties, and their responsibility for those actions, could well be enormous. At the same time, however, the judge is called to decide the case by articulating a general rule, which can be applied in other, similar cases. That general rule necessarily picks out certain features of the case as relevant and plays down others. In making these selections, the judge is both forging and expressing the values of the community and determining the fate of the particular litigants before her.

These aspects of the law-making process, I think, should be of interest to Outka. They force us to grapple with some important questions: In deciding a controversy such as that between the Wattses, in what respect do judges (who are persons) regard the litigants (who are persons) as their neighbors? Do they regard the litigants in their concrete uniqueness, in the midst of the particular circumstances that cause them distress, or do they regard them in the aspects of their situation that are shared in common with others, or at least with a significant segment of the community?

Noonan argues, rightly, I think, that a legal system needs to attend to both general rules and specific persons in order to function well. Paying exclusive attention to particular persons and our response to them strangles justice with either favoritism or hatred. There is a reason that a just judge is said to be "no respecter of persons"; justice cannot be done if our friends are always right and strangers and enemies are always wrong. At the same time, rules can become hardened and can be applied mechanically, in a way that turns them into masks that hide the humanity of the person before the bench. They can blind us to the true nature of the moral situation. Noonan's classic example, of course, is the way in which African Americans were classified as property before the civil war.[30] But there are other, less extreme examples. Noonan argues, for example, that the practice of headnotes in commercial case reporters and student study guides to strip all the facts out of a case, even the names of the parties, verges on submerging the particular person in the impersonal rule.[31]

Consider the statement of the facts in the Westlaw summary of *Watts v. Watts:* "Unmarried cohabitant brought action for accounting and share of accumulated property under theory of express or implied-in-fact contract, and theory of constructive trust based upon unjust enrichment." Does the label "unmarried cohabitants" fully capture the status of the Wattses vis-à-vis each other? Twelve years, two children, many joint tax returns? All those dinners cooked by Sue Ann for all those sweaty workers in James's start-up landscape business? Technically, of course, the term "unmarried" applies to the Wattses. But the other facts left out as irrelevant are, in fact, relevant both to justice and to the ultimate disposition of the case.

It seems to me that in affirming a theocentric account of universal love, Outka will need to affirm the importance of both particularity and generalizability in the course of attending to the neighbor and her situation. We are all unique, yet we are all human beings commonly made in the image and likeness of God. As Noonan's work demonstrates, a commitment to universal love requires appellate judges to recognize the specific persons whose cases are before them as unique individuals. It also requires them to be alert to the ways in which the legal categories they inherit can function to dehumanize those persons, and thereby prove themselves to be in need of rejection or reform. At the same time, however, by virtue of their role-related obligation, in deciding these specific cases, judges need to mark out a general path of action for others in the community to follow.

But how do we or should we account for both aspects of our neighbors in our decision making? I think the common law does a reasonably good job of accounting for both. In deciding a case like *Watts v. Watts*, the court must articulate a rule, which requires it to pick out some circumstances of the parties as relevant, and to discount others in ways that render them irrelevant. That rule, which will take on a life that is detached to some degree from the case, will go on to be applied to future cases. It is important to note, however, that the discounting and the detachment are always provisional, at least in principle. The rule is articulated in the context of the narrative of the case, which officially does continue to bear the name of and point to the stories of the parties who litigated it. It is more accurate to say that the rule is, so to speak, semi-detached from the case that prompted its formulation.

The case, as precedent, does not disappear. It is not consumed by the rule. It is preserved as the context that makes the rule intelligible. The rule is always subject to the possibility of being qualified or modified with reference to the circumstances of a later case, if the judges deciding it choose to distinguish the original case on the basis of differing facts now found to be salient. Human beings and their stories are unique, but they have some capacities, needs, and temptations in common. We may not be able fully to sort out the relationship between the particularities of individuals and common human nature, but we can ensure that our rules, and the persons whose situation prompted their development, go forward together.

What should we think about how universal love applies in a case of conflict between two neighbors? As Outka recognizes, the classical Christian text on love of neighbor, does not directly address this question. Outka asks, "When two or more persons are affected by one's action, does the claim [of the dignity of the human person] furnish any guidance? What especially of situations where the well-being of various persons conflict and choice is unavoidable?"[32] In considering the matter of conflict between neighbors, the Christian tradition, from Augustine to Paul Ramsey, has focused on questions pertaining to the use of violence to defend one neighbor wrongly attacked by another. The parable is altered to ask what the Good Samaritan would have done if he had come upon the scene a little earlier, as the robbers went about their "fell work."[33] While Outka recognizes the importance of these questions, he also urges us to move beyond them to consider situations of conflict between neighbors that do not involve violence.[34]

In my view, one way to grapple with the nonviolent conflicts between neighbors is to look at them through the prism of the judicial task. The question of whether love focuses upon regard for the neighbor in her unique particularity, or in the more universalizable aspects of her situation picked out by rules, is intimately entwined with the question of how love requires us to address conflicts among neighbors. In deciding a controversy between neighbors, are judges to do justice to the specific parties before them, in all their particularity, or to formulate a rule that will best serve the community, in particular to guide the behavior of similarly but not identically situated neighbors? In some cases, the appropriate solution to the particular case may also best serve the common good. But that is not necessarily so. In some cases, there might be tension between the two goals.

To illustrate and analyze this tension in neighbor love, let us return to the case at hand. Recall that the judges of the Wisconsin Supreme Court are charged to decide the claims of the Wattses, and that those claims are constituted in the midst of their specific situation. But the rule the court announces will bind other people in Wisconsin, shaping the way they live their lives and make their decisions. These people include not only the class of men and women who might or might not get married, but also all the other citizens of Wisconsin. These citizens, through their legislature, adopted the relevant legal framework on marriage and family law. They also pay the taxes that support the judicial resolution of disputes.

In short, the Wisconsin Supreme Court was not deciding this case in a legal vacuum; it was making its decision in view of the normative framework that it discerned in the context of the Wisconsin Family Code. According to the court, the state legislature emphasized the importance of *legal marriage* in formulating and revising that code. More specifically, the court found that the legislative purpose animating the code was "to promote the stability and best interests of marriage and the family.... Marriage is the institution that is the foundation of family and society. Its stability is basic to morality and civilization, and of vital interest to society and the state."[35] The court further interpreted the state's abolition of common law marriage, along with its denial of legal status to marriages that do not conform to the statute, as proof of the legislature's judgment that legal marriage is crucial to the well-being of society.

Thus the Wisconsin legislature came to the conclusion that legal marriage is the best foundation for the well-being of most of the population. In light of that conclusion, and its duty of deference to the legislature in interpreting the statute, the Wisconsin Supreme Court judged that it had a fundamental obligation to decide the case in a way that teaches that legal marriage is preferable to less formal arrangements, and to encourage people in the Wattses' general situation toward formalizing their relationships. At the same time, the court noted that fornication and cohabitation are not against the law in Wisconsin. Although the living arrangements of the Wattses were not favored by the law, they did not violate it, either. Somewhat surprisingly, the court did not mention, much less belabor, the fact that the Wattses had lied about their status on certain official documents, such as their state and federal tax returns. Nor did it observe that such lies were almost certainly financially beneficial to them.

In cases such as this, then, the faces of those whose situation calls for a remedy are vividly before the judge, while the faces of those whose lives will be affected by the new rule are at best indistinct and hazy. In my view, the insights of theological ethics can help advance our understanding of the legal situation by framing it in terms of the claims of near and distant neighbors.[36] What do the demands of impartiality, shaped by the insights of universal love, require in such a context? As Outka notes, the requisite impartiality will be concerned with "substantive fairness," not merely with rigid adherence to procedure.[37]

What, then, does substantive fairness require of the *Watts* court? What substantive interests need to be protected? To whom do they belong? Reframing the question in this way allows us to see that the conflict is not merely between two sets of people, near and distant neighbors, each with discrete and possibly opposing interests. Rather, the conflict is also and even primarily between different functions of the law: on the one hand, the remedial function (cleaning up the shards of the Wattses' broken relationship), and on the other hand, the pedagogical and channeling functions (teaching and incentivizing other people not to put themselves in the same position as the Wattses did).

All three functions are substantive, in that they all further substantive interests of society's members. All members of society, furthermore, have an interest in each of the functions being exercised in a vigorous and judicious manner by the courts. To put it another way, the Wattses are not the only ones who have an interest in their particular dispute being settled fairly; we all have that interest, because the remedial function of the law is important to the entire community.

By framing the potential conflict not as one between near and distant neighbors, but as between the remedial and the pedagogical functions of the law, we may, I believe, make substantial progress toward ameliorating it. Let us begin by looking at the broken relationship of the Wattses. How ought it to be remedied, with the very imperfect tools available to the court system? First, it seems clear that Sue Ann and James intended to live together *as if* they were participants in the social institution of marriage. Given that this is the case, it seems as if both ought to have expected that they would separate *as if* they were leaving that institution.[38]

The keywords, of course, are "as if." They never went through with the procedure specified by Wisconsin law as necessary to enter into the state of matrimony. Who is responsible? As tempting as the narrative makes it to absolve Sue Ann from responsibility, we cannot do that without infantilizing her. Nonetheless, we can certainly insist that James is just as responsible for the situation as is Sue Ann.

If we look only at their relationship, what does substantive fairness require? As the court itself noted, letting him keep all the money when both parties are equally guilty of flouting the technical requirements of legal marriage is substantively unfair. James would get a windfall at Sue Ann's expense. He would be rewarded for their mutual walk on the windy side of the law, while she would be punished.

What about the pedagogical function of the law? Does denying Sue Ann recovery teach others about the foundational value of legal marriage, and channel them into that institution? Initially, that might seem to be the case. We can envision the cautionary tale: "Make it legal, or end up alone and penniless like Sue Ann!"

But thinking a bit more deeply, in my view, suggests that denying Sue Ann recovery is not likely to have the desired pedagogical effect, for two reasons. First, the case is about what happens when two people break up, not what happens when they get together. How many people, especially young people, are likely to decide whether or not to get married legally by considering what happens if they eventually fail at their common life together?[39] Some people, of course, may think that far ahead. But how many? The incidence of prenuptial agreements might give us a rough idea of the numbers of people who consider the potential breakup of their future union before entering into it. As of March 2010, only 3 percent of individuals with a spouse or fiancée had a prenuptial agreement. That number, while up significantly from the 1 percent reported in a similar study in April 2002, is not a sign that most people are thinking ahead to divorce when planning a marital or quasi-marital partnership.[40] Second, and more crucially, the incentives associated in a rule that would deny recovery to those in Sue Ann's place actually cut both ways. If such a rule were adopted, a woman in Sue Ann's situation might be inclined to insist on a legal marriage before entering into a marriage-like relationship. But a man in James's position would be equally inclined to avoid formalizing the arrangement.

The incentives that count most, it seems to me, are the negative and positive incentives *to marry*, not those that pertain to what happens after a separation whose possibility both parties are likely to discount heavily when moving in together. In days past, many incentives to marry were negative in nature. For example, fornication was not only subject to moral disapprobation, but also illegal.[41] Laws such as these have disappeared from the statute books over time, as the *Watts* court notes. There are still, however, many positive incentives for couples to marry legally. For example, both state and federal law grants tax benefits to married parties, and banks consider the income of both parties in establishing credit ratings and deciding whether to loan money. It would not be difficult to encourage legal marriage—and discourage quasi-marriages such as the Wattses'—by requiring couples seeking financial and other benefits associated with marriage to provide a copy of their marriage certificate. It appears likely that James and Sue Ann would have regularized their situation in order to obtain the tax benefits had they not been able to obtain them simply by lying about their marital status.

An Asymmetry of Agency

The bulk of Gene Outka's essay on "Universal Love and Impartiality" is an attempt to identify the similarities and differences between self-love and love of neighbor for purposes of applying the command to love universally. It would seem, at first glance, that this effort is not relevant to my analysis of what judges should do when confronted with the claims of two battling neighbors, even as they take into account the interests of many neighbors who are more distant from the case. Nonetheless, I think his analysis is deeply relevant because it helps explain the limits of what law can do to remedy situations marred by disappointment and sin. While constraints of space prevent me from fully examining this point, I think it would be useful to outline its kernel. The analysis points, I think, to an additional way in which the insights of theological and philosophical ethics may shed light upon the decisions made by courts.

Briefly, Outka argues that there are several asymmetries between what I can do for my neighbor and what I can do for myself, some of which center on the phenomenon of human agency. I am responsible for my own acts and, ultimately, for my own response to God's call. I am also responsible for carrying out my unique life plan, in the form of pursuing my own vocation. There are corresponding limits, as Outka argues, based in both principled and practical considerations, to what I can do for my neighbor.

Outka observes, for instance, that I can commend love of God to my neighbor, but I cannot love God on my neighbor's behalf. Building upon Outka's observation, it also seems evident that I cannot force a neighbor to simulate the attitude or acts of love toward either God or a fellow human being. Of their nature, such acts must be performed freely. I can urge my neighbors to love each other, but I cannot force them to do so. Furthermore, I can take full responsibility for executing my life plan, but I cannot assume the same level of control over my neighbors' life plans. I can facilitate their vocations, but I cannot fulfill them.

How do the limits of what one agent can do for another affect our understandings of the limits of law in addressing human conflicts? In my view, they explain the degree to which the law is hampered in providing a remedy in the face of human sin and the actions that flow from it. Consider, again, the situation of the Wattses. The ideal resolution of this situation, of course, would be for Sue Ann and James to have a conversion of heart, and to recommit themselves to their love, to their children, and to their joint life plan. It is only that sort of conversion that would meet their mutual expectations, based on mutual promises to live as if they were married to one another.

But it is beyond the power of the law to produce the ideal resolution of this situation. Generally speaking, courts do not order specific performance with respect to personal services. In fact, they are notoriously leery to do so, in part because of the theoretical worry that doing so comes too close to ordering a de facto arrangement of slavery, and in part because of the practical worry that persons who are forced to perform particular functions rarely do so in a way that will meet the needs of the one exacting those functions from them. What, then, are the tools at its disposal? In some cases, it might issue a negative injunction, preventing a breaching party from assuming other obligations that are inconsistent with its contractual obligations. In other cases, it might order the breaching party to transfer property or money to the nonbreaching party. But the command to transfer money is not and can never be the equivalent of a command to transfer the loyalties and love of one's heart. That command is beyond the purview of the legal system.

In appealing the dismissal of her case to the Wisconsin Supreme Court, Sue Ann Watts claimed that any one of the following five legal theories would justify giving her relief on the facts she averred:

1. *Application of divorce laws.* Sue Ann claimed that she was entitled to straightforward division of the assets under the applicable provisions pertaining to divorce under the Wisconsin Family Code.
2. *Marriage by estoppel.* Sue Ann put forth a novel theory of "marriage by estoppel" in order to receive the same division of assets indirectly. In essence, she claimed that although they were never legally married, justice required that James be "estopped" from denying the fact of their marriage in the context of Sue Ann's claim to an equal share of his assets.
3. *Contract.* Sue Ann argued that she was entitled to recovery under a theory of an express or implied-in-fact contract between her and James, in which they agreed to distribute their assets equally in the event of a separation.
4. *Unjust enrichment.* Sue Ann argued that he was unjustly enriched, and that she was entitled to restitution based on the reasonable value of her services to him and his projects over the years.
5. *Partition.* Sue Ann, she argued that she and James had engaged in a joint venture, and that she was entitled to partition of the assets of that joint venture.

What were the respective views of the parties toward the five theories? Sue Ann would have preferred recovery under the first or second theory, since either would give her half the assets. The third theory would be acceptable, provided she could prove that the terms of the contract included a provision for equal division of assets. The fourth theory would be suboptimal, although better than nothing. It treats her as a wage laborer rather than as a full partner. Moreover, the reasonable value of services characteristically provided by women is very low. The fifth and final theory would provide an acceptable recovery to Sue Ann.

James, of course, resisted the applicability of any theory. He argued that both the first and second theories would erode the legislative policy privileging marriage. The third, fourth, and fifth theories, in his view, should also be rejected by the court on the grounds of public policy. In addition to arguing that these theories would also undercut the preferred status of marriage, James strongly implied that it would enlist the court in the unwise and distasteful enforcement of a "meretricious" contract, in which one of the items of consideration was sexual relations. The Latin word *meretrix* means "prostitute." By arguing that Sue Ann and he were involved in a "meretricious" contract, he was associating his life partner of twelve years and the mother of his two children with a woman who provides access to her body for money, not love. Doubtless the legal strategy was his lawyer's idea, not James's own. Nonetheless, it would be interesting to know whether he approved of it.

What did the court do? In essence, it split the difference. It did not allow the first or second theories to go to trial, agreeing with James that to do so would undercut legislative policy favoring legal marriage. It did, however, allow Sue Ann's claims to go forward under the third, fourth, and fifth theories, for four reasons.

First, the court noted changing mores on premarital cohabitation, concluding that their arrangement did not violate the common morality. Second, it observed that numerous courts "distinguish, however, between contracts that are explicitly and inseparably founded on sexual services and those that are not." A bargain "is not illegal merely because there is an illicit relationship between the two so long as the bargain is independent of the illicit relationship."[42] Third, the court recognized that the result of the judicial system's wholesale refusal to intervene in disputes between unmarried cohabitants would be unfair and harsh. One party would inevitably get an undeserved windfall. The other party, no more guilty than the first, would inevitably be correspondingly penalized. Even granting that the Wattses behaved irresponsibly by holding themselves out as married without benefit of actually being married, they were both equally irresponsible. Fourth, and finally, the court observed that this situation could "encourage a partner with greater income potential to avoid marriage in order to retain all accumulated assets, leaving the other party with nothing."[43]

What was the result? The Wisconsin Supreme Court remanded to the trial court, allowing the case to go forward on the contract, unjust enrichment, and partition claims. After a trial, the jury found that Sue Ann and James did in fact have a contract, but awarded her no damages based on that contract. Instead, they gave her recovery on the theory of unjust enrichment, in effect requiring James to compensate her for the reasonable value of the services she rendered.[44] Sue Ann received an award of

$113,090.08. According to Sue Ann's expert witness, James's net worth had increased by $1,113,900.88 during their time together.[45] In the end, she was treated as a wage laborer, rather than as an equity partner in the life they created together. What was the difference? In addition to the insult, about half a million dollars.

5

Compassionate Respect and Victims' Voices

Engaging Margaret Farley

BIKING THROUGH THE Stanford University campus in the hours after midnight in January 2015, two Swedish graduate students came upon a man sexually assaulting an unconscious twenty-two-year-old woman behind a dumpster.[1] The quick-thinking young Swedes detained the assailant and called the police. As a result of their intervention, Brock Turner, a twenty-year-old Stanford undergraduate and member of the university's swim team, was arrested and charged with two counts of rape and three counts of felony sexual assault. The rape counts were later dropped, but in March 2016, a Santa Clara County jury found Turner guilty on the three remaining charges, which included one count of assault with intent to commit rape, one count of sexually penetrating an intoxicated or anesthetized person, and one count of sexually penetrating an unconscious person.[2]

What is an appropriate sentence for such a crime? The prosecutors asked for six years in state prison. Yet in April 2016, Santa Clara County Superior Court Judge Aaron Persky imposed only a six-month jail sentence followed by probation, conjoined with an obligation to register as a sex offender.[3] Judge Persky justified his decision by observing: "A prison sentence would have a severe impact on him. I think he will not be a danger to others."[4] The lenient sentence precipitated a backlash of outrage not only from feminist scholars and victims' rights advocates but also from men and women from all walks of life. In fact, over a million persons signed an online petition demanding Judge Persky's recall.[5]

A crucial catalyst for the outrage was the powerful victim impact statement delivered by the violated woman in open court after Judge Persky handed down the sentence. To protect her privacy, the victim went by the name "Emily Doe." Addressing her attacker directly, Doe rebutted his excuses point by passionate point, as the following excerpt illustrates.[6]

> Lastly you said, I want to show people that one night of drinking can ruin a life. Ruin a life, one life, yours, you forgot about mine. Let me rephrase for you, I want to show people that one night of drinking can ruin two lives. You and me. You are the cause, I am the effect. You have dragged me through this hell with you, dipped me back into that night again and again. You knocked down both our towers, I collapsed at the same time you did. Your damage was concrete; stripped of titles, degrees, enrollment. My damage was internal, unseen, I carry it with me. You took away my worth, my privacy, my energy, my time, my safety, my intimacy, my confidence, my own voice, until today.[7]

Emily Doe's perspective on the situation, however, was not the only one proffered to the court. Dan A. Turner, the father of the defendant, wrote a letter to the judge, urging leniency for his son:

> As it stands now, Brock's life has been deeply altered forever by the events of Jan 17th and 18th. He will never be his happy go lucky self with that easy going personality and welcoming smile. His every waking minute is consumed with worry, anxiety, fear, and depression. . . . These verdicts have broken and shattered him and our family in so many ways. His life will never be the one that he dreamed about and worked so hard to achieve. That is a steep price to pay for 20 minutes of action out of his 20 plus years of life.[8]

Needless to say, this description of the assault as "20 minutes of action" further inflamed victims' rights advocates, who saw it as a shockingly cavalier description of a brutal attack with *lifelong* effects on the victim.[9] Viewed more charitably, however, the defendant's father was not attempting to minimize the harm to his son's victim; rather, he was pleading that his son's entire identity and future not be entirely defined by this one deplorable action. He was asking for the court's empathy—and for mercy for his son.

Should Emily Doe's harrowing account of her violation have received more weight in Turner's sentencing? Did her particular experiences shed light on the nature and gravity of his crime? Or was it ultimately irrelevant to the decision at hand, which properly focused on *Turner's* mental state, especially signs of diminished culpability, remorse, and prospects of future rehabilitation? The answers to these questions are neither easy nor uncontroversial. In fact, as I will discuss in more detail later in this chapter, the U.S. Supreme Court issued two sharply conflicting decisions on the use of victim impact statements within a span of a few years.

From an ethical perspective, the controversy surrounding the use of victim impact statements issues in criminal sentencing raises a cluster of issues around the role and relative priority of experience in moral decision making. It forces us to critically evaluate the role of experience in assessing the nature and gravity of a particular act from a moral perspective, as well as to consider whose experience counts most in that assessment. Moreover, the controversy raises questions about compassion and empathy: how does empathy with the painful experiences of another shape our moral and legal obligations; and second, in cases of conflicting experiences, who ought decision makers empathize with and why?

No Christian ethicist has done more to highlight the role of experience in moral discernment than Margaret Farley. At the same time, Farley is not naïve about the challenges that experience poses for moral reflection. She insists upon the need not only to attend in compassion to the suffering expressed by others, but also to pay attention to their objective circumstances. Furthermore, Farely is acutely aware that different people may experience situations differently. She knows that the question whose experience counts for what purposes is not resolvable simply by an appeal to experience. It requires reflection upon the nature of moral discernment, as well as sensitivity to the blind spots in our ongoing tradition of moral discernment. The answer to the question whose experience counts turns in part on whose experience has been unjustly excluded from the moral and cultural conversation thus far. In this chapter, I will explore and extend Farley's account of compassionate respect and the role of experience in moral discernment, by bringing it into conversation with some of the issues surrounding the use of victim impact statements in criminal sentencing. In my judgment, that conversation is mutually fruitful. On the one hand, Farley's normative reflections highlight the countervailing moral considerations involved in this use of such statements. On the other hand, the highly specific context of criminal sentencing facilitates the appropriation and extension of her insights, in order to begin resolving some of the abstract tensions that she identifies.

Margaret Farley on Compassionate Respect

Margaret Farley has devoted her academic life to overcoming a series of false but tempting conceptual dichotomies in ethical analysis. She calls upon her readers to hold together the insights captured by both sides of an apparent polarization, such as between mercy and justice, experience and reason, or feeling compassion and showing respect for autonomous personhood. Her consistent aim is to resist oversimplification, in favor of developing a rich and complex moral compass that can provide true guidance to persons who find themselves in complicated situations. Farley does not pretend that her ethical framework will yield clear and certain answers in every conceivable case; indeed, she would see any attempt to provide such answers as hubristic. For Farley, moral wisdom is always accompanied by the "grace of self-doubt," which does not mean a paralyzing inability to make a decision but, rather, an active and engaged epistemological modesty, which is willing to consider new sources and insights that bear on complicated moral problems.

Echoing her mentor James Gustafson, Farley recognizes experience as both a source and a test for moral norms. She writes, for example, that "some things are important for moral discernment that simply cannot be known without experience—things like the limitations and possibilities of ourselves as moral agents, the dimensions of suffering and diminishment, the ways to hope and to love, the parameters of intimacy, the multiple consequences of injury and injustice."[10] At the same time, however, Farley refuses to insulate *anyone's* experience from reflection, rational critique, or challenge. While Farley is sympathetic to many elements of the "ethic of care" proposed by important strands of contemporary feminist thought, she insists that an ethic of care cannot be untethered to an accurate perception of those who receive care.[11] One's own experience of compassion—and subjective sense of what compassion requires—is not self-justifying. True compassion must be integrally and reciprocally related to respect for the person toward whom it is directed. "Compassion . . . awakens in us a moral response, but respect, too, can sharpen the focus of what we see and keep our compassionate responses fitting and true."[12]

Who are the persons for whom we care? What does it mean to respect them? Here, too, Farley resists dichotomies. She is equally opposed to a wooden moral universalism and a postmodern dissolution of moral norms into a contest of unnormed interests and desires. Despite her insistence on the importance of taking the experiences of particular persons seriously, she maintains that there are important universal truths about human beings that merit defense.[13] Yet these truths are themselves complicated and they resist dichotomies. Respect for particular human beings requires respect for both their nature as embodied beings and their own purposeful willing or choosing. It also requires taking due account of the fact that each human being is called to relationship and sociality. Farley rejects any effort to "pit individual good against the good of the community, when what is at stake is the fundamental dignity of the individual."[14] She also refuses to define the well-being of persons apart from their network of relationships and commitments. "To care for a person adequately and genuinely as a person is to care for her in relation—in the context of the story of her relationships, past, present, and future."[15]

In short, Margaret Farley sees both compassion and respect as flowing from our obligation to love our neighbor, whose autonomy, relationality, and embodiment generate objective requirements that shape both the content and the direction of our care. She would be the last to deny the tension involved in negotiating these requirements in particular cases. Indeed, Farley's book *Compassionate Respect* illuminates these tensions in the context of medical-moral decision making, when respect for a particular patient's autonomous decision making and self-determination conflicts with providing treatment that best serves the individual's objective well-being.

As difficult as these conflicts may be when grappling with the needs and desires of single individuals, however, they become exponentially more complicated when dealing with the needs and desires of multiple individuals—all of whom lay claim to our compassion and respect. As we saw in the previous chapter focused on the work of Gene Outka, discerning the requirements of both love and justice as they applied to the conflict between James and Sue Ellen Watts is exceedingly difficult. That difficulty is exponentially compounded when the decision maker is a court that is not only settling the Wattses' situation but also setting precedent for unseen and unnamed parties in similar situations. Dialogue with the *Watts* case challenged, clarified, and deepened Outka's understanding of equal regard, which in turn illuminated key aspects of the case itself.

In my view, it is similarly profitable to place Margaret Farley's work in conversation with the debate about the use of victim impact statements.

Most broadly, her emphasis on the dignity of all human beings presses us to consider the legitimate needs of both the victim and the defendant. In addition, her cautious appropriation of critical theory, especially feminist theory, gives us reason to scrutinize the channels in which compassion flows—or fails to flow—to both victims and defendants in the highly fraught situation of a criminal trial, particularly a trial involving sexual assault. Finally, her emphasis on both the importance and the limits of experience as a moral source encourages us to think carefully about the purposes to which we put accounts of experience.

Challenges to Respect

What does it mean to show appropriate respect to all parties in a criminal case? As the controversy over Brock Turner's sentence suggests, those who advocate for the exclusion of victim impact statements maintain that the focus in criminal sentencing must remain squarely on the defendant. They contend that the introduction of victim impact evidence undermines justice by shifting the attention away from the background, circumstances, and character of the person about to be sentenced. In contrast, those who argue for the admission of victim impact evidence believe that the laudable concern for defendant's rights has occluded the dignity and needs of the victim. They call for "rebalancing" the criminal justice system so that the victim's voice receives the attention and respect it deserves.

To address this question, it is first necessary to think critically about fundamental categories. Victim impact statements present a vivid account of suffering. It is tempting, but ultimately misleading, to use the categories of "sufferer" and "victim" interchangeably. Victims are those whose legal or moral right has been infringed by another moral agent. Most, if not all, victims experience suffering as a result of that deprivation. Yet the category of "sufferer" is broader than that of "victim." Most obviously, the family, friends, and neighbors of the victim may suffer greatly. Yet matters are more complicated than they first appear. Defendants about to be condemned to death row or to a long prison sentence do not appear to be victims, only victimizers. Nonetheless, they may very well experience psychological suffering at the prospect of their grim future.

At first glance, the categories of "victim" and "victimizer" seem both straightforward and helpful. Yet deeper scrutiny suggests that both categories can be used in ways that occlude the dignity of those to whom they are applied. The philosopher Elizabeth Spelman has insightfully examined three ways in which observers commonly configure those who are seen to be suffering, all of which are highly problematic for the sufferers.[16] The first configuration treats sufferers as participants in a tragedy. Spelman perceptively notes that the internal logic of the tragic genre focuses attention and sympathy on tragic heroes, rather than on those who are damaged by the flawed perception and agency of such men and women. Spelman trenchantly argues, for example, that referring to the American institution of slavery as "our national tragedy" does not expose and assign culpability for the raw suffering of the enslaved. Instead, the label keeps the flattering spotlight on the founding fathers, configuring them as good men marred by a tragic flaw.[17]

In the context of a criminal trial, defense lawyers sometimes try to present the crime as a tragic occurrence that destroyed the lives of both victim and perpetrator. In fact, this strategy can be identified in the defense mounted on behalf of Brock Turner, including his father's statement to the judge. Yet as Spelman's work suggests, configuring the event as a tragedy makes the defendant, as a tragic hero, more interesting and compelling than the woman he violated. Turner is depicted as a promising young man whose life was derailed by a tragic mistake; Emily Doe is reduced to being the nameless and faceless cause of Turner's downfall. Her suffering is simply a piece in the larger and more interesting story of how "twenty minutes of action" thwarted his life.

Spelman identifies a second way in which the suffering of others can be misused. She observes that those resisting one cause of suffering can reduce those who have suffered on different grounds to "spiritual bellhops." She takes as her example the practice of many nineteenth-century white feminists who claimed that the oppression they faced because of sexism was analogous to the oppression caused by slavery. Rather than listening to the agonizing particular experience of enslaved men and women, suffragettes conscripted it for their own purposes. They used the label of "slavery" to carry their own pain to greater prominence. The oppression of people of color was of concern to them only instrumentally, as an effective vehicle to challenge the oppression of women.[18]

This temptation tends to trap prosecutors more than defendants. In a crucial sense, victims are instrumental to the state's larger purposes of defending the rule of law by punishing a lawbreaker. Prosecutors do not work for victims, but for the people as a whole. They need to make strategic decisions, such as which cases to take to trial, which to settle in plea bargains, and which to drop entirely. The suffering of the victim is but one factor to be incorporated in such decisions. Furthermore, victims take their place in a criminal trial not as protagonists but as witnesses for the prosecution. Consequently, as many victims of sexual assault have been shocked to discover, their own credibility frequently becomes an issue in the courtroom. Very frequently, it is the treatment that victims receive at the hands of the state's lawyers—not the lawyers for the defendant—that causes the most consternation.

What exactly is the relationship between suffering and victimhood? As I have indicated, it is possible to treat victimization as one cause of suffering, and victims as a particular kind of sufferer—those who experienced unjust lost at the hands of another. Unfortunately, the label of "victim" is at least as fraught as that of "sufferer," in ways that become acutely important in the context of a criminal trial. In her important work on the use of victim's stories to advance the cause of human rights, Diana Tietjens Meyers argues that the dominant conception of victims is far too rigid.[19] To trigger popular imagination and sympathy, victims must sort themselves into one of two approved categories that guarantee a certain type of innocence: either they can be *pathetic victims* who contributed in no way to their own plight or they can be *heroic victims* who resisted that plight with every ounce of energy they possessed.[20]

Meyers's analysis offers a cautionary insight into the way victims are commonly categorized in the context of criminal trials. Quite obviously, the socially dominant requirement of innocence excludes convicted felons from concern about their plight. It does not allow us to look past their own wrongdoing to see them as victims of an unjust punishment (e.g., the death penalty), or even a just punishment administered unjustly (e.g., incarceration in a brutal and brutalizing prison setting). Moreover, the dominant binary characterization of acceptable victimhood often excludes not only criminals but also the targets of criminal activity. This is particularly the case is sexual crimes, when questions are raised about whether the target of the assault contributed to her own ill treatment. Consider this passage from Emily Doe's statement:

> I was pummeled with narrowed, pointed questions that dissected my personal life, love life, past life, family life, inane questions, accumulating trivial details to try and find an excuse for this guy who didn't even take the time to ask me for my name, who had me naked a handful of minutes after seeing me. After a physical assault, I was assaulted with questions designed to attack me, to say

> see, her facts don't line up, she's out of her mind, she's practically an alcoholic, she probably wanted to hook up, he's like an athlete right, they were both drunk, whatever, the hospital stuff she remembers is after the fact, why take it into account, Brock has a lot at stake so he's having a really hard time right now.[21]

Margaret Farley has not thus far considered the specific question of how to treat victims' voices in the context of criminal trials. Yet it is clear that her understanding of respect for human dignity would lead her to take Meyers's concerns about the categorization of victimhood very seriously. Farley's view of human beings as capable of both wounding and being wounded would impel her to resist qualifying victims for attention and concern on the basis of their purity. Furthermore, Farley's holistic understanding of respect for human dignity would render her quite sympathetic to Meyers's proposal to replace the dominant binary framework that maintains that all victims worthy of sympathy must fall into the categories of innocent victims or heroic victims.

Instead, Meyers develops a "burdened agency" criterion that take into account the fact that most victims do not operate in anything approaching a situation of total freedom. More specifically, she proposes that we refrain from applying abstract and timeless moral norms to persons caught in situations of great duress, but instead try to formulate expectations about how it might be reasonable for vulnerable persons to act in the "warped action spaces" in which they actually find themselves.[22] Meyers claims that the burdened agency criterion not only expands the number of victims who merit sympathy and concern, but also benefits victims who do fit into the traditionally acceptable binary categories. It allow pathetic victims to be agents, even as it also permits heroic victims "to be human—that is, to suffer and despair, even as they lead and triumph."[23]

Farley would, I think, welcome this nuanced account of accountability and vulnerability. At the same time, I believe that she would press Meyers to more fully uncouple innocence and qualified victimhood. More specifically, Meyers does not jettison the requirement of innocence for qualified victimhood; instead, she redefines it. Victims who act according to the criterion of burdened agency are innocent; they deserve our help. Those who do not so act, Meyers implies, are the true "undeserving victims"—a category that continues to exist in her framework, although it includes fewer people than encompassed by the dominant framework.

I suspect that Farley would resist the categorization of some people as "undeserving victims," in part because of her commitment to mercy, as well as to justice. Farley writes that

> [l]ike God's mercy, genuine human mercy is formed by respect for what God has made—for human freedom, relationality, embodiment, historical and cultural formation, uniqueness, and the potentiality of fullness of life in an unlimited future. Like God's mercy, genuine human mercy is made true by its justice. Mercy and truth, each informing and unleashing the other: this is the mercy that God invites and commands.[24]

Farley emphasizes that mercy toward wrongdoers cannot undermine justice. To the extent that it is rooted in God's mercy, however, human mercy must never write off the possibility of repentance, forgiveness, and redeemed relationship. No matter what an individual has done in the past, he or she retains dignity as a child of God. Consequently, Farley would likely resist any suggestion that persons who acted inappropriately, or morally wrongfully, even according to Meyers's lenient standards of burdened agency, should simply be abandoned to stew in their own bad decisions. A young woman who gave an inebriated consent to a sexual relationship at a fraternity party may not be a "pure" victim on either the traditional standard or Meyer's "burdened agency" standard. Yet that does not mean that we withhold either our sympathy from her or our critical scrutiny from the man who took advantage of her vulnerability. At the same time, morally critical scrutiny of the assailant's actions cannot mean indifference to his fundamental welfare, either. We can insist that he be appropriately punished while taking steps to ensure that the punishment does not degrade his humanity or deprive him of an opportunity to set his life on a better course.

Challenges to Compassion

In 1987, in *Booth v. Maryland,* the U.S. Supreme Court held that it was unconstitutional to introduce victim impact statements in the sentencing phase of capital cases. The statements in question described "the personal characteristics of the victim and the emotional impact of the crime on the family." They also "set forth the family members' opinions and characterizations of the crimes and the defendant." The Court held that such statements violated the Eighth Amendment because "this information is irrelevant to a capital sentencing decision, and . . . its admission creates a constitutionally unacceptable risk that the jury may impose the death penalty in an arbitrary and capricious manner."[25] Two years later, in *South Carolina v. Gathers*, the Court held that descriptions of the personal characteristics of the victim are inadmissible if they "cannot be said to relate directly to the circumstances of the crime," and in particular if they pertain to matters about which the defendant was unaware at the time of the crime.[26] Shortly afterward, however, the Court reversed course. In 1991, in *Payne v. Tennessee*, the Court held that the Constitution erected "no per se bar" to presenting statements to a sentencing jury in a capital case that describe the personal characteristics of the victim and the impact on the victim's family of the murder. In a nutshell, *Payne* overruled both *Booth* and *Gathers*. As Justice Thurgood Marshall pointed out in his dissent, no new legal or empirical arguments had emerged in the intermittent period. The only thing that had changed was the composition of the Court.[27]

Victim impact statements have strategic importance. They are meant to elicit a compassionate response from those who hear them, particularly the sentencing judge or a jury. They are meant to give their audience some sense of the suffering that the victims have endured because of the action of the defendant. Yet as Margaret Farley has cautioned us, compassion is not an automatically unproblematic response; it can be misshapen, misdirected, or even blind. Her warning is particularly important in the context of criminal trials. I now want to suggest that giving distinct consideration to the *subjects of compassion*, the *objects of compassion*, and the *act of compassion* itself help us understand the potential pitfalls in the use of victim impact statements in the context of criminal sentencing. Moreover, this tripartite analysis can shed light on the conflicting opinions on this question issued by the Supreme Court within a very short period of time.

Subjects of Compassion

Individual persons, with unique life histories, feel compassion. Our own experiences—experiences of suffering, loss, fear, diminishment, and sorrow—harrow our souls and shape our imaginations. They also provide a basis for empathizing with others undergoing experiences that we can recognize as similar in some sense. Everyone suffers. And our own experiences of suffering can provide a basis for solidarity and an impetus toward moral and political reform. We act so that others will not have to suffer in the same way we did.

Personal experience can also provide a secure foundation upon which to build analogical and imaginative extensions of empathy. By talking to other people and reading about their lives, as well as reading great literature, we can incorporate vicariously the experience of others in our moral universe. Yet it can also impose a virtually impregnable barrier to compassion. If we uncritically treat our own experiences as normative, we can be tempted to discount the vision and voices of other persons with other experiences. We can disregard their suffering, telling ourselves that if they had only behaved more like we do, it could have been avoided.

The word "compassion" comes from the Latin word *compatior*; it means "to suffer with" another. Compassion, in the first instance, requires an acute awareness of the fact of the other's suffering, which can emerge from direct observation, first-person accounts by the sufferer (such as victim impact statements), or third-person descriptions of the sufferer (such as newspaper reports). Second, feeling compassion requires us to extend a bridge of understanding and connection. But what is the purpose of that bridge? Meyers notes that we can identify with the plight of another for at least three purposes:[28] We can put ourselves in their shoes for purposes of "sizing them up"—for purposes of objectively evaluating the situation that prompted them to act. We can empathize with them, creating a bond in order understand their plight more fully; this requires "navigating between imagining the other's first person-perspective and gathering relevant information about her from your own third-person perspective."[29] Finally, we can sympathize with them—which Meyers defines as adding a desire to help to the exercise of empathy.

Meyers's distinctions, in my view, help us recognize an implicit controversy about the use of victim impact statements in criminal sentencing that deserves explicit attention. The fundamental task of a sentencing jury is, in fact, to "size up" the defendant to mete out a just punishment. It is not to empathize with either the victim or the defendant as a friend would do, nor to sympathize with the individual in order to help him or her as a therapist or social worker would. The subjects experiencing compassion—in this case, the members of the jury—are constrained by their role-related obligations. Those who worry about the use of victim impact statements in criminal sentencing worry, I think, that such statements will create the wrong sort of bridge of empathy between the jurors and the victim, a bridge that misleads them about their appointed task.

Objects of Compassion

For whom do we feel compassion? Elizabeth Spelman perceptively contends that "[s]uffering is the human condition in the sense that those whose suffering we take seriously are those whose humanity we take seriously and vice versa."[30] Furthermore, she notes that taking someone's suffering seriously means taking that person's own view of suffering seriously. While Spelman believes that it is possible for human beings fruitfully to treat others as objects of compassion, she also notes that "humans are ingenious in devising ways to deny such shared status even while appearing to affirm it."[31]

In the context of the courtroom, this destructive ingenuity can adversely affect both victims and defendants. The prospect of being a victim of a violent crime is horrifying; that horror can create a barrier to compassion between jurors and victims. To avoid the necessity of confronting their own potential vulnerability, jurors may find ways to treat the victim as somehow culpably other than themselves. They can then say that what happened to the victim would not—indeed, could not—happen to them. A different but equally effective barrier against compassion operates with respect to defendants, particularly in the context of criminal sentencing. Configuring the defendant as a monster rather than a man or woman impedes the sort of imaginative identification that would facilitate compassion. As Meyers argues, "Fear of being victimized obstructs empathy with victims while also casting a shadow on the humanity of perpetrators."[32]

The first key issue in the Supreme Court discussion of the use of victim impact statements is implicated in the foregoing reflections on the objects of compassion. The crime of murder squelches out the life of a human being. The ensuing loss can be viewed in two ways. On the one hand, the life of the murder victim is of equal fundamental dignity with the life of every other human being, at least according to the values of a liberal democracy such as the United States. Age, beauty, occupation, and wealth neither increase nor decrease that fundamental dignity. On the other hand, the murder victim is a unique person, whose life might have taken a better or worse trajectory and might have been more or less enmeshed in the lives of other people in the community. Snuffing out the victim's life has particular ramifications because it wounds particular friends, relatives, and colleagues whose lives were intertwined with that of the victim.

Consequently, those who advocate for broader use of victim impact statements in criminal sentencing aim to honor the particularity of victims' lives. Chief Justice William Rehnquist observed that the contested statement in the *Booth* case "showed that the victim was an out of work, mentally handicapped individual, perhaps not, in the eyes of most, a significant contributor to society, but nonetheless a murdered human being."[33] They strive to emphasize that murder victims are not simply abstract, nameless, faceless, persons but, rather, unique and irreplaceable members of our community. They want to make concrete not only the specific nature of the frequently horrific murderous activity (which is allowed in sentencing) but also its specific consequences for those left behind.

The murder at the center of the *Payne* case, for example, involved a brutal stabbing of a twenty-eight-year-old mother, her two-year-old daughter, and her three-year old son. The mother and daughter died. Miraculously, the little boy, whose name was Nicholas, lived through the ordeal, after holding his own intestines inside his abdomen as he was loaded into the ambulance. He went to live with his grandmother after leaving the hospital. One statement at issue was the grandmother's testimony about Nicholas's emotional state: "He cries for his mom. He doesn't seem to understand why she doesn't come home. And he cries for his sister Lacie. He comes to me many times during the week and asks me, Grandmama, do you miss my Lacie. And I tell him yes. He says, I'm worried about my Lacie."[34]

By contrast, those who resist the broader use of victim impact statements do not deny the pathos of such stories. Yet they are worried that the widespread use of such statements will undermine the equal dignity of all persons, by facilitating a sentencing pattern that punishes the murder of society's "haves" more seriously than the murder of its "have nots." They would, of course, concede that human beings have different gifts and talents, which result in different levels of recognition and compensation in social and economic life. Those differences, they would point out, are at least partially accommodated in civil suits for wrongful death. The point of a criminal trial, they would contend, is to vindicate the equal importance of our common humanity—the murder of a pauper should be treated the same as the murder of a prince. Moreover, those who worry about protecting fundamental human equality in the courtroom context are sensitive to the ways in which that equality is already threatened, because of many types of unjust discrimination, particularly but not exclusively racism. No matter what their own race, defendants who have killed African American victims receive lighter sentences than those who kill white victims.[35] Other studies have shown that African American defendants receive harsher sentences than white defendants charged with the same type of crime.[36]

Justice Lewis Powell wrote for the majority in *Booth*, which *Payne* overruled. The murder in this case was especially ghastly: an elderly couple were bound, gagged, and stabbed repeatedly in the chest with a kitchen knife by drug addicts seeking money to purchase heroin. The victim impact statements testified to the love and esteem that family members and friends felt for the victims, who were pillars of the community. Yet Powell was worried about the institutional ramifications of allowing evidence of the victim's character to be introduced in the sentencing process in our adversary system: "Putting aside the strategic risks of attacking the victim's character before the jury, in appropriate cases the defendant presumably would be permitted to put on evidence that the victim was of dubious moral character, was unpopular, or was ostracized from his family."[37]

Acts of Compassion

Even the act of compassion itself is difficult to pin down. Philosophers distinguish among different terms used for feeling suffering with a fellow human being, which depend upon how deeply the person exercising compassion embeds herself in the world and worldview of the other person. Compassion is always a dialogue between the self's view of the other's situation and the other's own view of that situation. In exercising compassion we attempt to "walk a mile in the shoes of the other," but this attempt can easily shift into a moment of judgment rather than fellow feeling. We can override their own feelings, by attributing to them what we would have felt in their place—a projected experience that is ultimately highly misleading. Sometimes we put ourselves in the shoes of another—but not in their bodies, minds, and hearts. We try out their situations—but not their selves. Persons with disabilities, for example, often complain that able-bodied persons give too low an evaluation of the quality of their lives. In other contexts, we put ourselves in the shoes of other persons to imaginatively decide what we would have done in their place. This imaginative decision, in turn, easily operates as an implicit judgment upon what they actually did. We assess ourselves more capable of responding appropriately than they were. Proceeding in this manner, the process of empathy can be doubly delusional; we overestimate our own ability to handle a situation, and we discount the challenges under which the other person was operating.

This troubling phenomenon of compassion sheds light on the second key issue in the Supreme Court discussion of the use of victim impact statements: whether capital sentencing needs to focus on the harm intended or foreseen by the defendant, on the one hand, or, on the other hand, can broaden to encompass all harm caused by the defendant's criminal act, whether or not it was intended or foreseen. The justices who oppose the introduction of victim impact statements take the first position; those who support their introduction take the second. In philosophical terms, this debate raises the question of moral luck. Consider an example: Should the drunk driver who hits and kills a young mother be susceptible to more punishment than the drunk driver who hits and kills a drug-addicted prostitute? Why should either be subject to punishment when a drunk driver who is pulled over before harming someone else gets off with a slap on the wrist?

The phenomenon of moral luck intersects with the act of compassion in complicated ways. It can channel compassion both toward and away from various parties to an incident. For example, the story of a dead young woman and her motherless children not only pulls at the heart strings, it can also create a barrier to empathy with the defendant, the drunk driver who killed her. Yet in other situations, the operations of moral luck may funnel compassion to the defendant. This redirection of compassion is particularly likely to happen in cases where moral sentiment and legal norms have been evolving in a more rigorous direction, as the Brock Turner case demonstrates. Jurors and even judges, particularly male judges and jurors, who think back to their own youthful behavior may extend compassion to him because they see their own long-ago misdeeds in his. Even if they have come to see that behavior as deeply morally problematic, they may empathize with him. They may want to validate—through him—the second chance that they themselves were given by virtue of being born in a different time.

Conflicts of Compassion

No human being is an endless well of compassion. As Elizabeth Spelman argues, compassion is an important but scarce social resource. Because compassion captures interest, which in turn attracts resources and galvanizes movements for change, it is a resource over which there is considerable competition. Whose pain moves us? How and why does it move us? The endless appeals of groups such as Save the Children, the ASPCA, or

Amnesty International show us that charitable groups are well aware of the need to spark compassion in a competitive world. Those who succeed have proven themselves not merely, or even necessarily, to have the most worthy cause. Instead, they have proven themselves to be more adept at rhetorical appeals.

The practice of rhetoric, however, is an art as well as a science—and some people are much better at it than others, by virtue of talent or training, or both. The formulation and presentation of victim impact statements presents a rich opportunity to practice the art of rhetoric. As Aristotle noted, persuasion is not simply a matter of the soundness of the reasons proffered in a particular speech (what Aristotle referred to as *logos*); it is also a matter of the attractiveness and credibility of the speaker himself or herself (*ethos*), as well as the ability to move the audience to feel sympathy with the speaker's point of view (*pathos*).[38] Those who defend the introduction of victim impact statements point out that the American legal system has always operated with lawyers of different levels of analytic and persuasive abilities. Yet those who oppose the use of such statements maintain that they will highlight the relative rhetorical powers of victims, thereby introducing a new locus of unfairness in the legal system. As Justice Powell wrote in *Booth*, "in some cases the victim will not leave behind a family, or the family members may be less articulate in describing their feelings even though their sense of loss is equally severe. The fact that the imposition of the death sentence may turn on such distinctions illustrates the danger of allowing juries to consider this information."[39]

To return to the Stanford rape case, it is important to recognize that the persuasive power of Emily Doe's statement was not separable from the advantages given to her by her social class and education. Either deliberately or instinctively, she framed her ordeal in a narrative structure, which included a state of initial flourishing, followed by a traumatic event—the sexual assault, followed by partially successful efforts at self-reconstitution and recovery. She rhetorically places her audience—the sentencing judge—in a position of either bringing the story to a satisfying completion by handing Brock Turner an appropriately severe sentence, or subverting that story by giving him a mere slap on the wrist. Would a woman without those advantages who had suffered similar abuse have been able to make her case so compellingly? As Diana Tietjens Meyers has observed, many persons who have suffered grave abuses do not naturally experience it in the narrative form so compelling to judges and juries.[40] The trauma has upended or undermined their orderly experience of the world. If they have not been fortunate enough to receive an education that allows them to impose an audience-friendly order on their presentation, their victim impact statements may fall on deaf ears.

Experience, Roles, and Institutions

Victim impact statements recount the experiences of our fellow human beings who have suffered in body, mind, and soul because of the unjust and unlawful activity of others. Some of the victims were directly and immediately targets of the criminal activity in question; others were victimized indirectly, by their ties of love, dependence, and loyalty to the direct victims. In some sense, of course, an essential premise of our system of criminal law is that our entire community is harmed by a crime. An injury to one member of the body politic adversely affects all members. This premise is inscribed in the caption of any criminal case; the complaining party against the defendant is the state or the federal government, not the victim or the victim's family.

Margaret Farley's writings impel us to take seriously the experience of all victims. Her insights call upon us to treat them with both compassion and respect. At the same time, however, she would never deny even the most brutal criminal status as a child of God, which confers upon each of us an unalienable dignity. And she would doubtless insist upon the importance of procedural protections for anyone accused of a crime, particularly in a nation such as the United States, in which race and social class can significantly affect a defendant's prospects for justice.

What does taking the experience of victims seriously require in the context of the deeply flawed American justice system? Farley's normative framework on compassionate respect, taken in conjunction with the foregoing reflections on the special issues raised by compassion for those harmed by unjust acts, might not give us a definitive answer. It could, however, lead us to approach the question in the following manner.

First, as a Christian ethicist, Farley would be acutely sensitive to the effects of both individual and social sin on the decisions we make. Sin affects our capacity to see and judge correctly. Consequently, I think Farley would press us not only to ask how our reactions to the experiences of others gives us moral insight but also to reflect upon how those reactions can blind us to what we need to see at a particular point in time. She would invite us to reflect critically on our sense of whose experiences count, and why they count, for the decision making at hand.

Second, Farley would be deeply troubled by the limitations on the practice of compassion to victims brought to our attention by Spelman and Meyers. We may lack compassion for others who are suffering because we have too small and cramped a basis for knowing what their situation really is. We may also lack compassion because we suffer from a failure of imagination; we cannot place ourselves in their situation in a way that makes their predicament vivid to us. Even if we understand, abstractly, how another's situation pains the person, we may be unable to feel empathy for that person, either because of the constrictions of our own heart or because somehow we have convinced ourselves that *his or her* pain does not matter.

Third, as someone committed to justice as well as mercy, Farley would take seriously the phenomenon of clashes of compassion as they now play themselves out in American courtrooms. Only a very wise, perceptive, and self-reflective person could sort through the competing currents of experience, victimhood, and compassion as they unfurl in a given case, making appropriate adjustments for the rhetorical advantages or disadvantages possessed by the various parties to a criminal trial. Unfortunately, those criteria are not mandatory qualifications for judges, nor are they requirements for citizens who serve on juries. Consequently, wisely and responsibly dealing with lapses of empathy and clashes of compassion in the criminal justice context requires designing a system that can be operated by people who are not always wise or responsible.

At this point we need to broaden our vision to consider questions not only of retributive justice but also of social justice. How can we channel considerations of experience, evocations of compassion, in ways that are likely to advance respect for persons and the common good? What system can we design that will minimize the chance for reliance on misplaced compassion, particularly in cases of conflict? These questions invite us to return to the work of both MacIntyre and Noonan, discussed in the first chapter of this book.

MacIntyre has defended the importance of institutions in allowing practices that support the virtues to continue on in time. He sees them primarily in instrumental terms. Institutions provide the external goods—money and power—that allow practices to continue from generation to generation. Because they trade in external goods, institutions, in his view, are susceptible to distortion and corruption. Individuals may be drawn to them for the money and power they offer, rather than for the goods intrinsic to the practices they support.[41] MacIntyre is surely right that institutions can be an impetus for corruption. Yet they can also be a barrier to it. At their best, institutions can help ensure that the practices they inculcate are structured in ways that safeguard against predictable forms of misbehavior, including but not limited to corruption.

Some branches of Christianity see institutional life as inherently pernicious, as the title of Reinhold Niebuhr's famous book *Moral Man and Immoral Society* pithily suggests.[42] Yet other branches, including the Roman Catholic tradition to which Margaret Farley belongs, proffer a more nuanced assessment of institutional life. She would not, of course, deny the temptations in institutional life, nor the many moral deficiencies in all human institutions. At the same time, I think, she would recognize some positive and protective features of institutional life. Ideally, a more-or-less morally sound institution will assist its members in growing in virtue relative to the practices it supports. Equally importantly, however, a well-designed institution also anticipates and militates against likely distortions of those practices, whether they are due to individual malevolence or simply to human weakness and limitations. While a sound institution points toward all forms of excellence as ideals worth striving for, it does not base its operational practices on the illusion that most participants in those practices have already achieved the ideal.

In my view, despite its many flaws, the American legal system strives to operate in a manner that is realistic about the normal run of human abilities, including but not limited to capacities for moral decision making. One way in which it does so is by sharply defining the role-related obligations of each party to a criminal trial. The responsibilities of a judge are strictly defined; he or she is obliged to ensure that the trial proceeds fairly according to the law. He or she is not meant to single-handedly bring about the correct result. This is not to say, of course, that fairly managing a trial requires being blind to the unique circumstances of the persons before the bench. In *Persons and Masks of the Law*, Noonan wrote about the dangers of judges placing "masks" over their own faces, as well as those of the other participants in a trial. Yet Noonan does not deny the other danger—that judges will be *unjust* "respecters of persons" by paying too much attention to those to whom they have a social or economic connection, or an empathetic bond based on perceived affinity. The development of these bonds is inevitable—judges are human beings, too. They also are highly educated, well paid, and accustomed to a certain amount of deference. The task of a sound legal institution, therefore, is to develop a framework that minimizes the danger of *prosōpolempsia* on the part of the judiciary—lifting up for favorable treatment the faces that matter socially or politically.[43]

Similarly, a jury is not a council of philosopher-kings. Its mandate is not to do justice in a broad and holistic sense but, rather, to apply the law to the facts as proved by the prosecution. A second way in which the legal system structures itself in light of a realistic anthropology is to carefully describe and delimit the material that can be presented to the fact-finder, particularly a jury. The material must be both relevant to the question they are asked to answer and not unduly prejudicial to the defendant.

In my own view, those who worry about the use of victim impact statements in the context of criminal sentencing (especially but not exclusively capital sentencing) have the better of the ethical and political argument. While it proclaims equal justice for all, our legal system remains deeply socially stratified, particularly by race and economic status. In such a context, the use of victim statements poses too great a likelihood that victims will be sorted into categories based on social worthiness, and the fate of defendants will become even more dependent upon the relative rhetorical skills of their counsel. In our own time, as in Cicero's, more money buys better rhetoric. It may be impossible to eliminate this feature of American legal institutions. It is certainly possible to avoid exacerbating its effects, by declining to give wider scope to the use of victim impact statements.

In response, those who advocate the broader use of victim impact statements in criminal sentencing point to the virtue of "balance."[44] They note that the past half-century has witnessed the growth of procedural protections for the accused. The Eighth Amendment to the Constitution safeguards the right of a defendant to have mitigating evidence about his character and background presented to the judge or jury before a sentence is handed down. While not directly attacking these protections, they contend that balance requires similar attention to the plight of the victims and their families. The *Payne* majority proclaimed: "We reaffirm the view expressed by Justice Cardozo in *Snyder v. Massachusetts*: [J]ustice, though due to the accused, is due to the accuser also. The concept of fairness must not be strained till it is narrowed to a filament. We are to keep the balance true."[45]

Yet striking an appropriate balance must pay attention to context and purpose. It is not the victim who is the defendant's adversary, but the State. As Justice John Paul Stevens wrote in his dissenting opinion in *Payne*, "The premise that a criminal prosecution requires an even-handed balance between the State and the defendant is also incorrect. The Constitution grants certain rights to the criminal defendant and imposes special limitations on the State designed to protect the individual from overreaching by the disproportionately powerful State."[46] In the context of a criminal trial, an *appropriate* balance is not an *even* balance.

This does not mean, however, that the experience of victims ought not to play an important role in the broader context of the criminal justice system. In my view, the experience of victims is most crucial in the development of statutory frameworks and the assessment of what a city should be prohibited or permitted. As I described in the first chapter, John Noonan has emphasized the significance of the experience of believers in the development of the church's moral teaching. An analogous phenomenon characterizes experience of both victims and perpetrators around violations of criminal statutes. Experience shapes the legal categorization of particular types of activity. In some cases, activity that used be characterized as criminal no longer is so, such as the use of contraception or the consumption of alcohol. Conversely, what used to be considered tolerable behavior is now legally prohibited. Spousal abuse is more likely to be treated with the severity it deserves, thanks to activists who shed light into the dark corners of domestic violence.[47] Moreover, driving while intoxicated, which was formerly considered a socially acceptable form of risk-taking, has now been reconfigured as deeply antisocial behavior. That reconfiguration is largely attributable to the tireless efforts of groups such as Mothers Against Drunk Driving, which publicized the destruction inflicted by drivers impaired by alcohol or other substances. The experience of victims and their loved ones should instruct lawmakers about the nature and gravity of the activity they criminalize.[48]

Yet as victims' advocates point out, much more needs to be done to help those whose lives have been devastated by criminal activity. And much more *can* be done that does not conflict with procedural protections given to defendants at criminal trials. More social resources should be devoted to crime prevention, as well as to providing a full spectrum of care to victims and their families. More specifically, the community should treat the occurrence of a crime as a failure to protect one of its own, which requires remedy and repair on everyone's part. The criminal law treats a crime as an attack on the common good. The community as a whole, therefore, should assume responsibility for restoring itself to wholeness by caring for the victim of the crime.

As one victims' advocate noted: "Victims of violent crime and their families pay taxes and vote, and they need to receive just compensation for what they went through."[49] At the very least, no victim of a crime should be forced to assume responsibility for his or her own hospital or rehabilitation bills. Victims should receive assistance in rebuilding their lives, including compensation for lost wages and assistance in finding new employment. Moreover, these resources can and should be made available to the many victims whose assailants are never found or brought to trial.[50]

To be the victim of a violent crime is to suffer an excruciating violation of body, mind, and soul at the deliberate will of another human being. To be related by bonds of love or friendship to someone who has been victimized is not only to walk through the valley of the shadow of death but also to endure the touch of moral evil. Margaret Farley's account of suffering does not minimize these experiences nor attempt to encompass them with a glib explanation. She recognizes that "there is still darkness beyond the power of our minds to penetrate." God's presence in the midst of such darkness can only be experienced as a "dread mercy."[51] Yet God is present with us, and we can be present with each other.

> Misery in the heart of the merciful does not "double" the pain of the world; it holds it all together, so that hearts break together in the sharing of one another's burden. Thus are the burdens lightened and transformed. For there is a love stronger than death, a crucified love that does not turn away from swords of sorrow, and that goes forth unconditionally no matter what the forces of evil may do against it. The point of the cup and the cross is not death, but that relationships can hold.[52]

6

Covenant Fidelity and Culture Wars

Engaging Paul Ramsey

JOSEPH SAIKEWICZ WAS born in Massachusetts on July 27, 1909. Profoundly mentally handicapped and unable to communicate verbally, he was placed in a state school at the age of fourteen. Five years later, he was moved to Belchertown State School for the Feeble-Minded, nestled in the rolling hills of central Massachusetts, where he spent the rest of his life. Mr. Saikewicz had an I.Q. of 10; his mental development never exceeded that of a three-year-old. He was not the sort of person destined to attract attention in this achievement-oriented world. Yet his name has become widely known in the realm of medical ethics and law. Joseph Saikewicz was famous not for what he *did*, but for what was done—and more significantly, not done—*to him* as he lay dying.

In 1976, at the age of sixty-seven, Mr. Saikewicz was diagnosed with acute myeloblastic monocytic leukemia, a disease of the blood that was inevitably fatal. The normal treatment for the disease was chemotherapy, which not only targeted the leukemia cells but also subjected the patient to significant side effects, such as severe anemia requiring multiple blood transfusions. Only 30 to 50 percent of those treated with chemotherapy achieved a period of remission, which typically lasted between two and thirteen months. Patients younger than sixty were more successful in both tolerating the treatment and achieving remission. Notwithstanding these somewhat sobering statistics, however, most patients suffering from this type of leukemia decided to undergo treatment.

Because Mr. Saikewicz was not able to make the decision for himself, the superintendent of the Belchertown State School sought the guidance of the Massachusetts probate court. After a hearing, the probate judge agreed with the report of Mr. Saikewicz's court-appointed guardian ad litem that Mr. Saikewicz should not be treated, in part because he would not be able to comprehend the fear and pain associated with chemotherapy and in part because the treatment offered only a limited and uncertain benefit The Massachusetts Supreme Judicial Court granted an application for direct appellate review, seeking not only to address Saikewicz's case but also to provide guidance for all other cases. It held that: (1) all persons, whether competent or incompetent, have a right to refuse potentially life-saving medical treatment under some circumstances; and (2) in determining whether incompetent persons should be given such treatment, the decision "should be that which would be made by the incompetent person, if that person were competent, but taking into account the present and future incompetency of the individual as one of the factors which would necessarily enter into the decision-making process of the competent person."[1] Ultimately, the Supreme Judicial Court found that its guidelines supported the decision to withhold chemotherapy from Joseph Saikewicz, who passed away peacefully on September 4, 1976, almost three months before the opinion supporting the decision was published.[2]

The *Saikewicz* case set off a firestorm of discussion, precipitating both eloquent defenses and withering critiques. One of the most trenchant analyses was produced by Paul Ramsey, who devotes to the case an entire chapter of *Ethics at the Edges of Life: Medical and Legal Intersections*, his last book on medical ethics.[3] Ramsey expresses deep reservations about both the intellectual coherence and the moral purposes of the "substituted judgment" standard imposed by the Massachusetts Supreme Judicial Court. Because no one can actually discern the wishes of the never-competent patient, he views the standard as a dangerous license for "competent persons to impose their own private standards of life on an incompetent."[4]

In its approach to legal cases and the moral norms inscribed within them, *Ethics at the Edges of Life* is ahead of its time. In my view, the book is a harbinger of the culture wars that fully inflamed certain segments of American Christianity a quarter of a century after it was published, and that show no signs of burning out by its fortieth anniversary in 2018. Ramsey's stance is combative; he subjects legal decisions to relentless and often withering critique from the perspective of Christian moral commitments. Fighting what he perceives to be a rear-guard action against the rise of secular individualism, Ramsey urges like-minded believers to develop the skills that will allow them to resist the quickly secularizing legal system on its own terms. As I will detail more fully below, the strategies he recommended in the mid-1970s became key elements of the cultural conservative playbook over the next several decades.[5] Yet Paul Ramsey was not always this sort of culture warrior. He did not always view the secular legal system as implacably hostile to Christian moral norms. In fact, he was at the vanguard of American theological ethicists who have taken the law seriously and even sympathetically as an intellectual conversation partner. Nonetheless, the way in which he chose to engage the law shifted substantially over time.[6]

In this chapter, I will trace and engage the evolution of Paul Ramsey's writings on the Christian ethics and law. In the first section, I will propose that his views of the relationship of law and Christian ethics can be roughly grouped into three overlapping periods: (1) "the love and justice" period, strongly influenced by Reinhold Niebuhr; (2) the "creation and covenant" period, heavily indebted to Karl Barth; and (3) the "Christian combativeness" period, which was shaped, I suspect, by Ramsey's own previous immersion in debates about just war theory.

A certain degree of restlessness characterizes Ramsey's attitude toward and approach to secular legal norms and decisions. He cannot settle down into any one framework for relating theological ethics to law. What accounts for this restlessness? In the second section of the chapter, I argue that it is largely attributable to a lacuna in his fundamental theological anthropology. As an ethicist, he is deeply concerned with the manifold ways in which human beings disregard their obligations to God and to one another. Yet he never straightforwardly addresses the role of law in grappling with human sinfulness. In very different ways, the models of "love transforming justice," "creation and covenant," and "Christian combativeness" struggle to grasp the complicated and often ambiguous way in which human law and legal systems must approach the challenge of containing, if not always constraining, sin.

The concluding section will return to the case of Joseph Saikewicz. I argue that the decision of the Massachusetts Supreme Judicial Court is defensible, even on Ramsey's own terms. In fact, in my view, the hermeneutic of suspicion he applies to the decision is more likely to erode than enhance the values he cares about most. Moreover, I will suggest that the real threat to the dignity of Joseph Saikewicz was not his doctors' decision to withhold chemotherapy at the end of his life, but society's decision to immure him and others like him in an institution like Belchertown in the first place. Questions of medical ethics are ultimately inseparable from questions of social justice.

Christian Ethics and Secular Law: Three Periods of Engagement

Ramsey's first period of deep engagement with the law is exemplified by *Nine Modern Moralists.* Published in 1962, the book includes materials that Ramsey developed in the mid- to late 1950s, particularly two chapters based on the Clarence D. Ashley Lectures on Law and Theology, which he delivered at the New York University School of Law in 1958. In these materials, Ramsey treats secular law as an illuminating source for reflections on Christian ethics, particularly its central problematic of the relationship of love to justice.[7]

In *Nine Modern Moralists,* Ramsey takes the position that Christian "love interpenetrates and invigorates justice at every point, and often refashions it."[8] He goes so far as to propose that from a Christian point of view, the just course of action cannot be defined without the input of love: "Where Christ reigns, *agape* enters into a fresh determination of what it is right to do." He immediately goes on to note, however, that "Christ does not reign over a structureless world or over men who are bereft of any sense of natural injustice."[9] For Ramsey, the structures of natural justice and injustice are generously revealed in human law, both the *ius gentium* and the positive law of particular political communities. Consequently, he begins to elide the idea of love transforming *justice* with the idea of love transforming *law*—both natural law and positive law.

In dialogue with the progressive Roman Catholic moralist Jacques Maritain and the secular legal scholar Edmond Cahn, Ramsey develops an inductive and flexible account of natural morality. From Maritain, he borrows the idea that we know the substance of the natural law not by deductive knowledge but by inclination. Drawing on Cahn, Ramsey is inclined to describe that inclination in negative rather than positive terms—as *dis*inclination. We encounter moral claims through a sense of *injustice,* rather than a sense of justice itself.[10] In Ramsey's view, it is impossible to encounter the natural law in pure, unadulterated form. We meet it as part of an admixture. A key site of our reflection on natural moral norms is the *ius gentium,* the law of nations, which displays to us the "natural or unwritten law itself as exceeding the very sphere of nature and as particularized by the conditions of social life."[11]

From Cahn, Ramsey adopts the idea that the case-based reasoning of the common law tradition operates as a "*prism* through which moral judgments can become clear."[12] Ramsey argues that the insights of these very different theorists actually converge: "For both of these legal philosophers decision-making . . . is at once natural and contextual or positive; and for both 'it is realistic to look at the law . . . as a rich repository of moral knowledge which is continually reworked, revised, and refined.'"[13] A natural sense of justice, or more accurately, injustice, animates that repository.[14]

Yet it is impossible to distill a pure form of that sense of justice, a fact which is of consequence for both the legal and the religious realms. Ramsey contends that the natural "sense of injustice" manifest in the secular Western legal tradition is inseparable from the Christian moral tradition as it has developed over the centuries. Ramsey maintains, for example, that it is impossible to answer conclusively whether the idea of human beings as rights-bearers stems from biblical reasoning or reason through inclination, or is attributable primarily to the insights of divine justice or natural justice. "[I]t is the great glory of the Western tradition of morals and law that these questions cannot be answered conclusively."[15]

Ramsey treats the fact the community's religious heritage shapes the moral sensibilities of its judges as largely unproblematic. He wants to preserve the possibility of "some direct relationship between the law and man's living toward the goal of responding faithfully to the faithfulness of God, or between the law and the measuring of human justice in terms of the redemptive justice of God."[16] It is appropriate for fundamental theological concepts of the dignity of the human person and the common good to seep into the secular law. Yet he also emphasizes that directly imposing biblical justice is a mistake. Civil society should not codify biblical law or a strict religious interpretation of natural law.[17] Taking as examples the Catholic position on contraception, the Protestant position on bingo, or the Sunday closing laws, Ramsey maintains that "so long as such wide diversity of sincere opinion on these matters exists in our society, the distinction between mandatory and permissive legislation, or between state-action and the voluntary acceptance of certain standards by any religious group and their imposition upon its membership by 'spiritual' sanctions, must plainly be made."[18] While it is one thing for a judge to be influenced by religious values, he must not "suppose that *as judge* he belongs more to his particular religious community of discussion than to the discussion and decision enshrined in law."[19]

In *Nine Modern Moralists*, then, the dominant view of the relationships between and among love, justice, and law are flexible and dynamic. Legal materials, especially case law, provide source material for Christian ethicists to identify norms of love transforming justice, in which the boundaries between the two realms are not always clear. Ramsey's proposed method for identifying norms is inductive and somewhat tentative; it consists of reflection on norms arising in the prism of an actual cases. Moreover, such reflection is not purely rational; it also requires attention to the inclinations and disinclinations animated by such cases.

At the same time, *Nine Modern Moralists* also includes passages pointing toward a different way of thinking about the relationship of Christian ethics and natural morality, which is organized around the relationship of covenant and creation. Ramsey writes:

> As Karl Barth might put the point that has to be made: natural justice or the requirements made known to us through fundamental inclination or disinclination are the external or natural basis, the precondition, and the possibility of Exodus into covenant; while covenant-righteousness is the internal basis, the true meaning and the final purpose of whatever utterances of essential human nature may be produced in man's intellect as he seeks to know the good.[20]

The Barthian relationship of creation and covenant grew in importance for Ramsey as his work on applied ethics continued and diversified in scope. It becomes a dominant image for working out the meaning of love transforming justice in the second phase of his work, as exemplified in *Christian Ethics and the Sit-In* and *The Patient as Person*.[21] By reframing love transforming justice in terms of creation as constituting the external basis of the covenant and humanity, Ramsey forges a more stable base on which Christian norms and the secular law can engage one another. At the same time, he risks losing the dynamic and tentative nature of the relationship between Christian ethics and the law that he worked out in *Nine Modern Moralists*.

The evolution in Ramsey's view of that relationship proceeds by a series of informal equivalences and substitutions. Tacitly assuming that the idea of love transforming justice is more or less encapsulated in the Barthian formulation of creation as the external basis of covenant, Ramsey frequently goes on to equate "creation" with the constructed political order, including the secular legal regime. Building on this equation, he then proposes that the secular law, almost as a stand-in for creation, should serve as the external basis of the covenant. He writes, for example: "The state and its law as an ordinance of creation, natural justice, human and legal rights, and social institutions generally . . . all are the external basis making possible the actualization of the promise of covenant; while covenant or fellow humanity is the internal basis and meaning of every right, true justice, or law.[22] More specifically, Ramsey tends to employ a two-step process in substitution "law" for "creation" in the Barthian formula. First, he uses the secular understanding of a *contractual* relationship as the external basis for the *covenantal* relationship that is its inner meaning and fulfillment. Second, he uses his understanding of covenantal relationships to critique and revise secular contractual norms. Love transforming and elevating justice, in other words, is transmuted into covenant's transforming and elevating contract.

Ramsey's writings on love, law, and justice during this second period have a decidedly optimistic cast, and the idea of covenant transforming contract nicely expresses this optimism. For example, his analysis of the movements to desegregate lunch counters and other public facilities in *Christian Ethics and the Sit-In* weaves together the theological duties of covenant fellowship, the legal duties of public accommodations, and the ethical imperatives of desegregation. In "The Created Destination of Property Right," the first chapter of *Christian Ethics and the Sit-In*, Ramsey maintains that the moral duty of those who offer their services to the public is illuminated by the "inn keeper's law," developed by Anglo-American common law judges. Notwithstanding the general norm of freedom of contract, this law prohibited inns and taverns from turning away anyone for whom they had room. They could not discriminate among the weary and vulnerable travelers who sought rest and nourishment. Ramsey maintains that "[t]he 'inn keeper's law' manifests the fact that the political order with its justice and its law and a man's proper relation to the things he owns are the external basis, the promise, the possibility and capability for covenant-community."[23] Like the "inn keeper's law," anti-segregation laws also reflect the fact that "a man has no natural right to attempt to be a man wholly in isolation from his fellow man in the use of the things he owns."[24]

With these examples in mind, Ramsey maintains that any view of law holding that "a man in isolation with his rights and his just dues comes *first*" is "a basically mistaken view of justice and of human rights, because it is a mistaken view of God's creation in man."[25] He thereby rejects any notion of "bargain" or "contract" becoming a surrogate for "covenant." Instead, Ramsey calls for the ideals of covenant to transform and elevate the requirements of contract law, as well as other types of positive law. Legally defined rights and relationships are the *external basis* for covenant, because they offer "the promise and the substantial possibility" of achieving fellow humanity.[26] In this second period in his thinking, therefore, Ramsey assumes that the demands and possibilities of covenant fellowship can be used to critique, refashion, and improve the secular legal system.

The first period of Ramsey's thought, the "love and justice" period, was characterized by a tentative and ad hoc method of correlating Christian moral norms to the secular law. In contrast, in the second period, the "creation and covenant" period, Ramsey tends to assume that Christians obtain knowledge of the requirements of justice by reflecting on the necessary social preconditions for covenant fidelity. Those reflections, in turn, can be used to critique the legal status quo. While Ramsey continues to sympathetically engage legal phenomena, such as the manner in which courts of equity can avoid the harsh dictates of courts of law, he now views them as vivid *illustrations* of his Barthian account of the relationship of covenant and creation. While continuing to view the secular law as an ally and a conversation partner for Christian ethics, he no longer views it as a quasi-independent source of *insight*.

At the same time, Ramsey is not only more optimistic about the possibility of *knowing* the good, in the second period he is also more sanguine about the possibility of *doing* the good. Whereas the early Ramsey was humble, if not hesitant, about the possibility of true social amelioration, in the "creation and covenant" period he urges Christians to follow the model of Martin Luther King Jr., in working to transform the society by transforming its legal norms. Yet Ramsey's optimism about the possibility of remaking secular law in ways that facilitate covenantal relationships was not long-lived. Quite the opposite. In fact, the third period of Ramsey's account of the relationship of Christian ethics and law is marked by a notable pessimism about the possibility of Christian love's transforming justice. Ramsey's approach in the third period, which I call "combative Christianity," is centrally exemplified by *Ethics at the Edges of Life: Medical and Legal Intersections*— a book in which he treats key aspects of the secular law as an outright threat to the most important commitments of Christian ethics.

What accounts for this sea change in Ramsey's approach to the secular legal system? In my view, it is attributable to *Roe v. Wade*, the Supreme Court's 1973 decision conferring broad constitutional protection upon a woman's choice, in consultation with her physician, to obtain an abortion.[27] The decision radically reconfigured American politics and gave birth to cultural conservatism as a moral and legal protest movement. Although the abortion rights movement had been active for at least a decade by the time *Roe* was handed down, many ordinary Americans saw the decision as a "bolt from the blue," radically modifying abortion law in all parts of the country. Furthermore, many legal scholars expressed skepticism about the jurisprudential basis of the decision, since it was rooted not in a single, clear textual provision of the Constitution Instead, writing for the majority, Justice Harry Blackmun anchored the right to seek an abortion in the "right to privacy," which he gleaned from the "penumbras" of the Bill of Rights. Roe did not mark the first appearance of the right to privacy. In previous years, the court invoked the right to justify striking down laws prohibiting the use of contraception by married couples[28] and later, the sale of contraceptives to married and unmarried persons alike.[29]

Many Protestant theologians, including Ramsey himself, had no objections to the use of contraception within marriage in service to responsible family planning. Yet they lodged significant moral criticisms against the sexual revolution, which they perceived as disastrously putting asunder the bonds of love linking sex, marriage, and children, and as irresponsibly prioritizing ephemeral individual desire. In their view, *Roe* further entrenched the individualism of the sexual revolution that had been ignited by the widespread availability of birth control to unmarried persons. More troublingly, the decision also extended that individualism in a lethal new direction, by giving women the unfettered choice to kill the unborn life within them.

Ethics at the Edges of Life is at once Ramsey's blistering prophetic indictment and his *crie de coeur* against the erosion of Christian moral values in American society. At the end of his first chapter eviscerating the Supreme Court's majority opinion in *Planned Parenthood v. Danforth*,[30] which rebuffed the state of Missouri's efforts to restrict the abortion right within the framework of *Roe,* Ramsey wrote the following:

> If the opinion dissenting from the Court's Bicentennial abortion decision does not, in future years, come to be regarded as one of the great dissents in the history of the United States Supreme Court, then our children and our children's children will not even have been cognizant of the fact that they have journeyed on into the setting sun of Western law and morality, not seeing the shadows. We may even now be living "between the evenings" (a beautiful—and I, believe, Jewish—expression for "twilight"). That's the sum of it.[31]

Ethics at the Edges of Life, in my view, is also both the herald and the vanguard of the American phenomenon we have come to recognize as the culture wars pitting social conservatives against social progressives. Nearly forty years after the book was published, Ramsey's criticisms have become truisms for socially conservative Christianity. He lambasts the "atomistic individualism" that led the *Danforth* majority to strike Missouri's law requiring married women to obtain the consent of their husbands, and minor girls to obtain the consent of their parents, before obtaining an abortion.[32] He contests the "Cartesian dualism" that supports the belief that the unborn and the mentally handicapped do not count as equally protectable persons, because their cognitive function is not sufficiently developed.[33] And he challenges the "Baconian project," which threatens to sweep aside duties to respect all human beings, especially the most vulnerable, in order to carry out medical research in service to technological progress.[34]

Moreover, Ramsey's strategic worries and recommendations are also strikingly familiar in light of the political battles that have transpired in the past few decades. In fact, one might say that they were nothing short of prescient. His close reading of the Supreme Court opinion in the *Danforth* case leads him to urge pro-life lawyers to bring test cases in order to determine precisely what restrictions on the abortion right will survive constitutional challenge.[35] He devotes an entire chapter to examining the status of pro-life physicians and nurses within a medical community that accepts the legitimacy of abortion, euthanasia, and other procedures.[36] Deeply worried that the next generation of pro-life men and women will be squeezed out of the health-care field, Ramsey argues for the development of vigorous individual and institutional conscience protections to provide them with *Lebensraum* for expressing their moral beliefs. His arguments closely overlap with those put forward forty years later by lawyers arguing in support of religious exemptions to the contraceptive mandate in the regulations implementing President Obama's Affordable Care Act.[37]

Moreover, and for our purposes more significantly, in this combative Christianity phase Ramsey not only expresses deep pessimism about the trajectory of Western moral sensibilities, he also urges those who share his pessimism to build legal ramparts protecting important values while they still have time. He writes: "Any grey area in the fabric of the law—in a matter so fundamental as the protection of life—tempts customary morality into that grey area and renders the fabric of morality correspondingly uncertain."[38] Recall that in his first period, exemplified by *Nine Modern Moralists*, Ramsey embraced gray areas and ambiguity in the law, viewing them as necessary for deliberation, discussion, and the gradual unfolding of insights about love and justice. In this third period, by contrast, he views these very same phenomena as dangerous for both Christian ethics and secular law.

For example, consider his argument in the second half of *Ethics at the Edges of Life*, which deals with end-of-life decision making. Ramsey proposes and defends a "medical indications policy" that argues that objective medical risks and benefits are the only salient factors in considering whether to pursue various options to prolong the lives of patients who have not already entered the dying process. While Ramsey intimates that competent patients do not have the moral right to refuse medically indicated treatment on purely subjective grounds, he does admit (somewhat grudgingly) that sound legal policy might allow them to do so anyway.

In any case, strong patients able to defend their own rights are not Ramsey's central concern. The focus of his attention is the fate of the weak and vulnerable. He fears that the introduction of any subjective element in medical decision making for severely handicapped patients will provide cover for invidious quality-of-life judgments. Such judgments stand in fundamental contradiction to the Christian belief that the lives of all human beings, no matter what their disability, possess sanctity and merit protection and care.[39] Consequently, he maintains that objective considerations about the potential effectiveness of treatment are the only legitimate considerations in legally sanctioned decision making about incompetent patients.

We are now in a position to see the tremendous shift in Ramsey's thinking about the secular law. In *Nine Modern Moralists*, Ramsey treats the secular law as a more or less equal partner in discerning the concrete requirements of love transforming justice. In *Christian Ethics and the Sit-In,* he views the law as a useful and fitting external basis for the commitments of fellow humanity. In *Ethics at the Edges of Life,* however, he configures the deliverances of the law as nothing less than a dire threat to Christian moral commitments. Consequently, Ramsey's method of encounter is both wary and critical. He describes his method and goals in the preface of the latter book:

> [W]hen I directly undertake legal analysis I mean at the same time to engage in ethical assessment of a court's or of the law's reasoning. I mean also to hold up these legal processes and the law's final authorization of important national policies as mirrors in which we can see reflected the state of moral questions as these are perceived today—mirrors in which powerful trends in the ethos of contemporary society can be clearly seen.[40]

In *Ethics at the Edges of Life,* Ramsey does not use his interactions with the law to explore the concrete requirements of Christian moral commitments. Instead, he treats those requirements largely as the *grounds* for his indictment of the deliverances of the secular law on matters of life-or-death decision making. He writes:

> I do not hesitate to write as a Christian ethicist . . . to invoke ultimate appeal to scripture or theology and to warrants such as righteousness, faithfulness, canons of loyalty, the awesome sanctity of a human life, humankind in the image of God, holy ground, *hesed* (steadfast covenant love), agape (or 'charity'), as these standards are understood in the religions of our culture, Judaism and Christianity. I do not hesitate to employ the norms of past Christian medical ethics, even while proposing their radical revision.[41]

Generally speaking, Ramsey is not interested in using the secular law as a positive impetus to search out what these norms mean in our pluralistic liberal democracy. In this book, he treats the secular law as holding virtually no wisdom about the positive meaning of religious moral claims. Instead, as the preface signals, the deliverances of Christian ethics serve as the basis for evaluating and critiquing legal norms and the policies they instantiate. It is important to note that the state of the secular law does in fact provide an impetus of a negative sort for the development of Christian ethics. The "radical revision" proposed by Ramsey in *Ethics at the Edges of Life* is the substitution of a more rigid medical-indications policy in place of the Christian tradition's more flexible distinction between "ordinary" and "extraordinary" means of life-prolonging treatment. Ramsey does not propose the substitution because he believes his proposed policy is more nuanced and accurate. Instead, he believes it is safer; it offers a more reliable bulwark against invidious quality-of-life judgments.

I claimed earlier that Ramsey is at the vanguard of the culture wars that erupted across in the United States around the turn of the twenty-first century. In fact, the language that best describes Ramsey's mindset in his "Christian combativeness" phase will not enter the stream of conversation for another two decades, with the publication of Pope John Paul II's encyclical *Evangelium vitae*.[42] Like the pope, Ramsey is convinced that American society is repudiating a "culture of life" that cares for the vulnerable in favor of a "culture of death" that only values individual achievement and worldly success. Consequently, he does not trust the doctors and judges who are at the leading edge in this sea change of values. He can only resist them:

> No one should discount the power of legal precedents to replicate themselves and even to generate kindred species. No one should be convinced by a *theoretical* counterargument that it is always possible to *stop* the extension of legal language and principles. People who do so reason, who say that a line can be drawn somewhere just ahead of us down hill, often themselves ten or fifteen years ago voiced the same counterargument—about a line then just ahead which is now behind us and no longer persuasive as a legal or moral norm.[43]

Sin, Justice, and Law

What accounts for this evolution in Ramsey's attitude toward the appropriate relationship of Christian ethics and the law? I suggest that an important reason for Ramsey's shifting position is his unwillingness to grapple straightforwardly with the relationship between sin and the law, and in particular with the role of *human* law in trying to corral sinful men and women into some sort of functioning political community.

In *Nine Modern Moralists*, exemplifying his "love transforming justice" period, Ramsey is at his most sensitive to the fact that human law needs to grapple in nuanced ways with the effects of sin on individual and communal life. The *ius civilis*—that is, a community's positive law—needs to take into account both the goodness of creation and the reality of sin and selfishness. Human beings commonly act from mixed motives. They are morally weak. The law cannot ask too much of them. Ramsey explores the proper limits of civil law by critically engaging Edmond Cahn's analysis of a nineteenth-century American case involving "lifeboat ethics" following a shipwreck.[44] When the crew members determined that the lifeboat could not carry everyone on board, they threw some of the passengers overboard in order to save the rest. Seaman Alexander Holmes made it safely home only to be charged with homicide. The trial judge instructed the jury that if no seaman could be spared, the proper course of action would have been for the passengers to draw lots.

Cahn argued that this instruction was too lenient: respect for human life meant that all the passengers should have died together rather than saving some by ejecting others.[45] Ramsey respects Cahn's commitment to radical human equality, but questions whether that commitment can be legally enforced. He cautioned that "[w]e need to examine with extraordinary care the relationship between this redemptive righteousness beyond the law and the good in law itself."[46] Ramsey recognizes, in other words, that law cannot aim at making saints. We cannot treat redemptive righteousness as the "direct aim or goal of the legal system," although it "may exert a transforming pressure" on lawmakers and judges.[47] Cahn's problem is that "he does not exercise due caution in importing this [divine righteousness] directly into the legal system as a rule of law in the case we have discussed."[48] Ramsey suggests that the judge's instruction did indeed open up "graceful possibilities"[49] that ought to have been considered by the castaways. Valuing life equally does not necessarily mean allowing everyone to die; it can also mean drawing lots to give each an equal chance at survival.

While Ramsey's analysis of the lifeboat case is realistic, it is not clear, in the end, that it adequately grapples with the reality of human sinfulness. Ramsey thinks that mandating that everyone go down with the lifeboat unnecessarily requires heroic self-sacrifice; his alternative of drawing lots saves lives while also preserving basic human equality. Significantly, however, Ramsey does not explore, much less defend, the jury's decision to convict the defendants of the lesser crime of manslaughter, rather than murder, as well as to recommend a light sentence (six months in jail and a twenty dollar fine). Yet the jury's leniency is understandable, and even justifiable, if we take into account the human situation east of Eden. In my view, even an acquittal would have been defensible—in fact, none of the sixteen other seamen were ever brought to trial. It may have been morally wrong for the sailors to throw the passengers into the ocean, but they did so under grave duress. It may be too much for the law to demand that people sacrifice their own lives rather than the lives of others in dire situations not of their making. It may also be too much to expect them to formulate a procedurally fair alternative. To acquit them of criminal charges does not endorse what they did—it is simply to understand that it is inappropriate for the law to demand behavior that is beyond the capacity of almost all the citizenry, especially on pain of punishment.

Yet Ramsey never directly and explicitly considers how lawmakers should take into account the persistent effects of human sinfulness. He never addresses the hard questions about when the law should intervene to punish sinful actions and when it should stay its hand. In part, I think, this gap in his analysis is attributable to the fact that the dominant image in *Nine Modern Moralists* is that of love transforming justice. This image is too easily and uncritically transposed into love transforming law. In Ramsey's view, this generally means raising the legal bar. In his "love transforming justice" period, Ramsey only dimly and sporadically recognizes that, in some circumstances, love will dictate leaving the requirements of law at a mercifully low level.

Unfortunately, the dominant themes and concerns in Ramsey's second period offer even fewer resources to grapple with the question of sin and positive law. Recall that in this period, he highlights the Barthian formula of treating covenant as the external basis of creation, and creation as the internal meaning of covenant; Ramsey's use of the creation–covenant framework discourages any sustained focus on the relationship between sin and law in two interrelated ways. First, it orients his understanding of the structures of creation eschatologically forward, toward fully redeemed human relationships, rather than centering attention on the here and now, characterized by a homely mix of good and evil motivations and actions. Second, it tempts him to read the nature, function, and purposes of God's covenant with humanity *back into* the actual contracts that human beings form with one another. But using God's covenant of faithfulness to human beings as the standard by which we measure how well social institutions structure human relationships in our sinful world is to miss the point that those institutions are designed to deal with people as the highly imperfect beings they are now, not as they will be when redeemed after the Second

Coming of Christ. Quite ironically, in his first period, as we have just seen, Ramsey lodged this very point against Edmond Cahn.

Tacitly expecting one or both contracting parties to behave as God does in the salvific covenant with humanity fails to take into account the significant differences between the two situations. The covenant between God and humanity is not the result of a bargain or an actual exchange. The terms of the covenant are not negotiable; they are not even offered on a "take it or leave it" basis. Instead, they are inscribed into the very nature of the covenant. By treating the key markers of creation as the external basis of the covenant, a covenantal relationship fuses status and contract—indeed, the status and roles of the covenant partners are inseparable from the covenantal obligations. Furthermore, the covenant is not adopted for mutual benefit. Instead, it is adopted for the salvation of humanity—the benefit of the weaker party. Human beings repeatedly and seriously breached the covenant, yet God covers the breach with grace—indeed, with the love of his own Son. Consequently, covenant faithfulness, or *hesed*, is not only modeled on God's tender concern for humanity but it also is supplied by God to cover the defects of the human partner. In essence, God is responsible for upholding both ends of the covenantal relationship.

In contrast, modern contract law assumes two autonomous parties negotiating the terms of their relationship for mutual benefit. The goods and services transferred from one party to the other and vice versa are the subject of a bargained-for exchange, whose terms are to a great extent subject to negotiation. The parties are assumed to be equal in status and ability to pursue their own goals. In the vast majority of situations, neither party is assumed to have a duty to actively and selflessly promote the good of his or her counterpart—although both parties are subject to a duty to conduct their bargaining and exchange in good faith.

Moreover, and more significantly for our purposes, God's grace may be sufficient to cover the breach of the divine covenant with humanity. Yet it does not fully heal the breaches in the contracts we make with each other—at least in this time short of the Second Coming. If one party breaches a secular contract, the other party characteristically does not "cover over" the breach in order to make the relationship whole. The nonbreaching party can bring suit against the breaching party. Very often, however, it is a second-best solution. There is no earthly way for the courts or anyone else to make the nonbreaching party whole again. Any monetary damages awarded to the nonbreaching party generally do not compensate for the hassle, the worry, and the litigation costs. They cannot make up for the nonmonetary value of being able to rely on the promises received in a contractual arrangement and plan accordingly, rather than scrambling to make other arrangements.

Ramsey does at times try to accommodate the phenomenon of sin and brokenness in human relationships within the creation–covenant model by reworking Reinhold Niebuhr's famous maxim: "Man's capacity for justice makes democracy possible; man's propensity to injustice makes democracy necessary."[50] In *The Patient as Person*, for example, he modifies the Niebuhrian framework to encapsulate his basic moral stance on nontherapeutic medical research: "Man's capacity to become joint adventurers in a common cause make the consensual relation possible; man's propensity to overreach his joint adventurer even in a good cause makes consent necessary."[51]

But Ramsey's appropriation of Niebuhr's formula raises more questions than it answers. How, exactly does the legal framework Ramsey endorses restrain sinful behavior in a "necessary" (and effective) manner? How does the same framework enable the possibility of fellow humanity in the manner Ramsey commends to us? In *Christian and the Sit-In*, the possible/necessary formulation tends to place the accent on the "possible." Ramsey explores how the "inn keeper's law," as well as the legal framework surrounding marriage, provides the structure in which covenant relationships can flourish. Law is seen as essentially positive in its functions; its demands can be made more stringent and universal in order to better approximate the demands of covenantal relationships. So, for example, extending the logic of the "inn keeper's law" to justify civil rights laws prohibiting discrimination on the basis of race in public accommodations is a way of bringing the external basis of covenant into closer alignment with its internal meaning.[52]

Yet, in Ramey's work on medical ethics in the "creation and covenant" period, the emphasis is on the "necessary" function of law in restraining impulses inconsistent with co-humanity. His fullest exploration of these questions comes in his treatment of the consent requirement as a "canon of loyalty" in medical research.[53] Ramsey argues that the consent requirement has intrinsic value: the compact between the researcher and the human subject of that research signifies their participation in a "joint adventure" for the benefit of humanity. Conversely, failing to obtain patient consent does not treat research subjects as equal partners in the project; it reduces them to mere means in the plans and activities of the medical researchers. At the same time, Ramsey considers a strong, even an absolute consent requirement to have an instrumental value. While there may be hypothetical situations where research conducted without obtaining consent does not undermine fellow humanity, Ramsey contends that researchers are more likely to make an error by holding themselves open to relaxation of the consent requirement than by an assessment of whether an exception applies on a case-by-case basis.[54]

More controversially, he applies his understanding of the consent requirement as a canon of loyalty between investigators and their research subjects to create an absolute bar to nontherapeutic research involving children. Precisely because children are not adults, they are incapable of giving valid consent to such research. Furthermore, in Ramsey's view, to engage in such research is to treat a child as if he or she is *not* a child, rather than as a vulnerable fellow human being who merits only our protection, not our exploitation.[55]

Ramsey's position on this question has elicited broad interest and criticism.[56] My purpose here, however, is to focus particularly on the manner in which the position he takes illuminates his understanding of the relationship between law and sin. In my view, three aspects of his approach merit attention. First, legal concepts do not significantly inform his judgment about what moral principles should govern in the context of nontherapeutic research. Rather, they are invoked on an ad hoc basis to justify a set of norms that have their source elsewhere. Second, the principles Ramsey advocates in this context have a double source: (1) his conviction of the equal dignity of vulnerable human beings; and (2) his sense that their dignity is under significant threat owing to the effects of sinful overreaching upon the research imperative of investigators. Third, in invoking legal concepts to make his point, Ramsey unfortunately tends either to disregard or to distort the nature, purpose, and function of those concepts. Ramsey presumes that the best way to deal with the dangers of sinful overreaching is to augment and strengthen the legal requirements that surround nontherapeutic research and human subjects. The tacit logic of his legal analysis seems to be this: the idea that creation serves as the external basis of covenant gets transmuted into the idea that law is the external basis of covenant—and in our troubling times, a more stringent set of laws can provide a sounder basis for covenantal relationships.

Let me explain. The fundamental concept that Ramsey uses is that of consent—it is informed consent that makes a patient a co-adventurer in a medical research project rather than a mere means to someone else's goals, however laudable they may be. Yet the concept of consent implicates two distinct areas of the common law: the law of battery (tort law) and the law of mutual agreement (contract law). Ramsey does not keep clearly in mind the specific purposes of each area, but instead mixes and matches to serve his own purposes. The law of torts, especially the law of battery, protects *negative liberty*—the right to be free of invasions of one's personal space. Contract law is designed to promote *positive liberty*—the right of persons to collaborate in order to bring about a desired future state of affairs.

Consent is necessary in the case of nontherapeutic medical research, for two distinct reasons. First, such research will frequently involve contact with the research subject's body, which would constitute battery without consent. Second, it will require the research subjects to comply with the terms of an investigative program—duties which cannot be imposed upon them without consent. Yet Ramsey blurs the distinct lines of legal norms by making the focus of his analysis the nontherapeutic nature of medical research. That focus is doubly under-inclusive.

In *The Patient as Person*, Ramsey begins his analysis in a seemingly promising manner. He notes not only that "no man is good enough to experiment upon another without his consent," but also that "no man is good enough to cure another without his consent."[57] Yet the justification he offers for these insights is not the importance of bodily integrity but, rather, the potential for harm and abuse. No human being, in other words, is good enough (morally) or perhaps good enough (technically) to force medical procedures upon others. Ramsey has not fully absorbed the nexus between the battery prohibition and bodily integrity. Consequently, in a later book, he can rather easily toy with the position that in some cases, competent persons can rightly be forced to undergo *therapeutic* interventions against their will—a position that is fundamentally inconsistent with battery's protection of bodily integrity against all invasions, not merely harmful ones.[58] He also does not grapple with the fact that most ongoing research projects on human subjects will require consent as a sign of commitment to a joint plan of action, whether it whether medical or nonmedical, therapeutic or nontherapeutic. People are required to consent to research projects not because they are joint adventurers in *nontherapeutic* research but because they are joint adventurers in *any form of research* and they need to commit to certain actions that will make the experiment yield helpful results.

It is this failure to keep in mind the dual nature of the consent requirements, as well as their broader applicability, that facilitates Ramsey's controversial approach to the use of children in nontherapeutic research.

Consider how the prohibition of battery operates more generally with respect to minors. Parents come into physical contact with their children, and allow others to come into physical contact with their children all the time. While it is right to prohibit contact that has a significant risk of harm, it is far too much to require all contact to a have clear beneficial outcome. A teacher physically moves a little boy blocking the view of the class aquarium. A parent dresses a nine-month-old baby as a pumpkin for Halloween. A grandmother schleps her sleeping granddaughter to the store to buy a newspaper. In each case, the physical contact is not harmful—but it is not necessarily motivated by a desire to benefit the child, either.

The same could be said of consent to research programs. Parents enroll their children in research protocols all the time. For example, schoolchildren regularly take standardized tests that chart their individual and aggregate progress in relationship to their curriculum. Mothers and fathers enroll children in nutritional studies and marketing studies of all types. They promise to take their children to certain events and keep track of certain milestones. It is not clear that participation in this sort of research is beneficial to the children. At the same time, it is likely not to be more harmful than alternative ways in which they would probably be spending their time.

If we look at the question of enrolling children in minimally risky medical research protocols with this broader perspective, it becomes clear that by their own internal moral logic, neither the prohibition against battery nor the requirement of informed consent justifies the absolute barrier that Ramsey advocates. Treating children as children means consenting to their being touched for a wide range of legitimate reasons—some of which have nothing to do with their welfare, at least directly. It also means enrolling them in socially beneficial activities that don't necessarily benefit them directly—although they don't appreciably harm them, either.

So the question to Ramsey can be sharply posed: Why struggle to create a separate and stringent set of legal and moral requirements that govern research in the medical realm? The answer, it seems to me, has to do with his increasingly pessimistic assessment of the moral tenor of that realm as a whole—not with his grasp of the inner logic of the legal norms of consent. And while that assessment operates tacitly in *The Patient as Person*, it becomes fully explicit in *Ethics at the Edges of Life*, which exemplifies his "Christian combativeness" period.

By the time he is writing *Ethics at the Edges of Life* in the mid-1970s, Ramsey believes his fears about cultural developments have been realized. After *Roe v. Wade* was decided, it was virtually impossible for Ramsey to treat American positive law as the external basis for covenantal relationships. As legal decisions subsequent to *Roe* expanded the abortion right and eroded protections for the very young and the very old, Ramsey found it increasingly difficult to draw the connections between Cahn's "sense of injustice" and judge-made legal norms that he found so fruitful in *Nine Modern Moralists*. So Ramsey was forced to shift approaches.

In so doing, Ramsey provided a blueprint for the legal response of American religious and social conservatives to the social upheaval of the 1960s. He provided, in other words, a vision of law's primary functions that would animate the conservative culture warriors for decades to follow. In this vision, the community's law needs to refurbished and repaired to accomplish three goals: First, the law needs to be *didactic*; it needs to proclaim the morally correct course of action. Second, the law needs to be *punitive*; it needs to condemn and punish serious violations of moral norms. Third, the law needs to protect socially threatened values by constructing a network of rules and regulations that function as a *protective fence*.

All three expectations for law are operative in *Ethics at the Edges of Life*. In his searching critique of *Planned Parenthood v. Danforth*, Ramsey is most concerned that the Supreme Court opinion sends the wrong moral message about human nature and human relationships.[59] He contends that in striking down spousal and parental consent requirements, the Court is communicating a problematic normative vision that treats pregnant women as isolated and autonomous—as *les femmes seules*. It is for this reason he is less than sympathetic to the majority's pragmatic point that women in good relationships will tell their baby's father or their parents without any prompting from the law.

The second expectation of the law is most prominent in his discussion of the Kenneth Edelin case, which involved a Massachusetts doctor who was tried for manslaughter after performing a late-term abortion on a seventeen-year-old girl in 1973.[60] Although the jury convicted Dr. Edelin, his conviction was set aside by the Supreme Judicial Court of Massachusetts on the grounds that there was reasonable doubt as a matter of law whether he killed a viable baby in the womb or suffocated a living baby after it had been separated from its mother's body. Ramsey acknowledges how the Massachusetts Supreme Judicial Court might well find that in such a case reasonable doubt existed as a matter of law, and thus overturn the jury's conviction. At the same time, his central concern is drawing and defending a legal line, enforceable with penal sanctions, that could offer some protection to late-term fetuses.

The third expectation of law, *fence-building*, is most evident in the second half of *Ethics at the Edges of Life*, which is devoted to end-of-life decision making.[61] In a move that he admits is a radical revision of Christian moral teaching, he argues that the traditional distinction between "ordinary" (morally required) and "extraordinary" (morally optional) means of prolonging life should be abandoned in favor of a "medical indications policy."[62] In his view, the traditional distinction leaves too much room for invidious quality-of-life judgments by allowing the decision maker to holistically evaluate the patient's life post-treatment. Moreover, by explicitly including factors such as the cost of treatment, it risks subordinating the dignity of the patient to the material interests of family members and other third parties. In Ramsey's view, the only way to abate these dangers is to formulate a policy that compares the effectiveness of various forms of treatments, while steadfastly refusing to compare the value of the lives that are treated. Back surgery should be performed on children born suffering from multiple physical and mental defects in addition to spina bifida, provided the surgery is likely to be in closing the open spinal column and averting further degradation. Very young and very old patients should receive the same treatment for cancer or heart disease as other patients, provided the procedure itself will do more good than harm, notwithstanding other aspects of their conditions.

In short, the "medical indications policy" functions rather like a barrier, designed to safeguard the equal dignity of all human beings against hostile incursions. Ramsey acknowledges that in principle, it could be morally permissible to give nuanced consideration to the way in which a patient's response to treatment might be adversely affected by other disabilities. Yet he worries about abuse. He resists giving too much weight to patients' subjective experiences of fear or pain as a counterpoint to the possibility of extending their lives. Moreover, he suggestes that rather than risking invidious comparison, it might be better to have a rule *requiring* mentally handicapped persons to receive the same treatment that persons of normal intelligence would choose.[63]

Ramsey's three demands of secular law later became the demands of conservative culture warriors on matters such as abortion, homosexual relationships, and withdrawal of artificial nutrition and hydration, and even contraception. In my view, all three demands fall short of the mark for much the same reason: each of them treats an act of law almost as if it were an act of magic, capable of instantaneously bringing about a desirable situation or eliminating an undesirable one. Yet a legal decree, in and of itself, has no practical effect. It has to be integrated into the decision making of the law's subjects, who need to be able to factor its command or prohibition into their life plans in some workable way.

So, it is understandable that Ramsey wants the law to proclaim the moral truth about the essentially social nature of all human beings, including and maybe even especially pregnant women. As I have argued elsewhere, the law has an important pedagogical function, even in pluralistic liberal democracies such as the United States.[64] Yet moral proclamation is not enough for moral pedagogy. The law must provide specific pathways that the law's subjects can choose—and thrive in—while absorbing the law's moral message. To be an effective moral teacher, the paths promoted by the law have to be livable by those to whom it applies. So mandating that life-saving treatment be provided to everyone according to a medical-indications policy is not a workable mandate unless it deals with questions of cost and care. Who will pay for these procedures? Where will people whose lives are saved live and be cared for? Similarly, it is undeniable that condemning wrongful acts is an important aspect of the law. But moral condemnation is not enough to prevent those acts. A workable condemnation needs to be enforceable by moral means, and not to create other perverse incentives for behavior equally harmful to the common good. The nation's experiences with Prohibition, and more recently with the war on drugs, provides ample evidence of the way in which criminal law is not sufficient to control behavior.

Finally, it is understandable that Ramsey would want to protect the equal value of human life by constructing a legal fence around it. The trouble, however, is that once we start thinking in practical terms, putting a fence around one value often leaves other values insufficiently protected. So, for example, it might be possible to uphold the equal dignity of human life by prohibiting physicians from giving patients any medicine that could possibly shorten their lives. Yet as Ramsey himself would recognize, such a rule would prohibit physicians from giving strong pain medication to dying patients, not in order to kill them but to make their dying process less dreadful. Moreover, even non-dying patients facing chronic and severe pain need to balance a number of issues in selecting pain medication; they may decide that more fully participating in life here and now is worth the side effect of a shorter life.

Ramsey's analysis and critique in *Ethics at the Edges of Life* is driven by what he believes to be *the* temptation to wrongdoing operative in American medical culture in that time: the temptation to devalue the existence of those who are seen to be useless, defective, or dying. The mistake he made, in my view, is that he failed to recognize that law always has to deal with more than one temptation simultaneously. Law does not only teach, or condemn; it also channels human behavior. Blocking off one a path that is threatened by one set of dangers may incentivize people to travel a different path that is not safe and instead beset with a different type of problem.

The Case of Joseph Saikewicz

Can we say anything at all that is helpful about the way Christian love might transform justice inscribed into law? Ramsey's approach through all three stages has been to frame the question in *vertical* way. In the best of times, Christian love elevates the claims of law, holding legal norms to a higher and therefore more stringent moral standard. In the worst of times, Christian love stands as a bulwark, blocking the law's precipitous fall to a lower moral level. Previous sections of this chapter have articulated the drawbacks associated with picturing the idea of love transforming law in a vertical way. Yet I do not wish to abandon the idea; rather, I want to reorient and reimagine the picture.

I would like to suggest that we might do better to imagine the operations of love transforming law along a *horizontal* rather than a *vertical* plane. A major task for Christian love in the legal realm, in my view, is to *broaden* the horizon within which questions of law and policy are considered. By so doing, it can identify previously invisible stakeholders and uncover previously unnoticed problems that deserve our urgent attention. To borrow from the title of Margaret Farley's recent book, I think a major task of Christian love is "changing the questions" that the legal system asks.[65]

The Saikewicz case provides ample illustration of my suggestion. The named plaintiff in the case is the superintendent of Belchertown State School—the institution where Joseph Saikewicz lived and died. Yet virtually no one who proffered a strong opinion on how he should have died expressed any interest whatsoever in the conditions under which he spent most of his life. Despite its unremitting focus on Saikewicz's equal dignity, Ramey's lengthy chapter does not even include a paragraph on the conditions in the state institution to which Saikewicz had been committed as a young boy. Ramsey was not alone in his omission.[66] In fact, the majority opinion issued by the Massachusetts Supreme Judicial Court also omitted any discussion of Belchertown State School. This omission was particularly noteworthy, since the school was at the time the subject of a consent decree, under the supervision of a federal district court judge.

In March 1970, the local newspaper, the *Springfield Union*, began a six-part series called "The Tragedy of Belchertown." It was written by Jamie Shanks, a staff writer who pressed beyond the institution's beautiful façade to investigate its living conditions. Shanks wrote that after entering Building K, which housed the profoundly mentally handicapped men, he encountered a "stench creates by 48 years of neglect, urine and human wastes." But he was most troubled by "the sight of the men—other human beings, but retarded—standing around naked or holding their pants up because the laundry ruined the fastener.... Physically grown men roll on a cold tile floor, sit in grotesque positions motionless, or rock rhythmically back and forth. Others are bent in strange poses on stark prison-made benches."[67]

Building K housed about 120 men, ranging in age from fifteen to over eighty. The men had no privacy; they slept in large wards with beds arranged head-to-toe, and divided by narrow aisles. The toilets had neither seats nor privacy dividers. There were two showers for all the residents. Three attendants were responsible for caring for all the men during the daytime, and only one attendant was on duty at night. The attendants often left the men nude because it was easier to keep them clean that way. Shanks crystallized his observations with a vivid and damning quotation from M. Phillip Wakstein, who worked as a regional administrator for the Massachusetts Department of Mental Health. "The only difference between Belchertown and Auschwitz is the lack of gas chambers."[68]

The exposé generated a defensive reaction from the administrators of the school, some administrative shuffling, but no real change. Finally, in 1972, a class action suit was filed in federal court in Boston.[69] The lead plaintiff was Benjamin Ricci, whose son Bobby had lived at the school since he was six years old.[70] After languishing for more than a year, the lawsuit finally ended up in the chambers of U.S. District Court Judge Joseph L. Tauro. In a virtually unprecedented move, Judge Tauro decided to check out the conditions at Belchertown for himself. On a warm day in May 1973, he took his law clerk, along with the Massachusetts assistant attorney general who represented the defendants, to make an unannounced visit to

Belchertown. What he found was a nightmare. "I saw a little girl drinking from a feces-filled commode; bare rooms with no partitions between the beds. People were lying on the floor half naked in their own excrement and urine."[71]

Shortly after the visit, the state wisely decided to settle the case rather than take it to trial. Judge Tauro presided over the settlement. For years he monitored compliance with the consent decree, which required the state to improve the living conditions at the school and ultimately to move as many residents as possible into community-based group homes.[72] The last three residents left Belchertown State School for a group home in Agawam, Massachusetts, in December 1992.[73] When he retired from full-time judicial duties forty years later, Jude Tauro considered his work in the Belchertown case to be the highlight of his professional life. "I don't mean to sound immodest when I say this," he says, "but what we did changed the earth for those people. They were the most helpless of the helpless."[74]

In *Ethics at the Edges of Life*, Paul Ramsey commendably attempts to defend the equal dignity of "the most helpless of the helpless." In my view, however, his efforts would have been more effective had he widened the vistas of his analysis. First, a longer historical perspective on the history of the treatment of the mentally handicapped in this country challenges Ramsey's assumption of moral declension in American life. Institutions such as Belchertown State School for the Feeble-Minded were begun in the early part of the twentieth century, with eugenic goals in mind.[75] Sequestering the mentally handicapped would prevent them from reproducing and contaminating the public gene pool. In the mid-twentieth century, the rationale for institutionalization shifted to protecting families, and safeguarding normally abled children, from the burdens associated with caring for them.[76] The situation began to change in the 1960s. President John F. Kennedy pushed through amendments to the Social Security Act that provided resources for the mentally handicapped.[77] In 1972, further amendments to the Social Security Act allowed states to obtain federal reimbursement for up to 50 percent of the costs of caring for the mentally handicapped, provided they met stringent quality controls with respect to living conditions.[78] Activists began to question the need for institutionalization, arguing that it would be both more humane and more cost-effective to enable the mentally handicapped to live as normally as possible within their communities.[79]

Second and relatedly, Christian love can transform law by taking a broader view of the question demanding ethical analysis. In *Ethics at the*

Edges of Life, Ramsey is writing in the area of medical ethics. As a theological ethicist, however, he ought to question the sharp delineation of this area from broader issues of moral concern. Medical ethics should not be treated as a rigidly defined or hermetically sealed field. Just as human beings are essentially social, all ethical questions are ultimately questions of social ethics. The question of how to respect the dignity of Joseph Saikewicz in his dying cannot be addressed without straightforwardly addressing the abusive situation in which he did his living.

Most obviously, respecting the dignity of people in the same position as Joseph Saikewicz means calling attention to the conditions in which they live, not merely scrutinizing the medical interventions provided or not provided to them when they die. Ignoring or avoiding the scandals surrounding Belchertown State School in discussing his case is to truncate and even distort the necessary analysis. Understanding the conditions in which Saikewicz lived sheds crucial light on the end-of-life decision. Given the reports about Building K, it is highly likely that he experienced inhumane treatment over the years, including forcible restraints and even physical abuse. Given Saikewicz's limited mental abilities, he would not have been able to differentiate between restraint meant to facilitate treatment and restraint meant solely to thwart or harm him. In short, given his background and history, Joseph Saikewicz would likely experience treatment as torture. In all probability, he would not understand the forcible administration of chemotherapy, and the infliction of its often devastating side effects, as a form of covenant fidelity. Given the very real doubts about the success of the treatment, we might well ask "whether this kind of artificial prolongation of life does not amount to human arrogance in the opposite direction, . . . and the required assistance of human life a forbidden torturing of it.[80]

No matter how well intentioned, Ramsey's "medical indications" policy is a mask he imposed on Joseph Saikewicz, who was not a "normal" sixty-seven-year-old, on the one hand, or a "normal" three-year-old, on the other. He cannot be reduced to these two neat component parts. Joseph Saikewicz was precisely what he was—an *elderly* man who had the *mental age* of a three-year-old. A normal sixty-seven-year-old man may undertake the rigors of chemotherapy to preserve his own life, knowing that the treatment may be less successful because of his age. He runs that risk (or not) for his own purposes. Parents will run larger risks, and accept more unpleasant treatment, on behalf of a three-year-old afflicted with leukemia, in large part because an entire life stretches out in front of the child. To value each life equally does not entail refusing to recognize that there are different seasons in life. The death of a toddler is a greater violation of nature than the death of a septuagenarian. That does not mean that the life of a toddler is of greater worth than that of a septuagenarian.

The trouble with Ramsey's approach, in my view, is that in protecting one aspect of Saikewicz's personhood—his equal identity as a creature made in the image and likeness of God—Ramsey risks undermining another aspect: Saikewicz's unique instantiation of that identity. Human beings are not fungible. Nor are they nameless, faceless dignity-bearers. They are no stopgaps on a slippery slope. They are individuals. It is the need to respect human dignity in the concrete—in the faces of particular men; that has led John Noonan to talk about the "masks" that hide specific persons and their own unique vulnerabilities and suffering. Christian love transforms law by clear-sighted recognition that even masks adopted for the most benign purposes can be suffocating and cruel. That is one lesson that the *Saikewicz* case can teach us.

PART III

Legal Categories and Theological Problems

7

Juridical Insights and Theological Disputes

Engaging Robert E. Rodes Jr.

LIKE JOHN NOONAN, Robert Rodes has seamlessly developed his work as a legal scholar within the framework provided by his broader theological commitments. Moreover, he practices the ideal of reasoning in the context of a full-bodied moral tradition that is defended theoretically by Alasdair MacIntyre. As MacIntyre would endorse, Rodes's work is holistic in that it stems from an integrated vision of the nature and purpose of human flourishing, a coherent account of why human beings frequently impede their own flourishing and that of others, and a realistic understanding of both the potential and the limitations of human institutions, including the institutions created and sustained by human law in all its forms and manifestations. The most succinct expression of the metaphysical worldview underlying his writings can be found in the Nicene Creed, which is professed by most Christian denominations, including the Roman Catholic community to which Rodes belongs.

At a symposium organized to discuss his work at the University of Notre Dame, where he taught for many years, Rodes reflected upon the thrust of his scholarly work: "My interest is that of a Christian looking at the role of the church in society, rather than a student of society looking at the effect of the church on society.... When church and society part company, I go with the church, and not with society."[1] One who reads this quotation out of context, without adequate acquaintance with Professor Rodes's work, might be tempted to think that it was dedicated to advancing the interests and perspectives of the institutional church, as he understands them, in a secular environment that is at best indifferent and at worst hostile to religious truths.

Nothing could be further from the truth. Rodes understands that the God who created us and the God who redeems us in Jesus Christ are one and the same. He therefore recognizes that the desire to know and love God, and to serve those made in God's image and likeness, is not limited by the boundaries of the institutional church, although the institutional church bears special responsibility for proclaiming Christ's teaching and making available his sacraments until the end of time. Moreover, Professor Rodes realizes that neither church nor secular society has been blessed with a perfect blueprint of what is to be done in building up the kingdom of God, which will be fully realized only at the end of time, in God's own time and manner, and by God's own grace.

In fact, Rodes's model of the Christian life is that of a *pilgrimage* toward the kingdom of God, a pilgrimage on which "we are called to pursue an unknown end by inefficacious means."[2] It is also his model of life in general; he believes that "the pilgrimage, along with its legal consequences, is intrinsic to the human condition. It does not separate Christians in particular, or even believers in general, from a mass population headed in some other direction."[3] Rodes's Christian faith in God's ultimate grace and mercy toward humanity is complemented by a healthy humility regarding the mystery of God's ways. That humility leads him to recognize and honor insight, compassion, and wisdom where he finds it, both in the secular world and in the church. It also leads him to apply his own insight, compassion, and wisdom wherever it is needed, both for the secular world and for the church.[4]

If we look at Rodes's body of work as a whole, we can divide it into three basic parts. First, he has investigated the relationship of the institutional church and the broader society in a systematic and detailed way.[5] Second, Rodes has devoted a great deal of time and energy to the task of bringing the perspective of Christian anthropology and eschatology to bear upon the legal enterprise. The fullest example of his work falling into this category is his book *Pilgrim Law*, which is the most comprehensive articulation of his Christian jurisprudence.

Equally significantly, Rodes has dedicated significant effort to using the intellectual skills he has acquired as a lawyer and a law professor to illuminate questions and controversies that have arisen in our time within religious communities, and in particular the Roman Catholic community.[6] Rodes argues, to my mind persuasively, that some "important theological concepts have an inescapable juridical dimension that must be recognized and addressed if the concepts are to be rightly understood."[7] Rodes is not attempting to reduce theology to law, any more than he attempts to reduce law to theology. He is suggesting, however, that greater sensitivity to the ways in which theological claims can at times function rather like legal claims will assist the religious community in grappling with them appropriately.

Leaving First Amendment scholarship to one side, it seems clear that most normative scholarship falling within the general genre of "law and religion" is similar in its thrust to the second group of Rodes's work. That is, most normative interdisciplinary work in this genre attempts to take theological insights into the nature of the person, the function of society, and the meaning of moral responsibility and apply those insights to jurisprudential questions. Theology, in other words, is conscripted to provide additional strength, purpose, and richness to legal studies. But as I have argued throughout *Ethics at the Edges of Law*, there is no reason to think that the process of interdisciplinary enrichment cannot go the other way. As the third group of Rodes's writings suggest, the sort of analysis characteristic of the legal profession can provide additional focus, precision, and nuance to theological studies. This directionality in interdisciplinary work in law and religion is not as prominent as its counterpart. It is, however, equally important.

In this chapter, I will concentrate my attention on material developed in Rodes's third group of writings. More specifically, I would like to explore three sets of categories that he has articulated over the years, which are rooted in an analytical perspective characteristic of law, and which are also useful for understanding theological disputes, as well as disputes about the implications of theological claims within religious communities.

1. Rodes's first set of categories distinguish among *epistemic, normative,* and *constitutive* legal pronouncements. These terms help identify three distinct functions of legal pronouncements within a complex and well-functioning legal system such as our own.[8]
2. Rodes's second set of categories focuses on the two ways in which law can instantiate moral values: it can do so *instrumentally*, by employing a system of incentives and disincentives, or it can do so *didactically*, by holding up a certain pattern of behavior as worthy of emulation.[9]
3. Rodes's third set of categories distinguish between *Erastian* and *High Church* Christians. He argues that these labels point to two fundamentally different ways of relating the church to the culture, both possessing sturdy roots in the Christian tradition.[10]

Although Rodes has developed these three sets of categories more or less independently of each another, I believe that their explanatory power is exponentially increased when they are combined. More specifically, one's attitude toward the relationship of the church to the secular society tends to influence one's view of the proper purposes and methods of secular law. To put it another way, Erastians and High Church Christians tend to give priority to different functions of pronouncements in the law, for reasons internally related to the way each understands the function of law in communicating the moral vision of the community. They also tend to emphasize a different method by which law accomplishes its goals.

My manner of proceeding will be as follows. In the first section, I will sketch Rodes's three sets of categories in some detail. In the second section, I will construct an integrated analytical framework that combines these three sets of categories. Finally, in the third section, I will test that integrated framework by using it to illuminate a controversy that played out a decade ago, which is a harbinger of contemporary clashes between religion and the secular order: In 2003, the Commonwealth of Massachusetts became the first state to make the rights and duties of marriage available to same-sex couples. In 2006, after protracted and fruitless negotiations with state officials, Catholic Charities of Boston decided to cease functioning as an adoption agency rather than continue to place a small number of hard-to-place children with homosexual parents. The tensions between religious belief, religious freedom, and public morality that played out in one state and in one time period may have broader relevance. In 2015, same-sex marriage became available across the country, thanks to the Supreme Court decision in *Obergefell v. Hodges*.[11] Many people have written about the clash that same-sex marriage has created between religious and secular values. My focus in this chapter will be slightly different: I will examine the way in which the clash between Catholic teaching and secular law provoked disagreement *within* the Catholic community itself.

Exploring Rodes's Three Sets of Analytical Categories

The First Set of Categories

Robert Rodes has argued that we need to distinguish among three functions of legal dispositions: the normative, the epistemic, and the constitutive. The *normative* function is what most non-lawyers associate with the role of law; normative pronouncements tell people what to do and what not to do, "with ancillary provisions perhaps saying what will happen to us if we fail to obey."[12] The classic example of the normative function of the law, of course, is found in the criminal code. Do not murder; do not rape; and do not steal. If you do commit such an act, and are found guilty of doing so by a jury of your peers, you will suffer a significant penalty, most likely imprisonment. To those who focus exclusively on this aspect of the legal system, it appears that the function of law is essentially negative; its role is limited to impeding potential malefactors from imposing their unjust will upon the rest of society.

Other functions of law are far more positive, or at least neutral. Rodes observes that law also performs a *constitutive* function; that is, it "creat[es] a state of affairs."[13] Two examples of how law does so are found in the law of property and the law of marriage. "The execution and delivery of a deed in proper from will make A the owner of what was formerly B's house. A marriage ceremony in proper form will make a couple husband and wife."[14] Constitutive legal dispositions are creative; they generate real relationships that were not previously in being and are not physically observable. Rodes states: "Constitutive legal dispositions do not as such impose obligations at all. Their effect is metaphysical or ontological. They tell you how to bring about some juridical state of affairs, some condition such as adoption, marriage, tenure of a public office, or ownership of a house, that is not physically observable, and that is subject to control by operation of law."[15]

In other words, one cannot, properly speaking, disobey a constitutive legal provision. If we fail to comply with the process it sets forth, we simply fail to bring about the set of relationships that provision contemplates. We do not become the legal owners of a piece of property, we do not become husband and wife, or we do not become the legal parents of a child born to someone else if we do not follow the specified procedures.

Third, legal pronouncements often have, or entail, an *epistemic* function, which Rodes describes as "involv[ing] an authoritative determination that such-and-such is the case, based on an investigation or a hearing of evidence by some person in authority, who then decides in good faith that it is in fact the case."[16] An obvious example is a jury verdict; other examples include legislative findings of fact used to justify the enactment of a particular law, or factual determinations by administrative agencies.[17]

Rodes argues that these three functions of legal pronouncements have analogies in how various pronouncements of the Roman Catholic Church function. This fact is not surprising to him; the church is a community, a "polity," and it must therefore have a structure that gives it organization and stability. Rodes writes: "The basic polity of the Church—that is, its government by pope and bishops—is established by divine positive law. The deployment of people and resources in accordance with that polity is done by human law, mostly that of the Church itself, although the state played a major part in earlier times, and has a minor role even today. At every level, the applicable laws combine constitutive and normative forms."[18]

The clearest place to see the intersection of the constitutive and normative functions is in the Catholic Church's law of marriage. The church teaches that natural law prohibits sexual relationships between persons of the same sex and between close relatives; these prohibitions are normatively recapitulated in the church's positive moral norms. Furthermore, they are incorporated in the church's constitutive norms; a purported wedding conducted in violation of these prohibitions does not result in either a natural marriage or a sacramental marriage.[19] In other words, these normative prohibitions relating to partners of the same sex and to consanguinity shape the constitutive requirements for marriage. There are also normative requirements relating to the performance of a sacramental marriage that are not constitutive, such as the requirement that a marriage between a Catholic and a non-Catholic receive advance permission from the bishop. If this requirement is violated, the resulting marriage is illicit, but not invalid.[20]

Finally, Rodes describes how the church exercises *epistemic* authority, both judicially and legislatively. One paradigmatic case of judicial epistemic authority is the proceeding for the annulment of a marriage, which makes the factual finding that a valid marriage either does or does not exist. A second paradigmatic case is the canonization process, which makes a determination about whether the candidate proposed for sainthood possessed the requisite degree of holiness.[21] The legislative exercise of epistemic authority, according to Rodes, lies in the determinations of the magisterium, the teaching authority of the church expressed by the Pope and the bishops. As Rodes notes, "[i]t extends to all questions of doctrine and morals, although in the practical application of moral principles its scope is limited by the coordinate authority of the state and of the individual conscience."[22] He observes as well that sometimes pastors are called to apply Catholic doctrine and morals to matters involving factors on which they have no special expertise, such as the appropriate minimum wage law.[23]

Rodes contends that various ecclesiastical pronouncements are fruitfully understood by analogy to legal pronouncements, not only in terms of their functions but also in terms of their limits of their authority. "Normative dispositions are binding [in conscience] if they are just, possible, and known."[24] An unjust law, in Catholic tradition, loses much of the binding force of law. If compliance with a particular legal disposition is impossible either physically or morally (e.g., one is compelled under grave duress to do otherwise), through no fault of one's own, then one cannot be bound in conscience to comply.[25] In contrast, purely constitutive obligations do not impose obligations at all; as Rodes says, "[t]heir effect is metaphysical or ontological."[26] For example, if a constitutive requirement for a valid marriage is a blood test on both parties, failure to obtain the blood test does not violate a norm—it simply means that the parties do not become husband and wife. They are not penalized; they simply do not assume the status of a married couple.

Epistemic pronouncements, as Rodes notes, "have the effect of justifying actions taken on the supposition that what they determine to be the case is in fact the case, and condemning action taken on the opposite supposition. In the Church, they have the further effect of calling on us actually to believe what they tell us."[27] According to Rodes, epistemic dispositions are binding only upon those "subject to the authority" of those making the disposition, "and who are not better informed on the matter in question."[28] He goes on to note that "[a]nyone who is better informed has a right to disagree, and may have a duty to act accordingly."[29] An example he gives comes from a court martial of a German submarine commander who had fired upon and sunk a plainly labeled hospital ship during World War I. The commander's defense, accepted by the court, was that the German Admiralty had informed him that the British were disguising troop ships as hospital ships. As Rodes notes, however, if the commander had had personal knowledge that this particular ship was, in fact, a hospital ship, he would not have been entitled to rely upon the epistemic determination of his superiors to justify sinking it.[30]

In sum, Rodes's distinction among the three functions of law, in both civil society and the church, recognizes that legal pronouncements create complicated patterns of relationship. The obligation that each form of pronouncement elicits depends upon its function and its implicit presuppositions. A sophisticated understanding of law, and of how communities are constituted in part by legal bonds, will recognize and preserve these distinctions among the functions of law.

The Second Set of Categories

Obviously, all three functions of the law pursue moral values, by facilitating their instantiation in a given society or social structure such as the church. Cutting across the three functions are two methods by which the law pursues value: the didactic and the instrumental. The *didactic* operation of the law, says Rodes, "is simply a matter of witnessing the moral standards, the moral reflection, and the social customs of the community."[31] The fact that the law prohibits some activities (e.g., mayhem and murder) and encourages others (e.g., marriage) publicly proclaims various aspects of the community's value system, even to persons who are not directly involved in those activities. Rodes notes that "[t]he law plays a role that some of the political theologians refer to as consciousness raising. And even without raised consciousness we prefer, other things being equal, to obey the law and think of ourselves as law-abiding citizens."[32]

The law achieves its goals *instrumentally* "when it affects people's behavior by deploying incentives and disincentives."[33] The design and implementation of these incentives can require thought and planning. As Rodes observes, they "can be simple and straightforward, rewards for good behavior and punishments for bad, or they can be complicated and indirect, as when we try to discourage the poaching of alligators by forbidding the sale of alligator bags or when we try to encourage investment by lowering taxes."[34]

The use of the didactic and instrumental methods cuts across the three functions of the law. For example, the paradigmatic example of the normative function of the law, a criminal statute, includes both didactic and instrumental components. A statutory provision against murder proclaims the inviolability of innocent human life, while the penal sanctions provide an incentive for those not convinced by the provision's moral vision to comply with its prohibition anyway. The institution of legal marriage is a paradigmatic example of the constitutive function of the law. Tax breaks given to couples who marry proclaim the centrality of this relationship to our broader social structure and provide an incentive to couples to get married rather than live together. Jury deliberations constitute a central case of the epistemic function of law. Rules of evidence specify what can be presented to the jury. The rule against hearsay evidence is instrumental; its purpose is to ensure that only reliable evidence be presented to the jury. A rule against compelling one spouse to testify against another, or prohibiting the introduction of evidence obtained under torture, is didactic; it communicates to the society that the fact-finding process cannot be conducted in a way that will destroy other values of deep importance to the community.

The didactic and instrumental methods can stand in harmony with one another;[35] at least as often, however, they seem to be in some tension. For example, Rodes remarks upon the tension between instrumental and didactic approaches to sexual behavior. Should the law encourage chastity, or should it provide free condoms to minimize the risk of AIDS and birth control to minimize the risk of pregnancy?[36] We are all familiar with the political battles that have at their root a desire to give priority to one or the other method in this context. It can be tempting to reduce one method to a mere tool of the other, but Rodes urges us to resist the temptation:

> Accepting one or the other offers a certain philosophical convenience, but either of them leads to an impoverished jurisprudence. To refer the whole enterprise to its didactic function tends to stifle creativity in the enforcement process. Once you have commanded what is right and forbidden what is wrong, and laid on the stocks and the lash for lesser infractions, the ax and the gibbet for greater ones, you can rest content with your fulfillment of the practical responsibilities of your profession. You can devote your intellectual energies to refining your values and their application to more and more complicated fact patterns. without regard to their realization in the world. On the other hand, referring everything to the instrumental function tends to obfuscate the applicable values. You tend to find more and more sophisticated ways of accomplishing things, while paying less and less attention to what it is you are trying to accomplish. The end result is apt to be a legal system that is all realizations and no values.[37]

In Rodes's view, therefore, we need to keep both methods in mind if we are to design an adequately balanced legal system. He contends that classical and medieval legal systems succumbed to the temptation to focus nearly exclusively on the didactic method. "The late fifth-century Theodosian Code bears witness to the last days of the Roman Empire, when the supreme authority could find nothing better to do with the legal system than sit in the midst of the growing chaos issuing more and more commands that fewer and fewer people obeyed."[38]

In contrast, most modem legal thought places almost exclusive emphasis on the instrumental method. "It concentrates on realizations with only token regard for the values being realized. It is dominated by technical metaphors such as Roscoe Pound's 'social engineering.' It licenses the deployment of more and more sophisticated legal technologies with less and less regard for what they are supposed to be accomplishing."[39]

The Third Set of Categories

Rodes's historical study of the relationship of church and state in England has led him to the conclusion that there are two basic strategies for relating the church to the world: Erastian[40] and High Church. According to Rodes, the *Erastian* approach is "based on a general unity of function between church and state"; it is operative when "Christianity is viewed as a social agenda and a lifestyle for whole peoples."[41] Rodes notes that Erastians emphasize filling the gaps in the social service work of the government, such as education, health care, and poverty relief.[42] Rodes observes that the Erastian approach has historically been concerned with inculcating ideals of sexual morality, although not without noting the "unfortunate" results of coercive measures in this arena.[43] Rodes also observes that social justice and civil rights have been matters for concern for the church on its Erastian side rather than for the state. "Either the values concerned, like chastity and temperance, have commanded a moral consensus that society was not prepared to enforce coercively, or they have formed part of a Christian agenda that the church was more willing to propose than the society was to accept."[44]

In contrast, Rodes denominates as *High Church* those who present an eschatological witness over and against society.[45] He uses the term "to cover any view of the church as an institutional embodiment of the transcendence, the otherness, of God, and of the divine judgment that attaches to every existing society for not being the Kingdom of God."[46] Centrally, High Church views do not see themselves as advancing a merely political program "The reason it is High Church is that it points to human purposes beyond the reach of society, and to social shortcomings for which society has no remedy."[47] High Church views, according to Rodes, tend to promote a vision of the institutional church as a sanctuary against the corrupt world. But there are times when the High Church approach does venture into political life: he notes that "High Churchmanship sometimes goes beyond an eschatological stance, but when it does, it tends to move toward a domination of civil society by ecclesiastical authority which is not acceptable either theologically or politically."[48]

Rodes recognizes that both approaches to the relationship between church and culture are necessary. He also sees that it is difficult to distinguish them at times; which one is more prominent may depend upon the way things are going in a particular society. "When a work is progressing nicely and attracting good support, utilitarian, Erastian perceptions of it are apt to be uppermost in people's minds. Conversely. when the effect on society becomes harder to achieve or more limited by considerations proper to the art of the possible, those involved in the work are more apt to content themselves with a non-utilitarian, High Church witness, and the mutual support that they derive from bearing that witness in common."[49]

Rodes also argues that these approaches take somewhat different forms in different cultures and their associated economic and political systems. Drawing upon the insights of Milovan Djilas, Rodes has maintained that the ruling class of both capitalist and socialist economies was composed of bureaucrats and managers, who alone were capable of providing the expertise that allowed such complicated economies to function.[50] Consequently, in our society today, "[m]anagerial Erastianism enlists the church in an extensive consortium of organizations and experts engaged in the solving of problems."[51] Spiritual concerns, maintains Rodes, can take too much of a back seat to the need to ameliorate social injustice and human suffering.[52]

What form does a High Church approach take in a capitalistic economic framework dominated by managers? High Church sensibilities tend to be the prerogative of an elite; "people who had enough education to appropriate a fairly complex set of theological doctrines, and who did not need to spend much time and thought on material needs."[53] Rodes contends that "[w]here Erastianism creates a danger of reducing the Word and the sacraments to the level of a class-bound secular agenda, High Churchmanship creates a danger of exalting some class-bound secular agenda to the level of Word and sacraments."[54]

Integrating the Three Sets of Categories

Robert Rodes has provided us with a set of helpful analytical tools with which to approach not only past disputes about how to instantiate the Gospel in a given culture but also current controversies that divide many Christian communities. I would like to suggest, however, that the power of these tools will be greatly increased if we make some effort to integrate them. More specifically, I think that Erastians and High Church people tend to give priority to different functions of the law, as well as to different methods for achieving its end.

This difference in priority ought not to be surprising. High Church people are acutely sensitive to the radical way in which the kingdom of God differs from all worldly kingdoms. While God's kingdom will be fully manifest only at the end of time, it is present among us in embryonic form in the church, particularly the sacramental life of the church. The primary task of believers, therefore, is to witness to the values of the kingdom of God, to prevent their submersion in the hopelessly compromised value system of the secular world. When they turn their attention to the secular world, High Church people tend to see their major role as proclaiming and protecting the basic insights of the natural law, which represents God's basic intent for the normative shape of human life and human society. They see those insights as under constant threat by secular values, and in need of constant reinforcement by religious believers, whose commitment to the natural law is fortified by situating it in its proper place in the divine plan, to which they have access through the divinely guided magisterium of the church.

In the context of their dealings with the secular world, Erastians tend to emphasize creation and incarnation rather than the eschatological consummation of the divine plan. They tend to focus on the many corporal and spiritual works of mercy that need to be performed here and now, rather than devoting too much attention to the nature and function of the eschatological kingdom of God. Moreover, they are not leery about cooperation with all people of good will, whether or not they are believers, because they emphasize our common character as children of the God who created, redeems, and sustains us all. They are more open to the discernment of the requirements of natural law inductively rather than deductively; they take seriously not only the moral wisdom of the institutional church but also the moral wisdom of ordinary people whom they consider to be of good character, whatever their professed belief systems.

So how would this difference in emphasis with respect to the relationship of the church to the world affect the way in which Erastians and High Church people approach Rodes's two other sets of categories? Let us begin with Rodes's distinction among the three functions of law—the normative, the constitutive, and the epistemic. In my view, Erastians are more likely to emphasize the normative aspect of law, while High Church people are more likely to stress its epistemic function. At first, this may seem counterintuitive: High Church people, after all, tend to be rigorists, while Erastians tend to be more willing to compromise with political necessity.

Yet a deeper consideration of the situation may reveal some surprising twists. It seems, to me at least, that High Church people consider it their primary duty to preach the kingdom of God, unseen but already present in embryonic form in our midst. They see their task as breaking through the confusion and self-deception caused by both individual sin and collective patterns of sin, in order to convey a clear and uncompromising understanding of God's loving plan for human life. To the extent that secular law touches upon matters determined by that plan (e.g., matters determined by natural law), secular law must also be clear and unequivocal about the moral truth. For many Catholic High Church people, the emphasis on the epistemological function of the law is consonant with their definition of law, which finds its roots in the *Summa Theologica* of Thomas Aquinas. According to Aquinas, the eternal law is nothing more or less than God's plan for the entire world.[55] Whereas nonrational creatures participate in the eternal law solely by instinct, human beings participate in the eternal law by using their practical reason. Natural law, for Aquinas, is nothing other than the human person's participation in the eternal law, in and through the exercise of his or her practical reason.[56] The making of positive law involves articulating the requirements of natural law for those who are unable to grasp them, and fleshing out those requirements in particular ways to fit the needs of a particular community.[57] Consequently, in a just community, the positive law should reflect the basic content of the natural law.[58]

The overwhelming priority for High Church people in both dogmatic and moral theology is purity and comprehensiveness of teaching. High Church people believe that no human measures are likely to be effective in bringing about the kingdom of God— that kingdom will be made manifest in God's own time. Consequently, they are less interested in moving incrementally toward a realization of the kingdom's values than they are in proclaiming those values in all their radicalism, all their fullness. In a nutshell, they are concerned with ensuring that the law reflects and proclaims the truths of the natural law—the epistemic function of law is primary.

In contrast, Erastians are centrally concerned with improving this world, despite its enduring imperfections. As Rodes notes, Erastians focus on "presenting and even implementing a practical agenda for the whole society, and for offering a lifestyle within the reach of people with average or below average spiritual capacity and moral fiber."[59] Erastians are concerned, therefore, with accomplishing certain pragmatic goals in order to better society, and moving persons and resources in order to accomplish those goals. Consequently, they are most concerned with the normative function of the law; they want to regularize means for ensuring that the basic social welfare needs of the most vulnerable members of society are met. Because they are more likely to see church and state as more or less harmonious partners in the betterment of society, they are more likely to see the secular legal system as one tool that can be used in accomplishing their goals. In a nutshell, the normative function of law is primary.

What about the constitutive function of law? In my view, it is a mediating category, which Erastians and High Church people both tend to interpret in terms of the requirements of the more extreme category that they favor. So, Erastians see the constitutive function of the law as one more tool to use on the pilgrimage to the kingdom of God, and in particular in providing for the basic needs of suffering and sinful people. They are more inclined, therefore, to recognize, organize, and attempt to ameliorate relationships and patterns of behavior that are already in existence, whether or not they are morally appropriate from the point of view of the kingdom of God fully instantiated. For example, Erastians would be more likely to create a category of legal prostitution, which would confer legal protection to a brothel on the condition that it met certain public health and safety requirements.

Erastians would indignantly deny the charge that such a strategy amounted to condoning prostitution; instead, they would argue that they were minimizing the unjust effects of a pattern of behavior that was impossible to eradicate from human society. Similarly, Erastians would be more likely to endorse the creation of institutions and bonds that facilitated responsibility and mutual care among human beings, no matter how fallen. The creations of legal categories to cover same-sex marriage, polygamous marriage, or even "marriage lite" (a set of defined but limited responsibilities for those who have decided to live with one another without benefit of marriage) would be justified by Erastians on the basis of the empirical evidence: if such institutions were thought capable of minimizing injustice by ensuring that parties actually were not penalized excessively for making and relying upon promises of some sort of support and protection to one another. It is not, of course, that Erastians are unable to appreciate the importance of upholding ideals in areas of marriage and sexuality; however, they would be more likely than High Church people to consider whether proclaiming the ideal was more likely than regulating the reality to produce a more just and humane set of relationships.

In contrast, High Church people will be more inclined to say, at the very least, that the constitutive function of the secular law should not undermine or contradict God's providential determinations about what is and is not the case. Marriage, for example, by God's metaphysical and moral design, simply *is* the lifelong commitment of one man and one woman. The constitutive arrangements recognized by the state and, a fortiori, by the church ought not to proclaim that the impossible is possible, no matter how much good might result from a pragmatic perspective. The most important task of the church is to proclaim the unadulterated truth. Ideally, the legal system would do the same in matters pertaining to natural law. If, however, Christians are unfortunate enough to be in a legal system where sin and self-deception have masked the requirements of the natural law, their primary responsibility is to proclaim those requirements clearly and without any appearance of compromise.

In an environment that they perceive as determinedly secular and therefore hostile to Christian faith, High Church people are especially reluctant to approve what the Catholic moral tradition has traditionally called "cooperation with evil"—the performance of an action that facilitates in some way the wrongful action of another. From their perspective, cooperation with evil is one thing in a society that as a whole honors and accept Christian values, including the basic requirements of natural law; it is different thing entirely in a secular society that treats those values with contempt or indifference.[60] Whereas Erastians tend to accept with resignation the inevitability of some form of cooperation with evil, High Church people are far more worried about its deleterious effect on the purity of the Christian witness.

The issue of cooperation with evil is instructive. The Catholic moral tradition has developed an elaborate, if not abstruse, matrix to help people differentiate between permissible and impermissible cooperation with evil.[61] Both Erastians and High Church people acknowledge the relevance of that matrix; nonetheless, they frequently come to different judgments about whether cooperation is acceptable.[62] Their differences, in my judgment, come down to different priorities: Erastians place a greater emphasis on performing the corporal works of mercy to assist people in need, and High Church people give greater importance to proclaiming the holiness of life in the kingdom of God. Erastian Catholics are likely to justify giving condoms to persons at risk of AIDS in sub-Saharan Africa under the principle of cooperation with evil, while High Church people are likely to resist such a program on the grounds that it could be construed as encouraging immoral sexual activity. According to Catholic teaching, this includes all homosexual acts and heterosexual activity outside of marriage, which are always inconsistent with the natural law. Many High Church Catholics would resist the use of condoms by a married couple, even to prevent the transmission of disease, because they believe that such use distorts the natural structure of the marital act.

Finally, and not surprisingly, Erastians and High Church people differ in the respect and emphasis each places on Rodes's two methods of law, the didactic and the instrumental. Needless to say, High Church people favor the didactic; they see the central job of the church's magisterium (and by extension, the secular government) as proclaiming the truth of the matter about various controverted moral issues. For reasons described, they are less concerned about whether the mere proclamation of the truth is the best method of bringing about the social reality they seek to bring about; it is God's job, not theirs, to render human fidelity to divine truth effective. In contrast, Erastians are more concerned with using the instrumental methods of the law to bring about incremental improvement in the human situation. If the best way to secure a particularly desirable state of affairs is not to preach about it, but to provide incentives to facilitate its implementation, so be it.

Erastians see High Church people as mesmerized by idealized visions of reality; because they are idealists, they ignore both the limitations of the real world and the possibilities for incremental improvement. High Church people, for their part, see Erastians as too focused on the gritty here-and-now immanent to give proper respect God's plan for human beings, as set forth in Scripture and (for Catholics) in the authoritative tradition as well. In the view of High Church people, the realism of Erastians leads them to settle for too little moral improvement.

An example of this difference in viewpoint can be found in different strategies pro-life Catholics have taken regarding abortion law in recent years. Erastians tend to favor incentives to reduce abortion rates, such as prenatal support, generous subsidies to unwed mothers, and high- quality public education from preschool to college. In contrast, High Church people tend to emphasize the unequivocal didactic power of an absolute prohibition. (It is important to note that most people in this camp do not favor criminal penalties targeting the woman seeking an abortion, but instead would criminalize the activity of the doctor performing the abortion.) Erastians have pointed out that the lowest abortion rates in the West are found in those countries that do not penalize abortion, at least in the early weeks, but instead provide incentives for a woman to carry her baby to term.[63] In response, High Church people often state that the fundamental purpose of the law is not primarily to be immediately and tangibly effective, but instead to proclaim the unequivocal dignity of unborn human life. From the High Church perspective, a legislative compromise may undermine the crucial didactic function of the law.[64]

A Test Case: Same-Sex Marriage and Catholic Charities of Boston

I would like to conduct a brief test of my theory that an integrated approach to Rodes's three sets of categories powerfully increases their explanatory power. The subject matter of my test will be the contretemps that developed in the fall of 2005 and the spring of 2006 over whether or not Catholic Charities of Boston should have continued to place children with homosexual couples as a condition of maintaining their status as a licensed adoption agency in the state of Massachusetts. In the end, Boston Catholic Charities decided to cease all work in the adoption area rather than directly contravene a directive from the Vatican prohibiting Catholic organizations from placing children with same-sex couples as adoptive parents. The tensions between the rights of same-sex couples and the freedom of religious institutions to operate according to their own moral beliefs played themselves out in Massachusetts almost a decade before they became pervasive in American culture.

In examining this controversy, my remarks will be narrowly restricted: they will not encompass the broader societal and religious debate over whether or not homosexual acts are morally justified. Quite obviously, if one thinks that the official teaching of the Catholic Church on this matter is misguided, one will have little sympathy for the ultimate decision of Boston Catholic Charities. My concentration, therefore, will be on the disagreements that developed between and among Catholics (and others) who do not see themselves as challenging the underlying teaching of the church on the morality of homosexual activity. These disagreements centered on whether respect for that teaching required Catholic Charities to cease its good work in placing children with adoptive families rather than place a small number of children with gay couples.

But first, some background. In the fall of 2005, the *Boston Globe* reported that Catholic Charities of the Archdiocese of Boston had placed thirteen children for adoption with homosexual couples.[65] These adoptions had taken place over an eighteen-year period, in which Catholic Charities had arranged for the adoptions of a total of 720 children.[66] The agency was between a rock and a hard place. On the one hand, the Commonwealth of Massachusetts required that all adoption agencies agree to abide by its nondiscrimination clause as a condition of licensure.[67] On the other hand, in 2003, the Vatican's Congregation for the Doctrine of the Faith issued a document on same-sex marriage and civil unions, which claimed that it was gravely immoral to place a child for adoption with a same-sex couple.[68] In a nutshell, then, the state seemed categorically to require Catholic Charities to engage in practices that the church categorically prohibited.

The controversy continued for approximately six months. The Massachusetts Catholic Conference formed a committee to review the issue in November 2005;[69] its work resulted in a statement issued on February 26, 2006, by the four Catholic bishops in Massachusetts.[70] They called upon state legislators to grant Catholic adoption agencies an exemption to the requirement of equal treatment of same-sex couples on the grounds of religious freedom This stance put them at odds with the board of trustees of Boston Catholic Charities, which had voted unanimously in December 2005 to support the continued placement of children with gay couples. In response to the statement, seven members of the board resigned.[71] Mitt Romney, the governor at the time, stated that he could not waive the anti-discrimination laws, and suggested that the bishops file a bill to that effect with the legislature.[72] State legislators informed church leaders that such a proposal had no chance of passing.[73]

All efforts to reach a political compromise failed. In March, the board of trustees of Boston Catholic Charities voted to end all adoption services.[74] In a joint statement issued on March 10, 2006, the organization's president, Rev. J. Bryan Hehir, and the chair of its board of trustees, Jeffrey Kaneb, acknowledged, "[W]e have encountered a dilemma we cannot resolve. In spite of much effort and analysis, Catholic Charities of Boston finds that it cannot reconcile the teaching of the church, which guides our work, and the statutes and regulations of the Commonwealth."[75]

The agency then began the work of transitioning its caseload, which included many hard-to-place children, to other adoption agencies, a task which it projected to be completed by the end of June 2006.[76] There was a great deal of public chagrin because no one doubted that Catholic Charities had proven itself to be a tireless advocate of children, particularly hard-to-place children. Patricia Wen, the reporter for the *Boston Globe* who broke the story the previous fall, wrote an article describing how the agency was preparing to end over a century of providing adoption services to the greater Boston area.[77] It reads like an obituary.

So how do Professor Rodes's categories, used in an integrated manner, help us to understand this heart-wrenching controversy? Let us begin with a High Church approach, which I believe is exemplified in the interview conducted by the *Boston Globe* with Archbishop Sean O'Malley immediately before he went to Rome to be created a cardinal by Pope Benedict XVI, in March 2006. When pressed to articulate the Vatican's concern in these matters, he emphasized the importance of a clear and unambiguous witness to the nature of marriage proclaimed by the church:

> I understand the Holy See's concern that in our works of mercy, in our social programs, that we must be consistent in teaching the Catholic faith in one voice. And certainly the church's teaching on marriage is very central to our beliefs and how we see that the institution of marriage in today's world is very much threatened on many fronts, and yet it is the very cornerstone of society. And the best way for a child to be raised is to be conceived and nurtured by committed, loving parents in marriage. And so, for the church, in our social services activities and other works of mercy, we need to be consistent. And it was your newspaper that pointed out the anomaly to us, and we have tried to deal with that.[78]

The overriding concern for O'Malley was the purity of the message conveyed by the participation of Catholic institutions in the adoption process. To him, the most important function of the secular law, especially in this time of moral confusion, was its epistemic function: it should embody the definition of marriage and family demanded by natural law and promulgated in season and out by the church. The constitutive function of the law—that is, the institutions and relationships that it brings into being—should harmoniously reflect and support its epistemic function. The clarity of the church's moral message, and the congruence of its charitable activities with that message, is particularly important, in view of the fact that the Commonwealth of Massachusetts has extended the definition of marriage to include same-sex couples.

More specifically, to those who adopt this position, the fundamental problem with the 2003 decision of the Supreme Judicial Court of Massachusetts declaring it unconstitutional to limit marriage to heterosexual couples[79] is epistemological, not moral. More specifically, the basic flaw in the decision is not primarily that it legitimates sexual activity between two people of the same sex. Rather, it is that it incorporates an incorrect definition of marriage, as something other than the permanent and exclusive union of one man and one woman.[80] Constitutively, then, the institution of marriage as defined by the Commonwealth of Massachusetts subverts the epistemic function of the law—its duty to embody the truth about the nature of marriage. Normatively, in this time of great epistemic crisis, it is of paramount importance that Catholic institutions behave in ways that testify to that threatened truth. What good is it, from this perspective, if Catholic Charities helps hundreds of children in crisis if it undermines the stable family life of thousands more in the process?

The Erastians would approach the situation from a very different vantage point, which is encapsulated in the title to a *Commonweal* editorial on the controversy, "Abandoned Children." Here are the first two paragraphs:

> In any given year, tragedy, family dysfunction, poverty, neglect, and abuse separate hundreds of thousands of children from their birth parents.
>
> When adoption cannot be arranged, many of these children find themselves moved from one foster family to another. Finding a permanent home for abused, handicapped, or troubled children is especially hard. In such cases, objections are rarely raised when prospective adoptive parents happen to be gays or lesbians. Whatever one's views about the morality of homosexuality, it is hard to understand how an orphaned or abandoned child does not benefit from being placed in a loving home.[81]

For the Erastians, the primary imperative for both the state and the church at this point in time was to help the vulnerable members of the community pick up the pieces after sin and misfortune have worked their ravages. The Erastians, in other words, are most concerned about the normative function of law: the law's purpose in this context is to ensure that children are cared for by loving families, accomplished by encouraging as many people as possible to respond compassionately to children in desperate need of a home. The constitutive function follows the normative function: if the only people willing to take a bruised or battered child are not exactly Ozzie and Harriet, so be it. It may not be perfect, but it's much better than the alternative of leaving hard-to-place children to languish in foster care. To those who take this position, the primary imperative is to care for the particular children now in our charge. To refuse to ameliorate their situation by placing them for adoption with a same-sex couple because of a general commitment to the social value of heterosexual marriage strikes Erastians as heartless.

I suspect that the underlying differences between these two groups can be accounted for by the differing perspectives on how to deal with tragedy. In the introduction to this chapter, I noted Professor Rodes's insistence that the ability to deal with tragedy is an essential feature of pilgrim law. He writes that "Christian jurisprudence . . . must bear witness to redemption, and, as far as possible, further it. It is here that pilgrim law provides an essential complement to natural law, which is prelapsarian in its outlook, and has no answer to anyone's failure to live up to what it prescribes."[82]

Broken families. Bruised children. Moral uncertainty. Practical uncertainty about the best way to pick up the pieces. All are aspects of the tragic nature of human life. Although we are redeemed from sin, we are not fully healed from its effects, individually or collectively. In this landmark debate about Boston Catholic Charities, Erastians placed their emphasis on picking up the pieces after tragedy has wreaked its devastation—they see the faces of the particular children languishing in foster care and in need of a loving home. They feared that the High Church people are pressing the requirements of natural law in the manner alluded to by Rodes: they have "no answer to anyone's failure to live up to what it prescribes."[83] And indeed, some High Church people may have been guilty as charged. But at their best, High Church people were arguing on behalf of prevention: in their view, the best way to prevent this type of tragedy from expanding its sway upon human life is by promoting and protecting the only institution that has proven more or less capable of raising healthy children under a variety of adverse social and economic circumstances: the traditional family.

Thinking of the debate among Catholics in Boston as a disagreement about the best way to respond to human tragedy does not, of course, resolve the debate, which has now moved beyond the Commonwealth of Massachusetts to the national stage. Furthermore, it does nothing to address the more wide-ranging debates that I deliberately set to one side in this chapter, such as the moral status of the traditional family itself.

Nonetheless, by conceptualizing the debate in this way we might be less inclined to demonize those who disagree with us on hard questions.

As the work of Robert Rodes shows, an understanding of the analytical categories applicable to secular law can help us understand the debates within Christian communities about their proper relationship to a broader, pluralistic culture. The next chapter will show that the substance of secular law can actually help Christian communities resolve debates about internal church discipline.

8

Second Chances and Statutes of Limitations

Engaging Walter Kasper

IN APRIL 2016, Pope Francis released *Amoris laetitia*, his long-awaited apostolic exhortation on family life, which marked the completion of the work of two international synods of bishops held in Rome in 2014 and 2015 to discuss global challenges facing the vocations of marriage and parenthood in the twenty-first century.[1] Despite its many insights, the document failed decisively to settle the question that had captured the attention of both the secular and the religious media: Will Catholics who divorced and remarried civilly without obtaining a church annulment of their first marriages continue to be banned from receiving communion? While *Amoris laetitia* appears to have opened the door to the reception of communion by persons in that situation, it does not grapple with the normative foundations for such a change in approach. Instead, it generally treats the opening as a matter of pastoral practice, and a retrieval of the importance of priests working with the people enmeshed in such situations to facilitate their own discernment about their particular spiritual situation.[2]

At the same time, there is some reason to think that *Amoris laetitia* does in fact mark a development in church teaching, rather than merely increased flexibility in pastoral responses to people in difficult situations. At a Vatican press conference introducing the apostolic exhortation, Cardinal Christoph Schönborn, a distinguished theologian who was editor in chief of the Catechism of the Catholic Church, stated that "there is an organic development of doctrine" in the document.[3]

If the development, in fact, includes an opening to the reception of communion on the part of the divorced and civilly remarried, what is its actual rationale? It is the task of Catholic theologians, of course, to help answer this question. In my view, one useful approach is adumbrated in the remarks of Cardinal Lorenzo Baldisseri, who was selected along with Cardinal Schönborn to introduce the document at the Vatican press conference. Baldisseri emphasized that the document needed to be interpreted in the context of the pope's constant emphasis on the importance of mercy in understanding the way in which God relates to human beings. Baldisseri also highlighted aspects of the apostolic exhortation that, in my view, are closely related to mercy. First, he emphasized the importance of the passage of time in marking human development and in measuring human relationships. Baldisseri noted that "the principle according to which 'time is greater than space' suggests that time is needed and there are different ways to find the best solutions to different situations."[4] Second, he drew attention to the exhortation's insistence that "no one can be condemned for ever, because that is not the logic of the Gospel."[5] Time is limited in its ability to keep repentant human beings separated from a merciful God.

Baldisseri's remarks in the press conference are provocative, but they are far from systematic. My goal in this chapter is to show how they can be expanded and ordered by drawing upon insights from both theological and legal sources. My theological conversation partner will be Cardinal Walter Kasper, and in particular his recent work on mercy. It is widely known that Kasper's approach has had a significant influence on the thought of Pope Francis. Not only did the pope give an enthusiastic endorsement to Kasper's book on mercy, he also invited him to address a meeting of the world's cardinals in preparation for the synods on the family.[6] In the first section, therefore, I will draw upon Cardinal Walter Kasper's book on mercy to develop a richer sense of what mercy means, and what it may require of the church in its pastoral care for divorced and remarried Catholics. Drawing insights from American civil law, the second section will address a key objection to Kasper's proposal that most divorced and remarried Catholics cannot be admitted to communion because their sin against the first marriage is a continuing sin. The supreme lawgiver for the Roman Catholic Church is, of course, Jesus Christ, who gave his life in order to give repentant sinners the opportunity for new life. In the brief third section, I reflect upon whether Jesus's teaching is consistent with my proposal.

What is it about the insights of secular law that might help address this question of discipline? Secular law can help us grapple with questions about when wrongdoing begins, when it ends, and how people can put it behind them and move on with their lives. In other words, secular courts have something to teach us about the practice of mercy—a subject to which Cardinal Kasper has given considerable attention.

Mercy as a New Chance

What does it mean for the church to situate its discernment about how to respond to the travails of its members regarding marriage and family life within the framework of mercy? Cardinal Walter Kasper helps us to address this question in *Mercy: The Essence of the Gospel and the Key to Christian Life*. Kasper argues that the topic of mercy has been "criminally neglected" in theological reflection, despite the fact that the terrible events of the twentieth century reveal the overwhelming need of humanity for the mercy of God and the mercy of one another.[7] Moreover, Kasper shows that this deepest of human needs corresponds to a fundamental truth about God's nature. God does not merely act mercifully from time to time; God *is* mercy. Kasper writes:

> Thus from the beginning of history, God's counteraction is at work against disaster. From the very beginning God's merciful action [*Erbarmen*] is powerfully effective. His mercy is how God provides resistance to evil, which is getting the upper hand. He does not do this forcibly and violently; he doesn't simply do battle; rather, in his mercy God repeatedly creates new space for life and for blessing.[8]

The vision of "new space for life and for blessing" is a key to understanding Kasper's view of divine mercy. While sin entails death, mercy enables new life. God does not merely pronounce forgiveness from a distance, leaving us to stew in our own misery. God gives us a *new chance*, and with it new possibilities for flourishing. As Kasper writes: "In his mercy, God grants humanity life and living space anew."[9] Forgiveness erases the sin; mercy enables new life.

Mercy is not simply one of God's marvelous qualities; according to Kasper, it is "God's defining attribute."[10] In fact, mercy is the divine characteristic in light of which all of God's other qualities must be interpreted and understood—including justice.[11] Moreover, and equally important, mercy provides the hermeneutical key to God's relationship with the world; it is nothing other than the "source and goal of God's activity."[12] "God holds the possibility of salvation open for every human being who is fundamentally willing to be converted and who is sorry for his or her guilt, even if their guilt is ever so great and their former life ever so botched up."[13]

Given his view of the nature of God, and the salvific action of Christ, it is not surprising that Kasper views mercy as central to the activity of the church; in fact, he calls the church the "sacrament of love and mercy."[14] Drawing inspiration from Pope John Paul II's encyclical *Dives in misericordia*,[15] Kasper argues that the church must "give witness to divine mercy" in a three-fold way: It "must proclaim the mercy of God; it must concretely provide people God's mercy in the sacrament of mercy, the sacrament of reconciliation; and it must allow God's mercy to appear and be realized in its concrete structures, its entire life, and even in its laws."[16]

It is not enough, therefore, for the church to proclaim God's mercy with words, or even to make God's mercy available through the sacrament of reconciliation. As the body of Christ, it must incarnate God's mercy in all aspects of its institutional life, including in its canon law. It must not cater to the respectable, the proper, and the prosperous. Like Jesus himself, it must reach out lovingly to the poor and the marginalized, especially to sinners. Kasper writes; "The most serious criticism that can be leveled against the church, therefore, is the accusation that oftentimes only a few deeds follow, or appear to follow, its words. The church is reproached for speaking of God's mercy, while it is perceived by many people to be strict, harsh, and pitiless."[17]

Kasper emphasizes that mercy does not undermine justice, but it fulfills and transcends it. It does this not by denying that a wrong occurred but by refusing to allow the wrong act to entirely define the wrongdoer, and resisting any effort to do justice by annihilating all hope of that person's future participation in the community.

Furthermore, canon law itself must be concerned with mercy, because mercy is part of canon law's ultimate purpose: fostering the church's active participation in God's saving plan for humanity. Prioritizing mercy in the interpretation of canon law, however, does not mean abandoning the law's objective character. Instead, we might say, part of the task of mercy is to invite us to fine-tune the application of the law by using the *aequitas canonica*: "[T]he point is to apply the objective sense of the legislation analogously in an often complex concrete situation so that the law's application truly is fair and just in the given situation."[18] Moreover, he emphasizes that canon law must be interpreted in particular cases "according to its authentic intention, that is, according to the οἰκονομία, the entire divine order of salvation."[19] Concretely, that means leaving people room for a new start and hope for a better future: "The judge will then render a fair judgment, but nevertheless not a judgment that functions like a guillotine, but rather a judgment that leaves open 'a loophole of mercy,' that is, that makes possible a new beginning for the other, if he or she is of good will."[20]

In his recent lecture on "The Gospel of the Family," Cardinal Kasper expanded upon his thoughts about the relationship of mercy, justice, and law to particular questions facing the Extraordinary Synod, such as how the church deals with divorced and remarried individuals.[21] Cautioning against reducing the problem to one of readmittance to communion, he stresses that the church must consider "pastoral care for marriage and family life in their totality," which must include thoroughgoing catechesis and marriage preparation beginning in adolescence.[22] Prevention of family breakdown, however important it may be, is not enough in today's situation. Kasper observes that "many deserted partners, for the sake of the children, are dependent upon a new partnership and a civil marriage, which they cannot again quit without new guilt. In such new ties they often experience human happiness—indeed a virtual gift from heaven—after previous bitter experiences."[23]

How should the church respond to such couples? On the one hand, Kasper recognizes that "[i]t cannot propose a solution apart from or contrary to Jesus' words," which form the basis for the church's teaching on the indissolubility of sacramental marriage.[24] On the other hand, Kasper cannot interpret Jesus's words apart from the entire context of Jesus's saving mission: "Mercy and fidelity belong together. Therefore, there can be no human solution that is absolutely desperate and hopeless. However far a human being may fall, he or she never falls deeper than God's mercy can reach."[25] For Kasper, this point is crucial. God's mercy is creative; it entails the opportunity for renewed life, including and especially a renewed and richer relationship with God.

With these principles firmly in place, Kasper proceeds with caution to the analysis of particular cases, which he divides into two categories: (1) situations in which the parties are convinced that their first sacramental marriage was invalid; and (2) situations in which the first sacramental marriage was valid, but proved intractably unworkable. With respect to situations in the first category, he calls for revision to the church's annulment practices and procedures, so that they better honor the personal dignity of those who participate in them, since "behind every process, behind every case stand persons who expect justice."[26]

It is Kasper's response to situations in the second category, however, that has generated the most attention and controversy. Kasper begins by pointing out that civilly divorced and remarried Catholics have been encouraged to receive spiritual communion at Mass, despite their irregular marital status. He then goes on to ask why they should be excluded from actual receipt of the Eucharist. "If we exclude divorced and remarried Christians, who are properly disposed, from the sacraments and refer them to the extra-sacramental way of salvation, do we not then place the fundamental sacramental structure of the Church in question?"[27] Allowing such persons to receive communion, Kasper emphasizes, does not mean that divorced and remarried persons can contract a second sacramental marriage during the lifetime of their first spouse. It is not a "second ship" after the shipwreck of their first marriage. It is, however, a "lifesaving plank" that is mercifully extended to a drowning person—"a plank of salvation through participation in communion."[28]

What does it mean for a divorced and remarried person to be "properly disposed" to receive communion? Kasper is no latitudinarian; a careful reading of his proposal reveals that he sets five criteria for the reception of communion: (1) the divorced Catholic is sincerely sorry that he or she failed in the first marriage; (2) a return to the first marriage is definitely not possible; (3) the second marriage cannot be abandoned without incurring new guilt; (4) the Catholic seeking communion tries to live out the second marriage in the context of faith, including by raising any children as Catholics; and (5) the Catholic longs for the sacraments of penance and communion as a source of strength.[29]

Under these conditions, Kasper proposes that the penitent, divorced, and remarried Catholic ought to be admitted to confession and communion. He maintains with passion, as well as rhetorical power: "If forgiveness is possible for the murderer, then it is also possible for the adulterer." The sacraments, he reminds us, are not "a reward for good conduct or for an elite, who exclude those who are most in need of them."[30] Despite its power, this rhetorical analogy has met with significant resistance among some moralists and canonists.[31] Because a sacramental marriage endures until the death of one of the parties, Kasper's critics insist that the church must treat the purported second marriage as entailing repeated acts of adultery. Consequently, they maintain that Kasper's analogy is inapt: the repentant murderer confesses a sin that is over and done with, while the divorced and remarried person confesses a sin that is ongoing and continuing, without a firm purpose of amendment. Consequently, the murderer is eligible for absolution, while the divorced and remarried person is not—unless he or she agrees to live with his second spouse without engaging in a sexual relationship. In short, Cardinal Kasper's critics believe that his proposal for readmitting divorced and remarried Catholics to communion is false mercy, because it does not take into account the demands of truth and justice.

A Way Forward: Insights from Secular Law

Is there a way out of this conundrum? I would like to propose a possible path, composed of two steps. First, I suggest that the term "adultery," as it is used in the contemporary context, is not the proper way in which to describe the sin of a divorced and civilly remarried person against his or her sacramental first marriage. Second, it is doubtless true that in many cases, the parties to a broken marriage have sinned against each other and against their bond of matrimony. I propose, however, that the church treat their sins against the first marriage as completed sins, and not as ongoing sins. By treating them in this way, it is possible for the divorced parties to a sacramental marriage to repent of their wrongdoing and to begin a new life with a new spouse. It is possible for them to have a merciful second chance.

The concept of "adultery"—and the wrong it works—has changed significantly over the centuries. In ancient times, adultery was generally seen to be analogous to a property crime—the violation of another man's property in a woman. In Mosaic law, as in early Roman law, a married man who had sexual relations with an unmarried woman was not committing adultery. Adulterous activity was problematic not only in itself but also in its consequences for the social and economic structure of the household. It rendered the lines of patrilineal succession uncertain, since a man would not be certain that any children borne by his wife actually belonged to him.

In our own era in the West, the concept of adultery refers centrally to the betrayal of one spouse by another. It applies equally to men and women. The sexual betrayal is one aspect of the phenomenon of adultery—but it is only one aspect. Adultery involves a multifaceted betrayal. While purporting to maintain a joint household and family life, the adulterous spouse is in fact diverting his or her sexual intimacy, emotional support, and perhaps even financial resources away from the joint project of the marriage.

In a typical case of adultery, the adulterer's behavior is often kept a secret from the other spouse, who often feels shamed and duped when the betrayal is discovered. Moreover, the betrayed spouse often experiences a sense of being used by the betraying spouse. While his or her partner has been looking outside the marriage for satisfaction, the betrayed spouse has been devoting his or her attention and energies to the marital partnership. Particularly if the innocent spouse is a woman who devotes herself to taking care of young children rather than participating in the workforce, she is relying upon the marriage for her financial security and material well-being. In our era, then, adultery involves three factors: (1) deceit; (2) physical and emotional betrayal; and (3) exploitation of the innocent spouse.[32]

It seems to me, therefore, that the term "adultery," does not rightly apply to a situation that arises *after* a married couple obtains a civil divorce and one or both parties remarry. Civil divorce is public; there is no deceit involved. Because the divorce dissolves the legal bond between the two parties to the original marriage, what happens after that point does not count as betrayal, strictly speaking. Finally, the divorce has put each party on notice that the other is no longer engaged in building a common life with the other. It has put both parties on notice that they have no expectation of sexual fidelity from each other. After a civil divorce, therefore, it is very difficult to think of even the innocent party as still *exploited* by his or her former spouse.

I think that it is deeply misleading to speak of one person acting "adulterously" toward his or her first spouse after they have been civilly divorced, because using that term in this situation does not account for key elements of the term's meaning. It is even more misleading, I think, to speak of a person who is divorced and remarried as committing adultery against his or first spouse when having sexual relations with his new spouse.

At this point, I need to emphasize two key points. First, it may very well be the case that one or both parties acted wrongly in bringing about the breakdown of their marriage. But once there is no realistic possibility for reconciliation in this lifetime, the wrong is a completed wrong, not a continuing wrong. Catholics, after all, do not believe that marriage extends into eternity. A marriage as a joint project between two people is over, therefore, when there is no possibility of its being revived in this life. Consequently, the wrongs committed by marriage partners against that marriage are completed once they are civilly divorced, and it is clear that their relationship is no longer salvageable.

Second, it is still possible to act wrongfully against one's former spouse after the divorce. It is not as if the divorce entirely erases the bond between the two parties. One party may, for example, have a moral obligation to pay alimony to support the other party, particularly if he or she dedicated his or her time to raising children. Every parent has continuing moral obligations, I believe, not only to one's children but also to their mother or father—one's former spouse. At the very least, and in all circumstances, I think that both parties have a continuing obligation to pray for their former spouses.

Neither of these two points, however, entails the claim that a divorced person commits a *further* wrong against his or her first spouse —or against his or her first marriage—by remarrying. By disentangling their lives, by separating each other with respect to bed and board, the civil divorce has made it clear that their joint marital project is finished and not to be resumed in this lifetime—or ever, since we know there is no marriage in heaven. When one or both parties remarry, they make new commitments to different people. But in and of itself, that new commitment does not do further harm to the first marriage. Because the first marriage cannot be revivified in this life, it is no longer susceptible to any further damage. Consequently, it accords with the facts about marital life today in the West to think, Cardinal Kasper suggests, that the parties to the first marriage can repent of any harm they have done and move on with their lives, grateful for God's forgiveness and mercy.

As a legal tradition matures, it adds nuance and complexity to its categories of offense, in order to better account for salient features of the cases it encounters. Consider, for example, the development in the crime of homicide in the Anglo-American tradition. As late as the eleventh century, all homicide was either murder or justifiable homicide. All murder was punishable by death. As time went on, distinctions were added to the law to save the less culpable "murderers" (e.g., those who had killed accidentally). Initially, ameliorating the sentence of such criminals was a matter of the king's favor. Later, as the law itself began to incorporate the categories that triggered a royal pardon, it became a matter of justice to treat intentional homicide different from accidental killing.[33]

So a legal system can and does develop over time to take into account morally salient factors. As the example of murder shows, this development can happen as society comes to a better understanding of the difference made by the mental state of the criminal (the *mens rea*). But development can also take place as society comes to a better understanding of the exact nature and scope of the wrong that it is targeting (the *actus reus*).

The first task facing any prosecutor is to determine the "unit of prosecution" for the wrong committed by the defendant.[34] This task is not always easy. Does a thief who takes six bracelets off of one dresser commit one crime or six? Does a father who hits his child with all his force three times commit one crime or three? Determining the answer to these questions requires attention to the purpose of the lawmaker. But it also requires courts to exercise practical wisdom, because legislative intent is not always clear. The challenge in defining the crime is more difficult when what is at stake is not merely an isolated action but more an organized pattern of behavior. For example, one might ask if operating an illegal tavern is one offense, or whether the offenses mount up with every drink poured or customer served.[35]

What, exactly, is the wrong committed by the divorced and remarried Catholic? The Catholic tradition has generally said that such a person commits adultery every time he or she has sexual relations with the second spouse. Although adultery was not widely criminalized in Europe, some American states, influenced as they were by Puritan moral codes, did make it a crime. In many cases, American courts did indeed see each act of adultery as a separate chargeable offense. And in many circumstances, that might make sense. But in circumstances involving longer-term second relationships (such as involved in divorced and remarried Catholics), some American courts reframed the charge so that it better fit the actual offense.

Consider, for example, the case *In re Snow*, in which the U.S. Supreme Court was asked to grapple with the question of how Mormon polygamy intersected with the laws against unlawful cohabitation.[36] Lorenzo Snow was a polygamist living in Utah. The federal prosecutor charged him with three counts of unlawful cohabitation for three successive calendar years. The Court held that the government could not arbitrarily divide a single, uninterrupted, three-year unlawful cohabitation into three separate criminal charges; the description of the crime needed to conform to the lived reality of the defendant.

A second polygamy case, *In re Nielsen*, makes the point even more clearly. The federal government charged Hans Nielsen with unlawful cohabitation and the separate crime of adultery. Rejecting the government's way of framing Nielsen's criminal activity, the U.S. Supreme Court held that adultery was a lesser crime included within of the crime of cohabitation.[37] The court looked at the big picture: it recognized that the problem raised by the Mormon polygamy cases was not only, or mainly, the sexual activity outside the first marriage considered in the abstract. For the American legal system, the fundamental problem was the fact that Mormon men saw themselves as entering an additional marital relationship, of which the sexual acts were only one part.

As *In re Snow* and *In re Nielsen* illustrate, one very ordinary challenge of every legal system is to describe the wrongful activity engaged in by the defendants in the right way—in a way that captures what they are actually doing, as human beings and moral agents. In some cases, properly describing the defendant's wrongful action requires looking beyond the isolated, individual acts they have committed and situating them within a broader pattern of purposeful activity. It requires, so to speak, recalibrating the focus of the law's lens to get a meaningful perspective on the scene.

It seems to me that this sort of recalibration of perspective could assist the church in understanding the situation of divorced and remarried persons. The proper description of their activity is committed *cohabitation*—it is simply inaccurate to portray a civilly divorced and remarried Catholic as engaged in multiple, disconnected acts of adultery. The parties to the second marriage are not skulking off to a hotel room to grasp a moment of irresponsible pleasure. They are engaged in an ongoing, committed, and organized life project, which includes but is not limited to sexual relations. That life project may very well involve further, ancillary commitments to children, to aging family members, and to one another in sickness and health.

In some respects, both moralists and jurists face the same challenge. To do their jobs well, both of them need to frame the question appropriately. They need to ask: What is the proper description of the activity we are charged with guiding and regulating? For the Catholic Church, at this moment in time, the issue at stake in the case of divorced and remarried persons is not primarily about sexual acts. Most fundamentally, it is about relinquishing one complex set of commitments and vulnerabilities that marriage brings, and taking on a new set of commitments and vulnerabilities, even while one's first spouse is still living. As the judgment in *Nielsen* intimates, the broader frame provided by the new relationship should be the focus of our attention and analysis.

At this point in the chapter, a reader might object that my insights from American law may be interesting, but they do not advance Cardinal Kasper's case for mercy for the divorced and remarried. In fact, some readers might claim that I am harming his case. Rather than saying that divorced and remarried persons sin in every sexual act they commit, my legal analysis commits me to saying that they sin in the totality of their cohabitation in the second marriage. If anything, that puts them in a worse position, since if that is the case, they cannot remedy their situation even by living together as brother and sister.

My response to this objection is to turn to civil law for further insight. With respect to the situation of the divorced and remarried, in addition to addressing the question "What is the wrong at stake?" we also need to ask "When does the wrong at stake begin and when does it end?" Does the wrong actually continue as long as the second marital relationship continues, provided the first spouse is still alive?

Not surprisingly, secular law has had to grapple with the general question of how long an offense continues in a number of cases. As we will see, the law recognizes that the mere fact that the effects of an offense persist throughout some length of time does not make it a "continuing offense." I think this recognition will provide some assistance to Kasper's approach. If an offense is completed, and therefore not continuing from a legal or moral perspective, its agent can repent of it effectively. To put it more concretely, if a man or woman's acts of wrongdoing against his or her first marriage are completed (say) at the time he or she contracts a second marriage, then he or she can effectively repent of those acts of wrongdoing and receive communion.[38]

As I have noted, a key barrier to admitting divorced and civilly remarried persons to communion is the canonical judgment that their offense against the first, sacramental marriage is a continuing offense. According to critics of Cardinal Kasper's proposal, it is this fact that distinguishes the situation of the murderer from that of the divorced and remarried person with respect to communion. The murder is completed; therefore, the murderer can repent of his or her sin and receive the Eucharist. The divorced and remarried person cannot, because the sin is ongoing rather than completed.

But why do we have to think of the situation in this way? Answering this question requires us to explore a more fundamental issue: How do we distinguish between completed wrongs, on the one hand, and continuing wrongs, on the other? A moment's thought reveals that the answer to that question is not self-evident. Why not, for example, view the murder as a continuing wrong? After all, the victim continues to be dead, and the suffering that loss inflicts upon his family, friends, and community continues for years. Why do not we say, for example, that the murder is an offense that continues for the expected lifetime of the victim?

As it turns out, the civil legal system recognizes that distinguishing instantaneous from continuous offenses is not always a simple and straightforward task.[39] Generally speaking, an instantaneous offense is a "discrete act" that occurs at a particular moment in time. The harm it causes occurs in that moment, and does not extend beyond it. A continuing offense differs in two ways: First, it generally involves an ongoing course of conduct. Second, the harm it causes persists over that period of time. *Both* prongs are necessary to the definition of a continuing offense. Consequently, the law recognizes that some conduct that counts as an ongoing course of criminal activity does not actually qualify as a continuing offense. "The hallmark of the continuing offense is that it perdures beyond the initial illegal act, and that 'each day brings a renewed threat of the evil Congress sought to prevent' even after the elements necessary to establish the crime have occurred."[40] At the same time, the courts have recognized that even "continuing offenses do not, in general, continue indefinitely."[41]

It is important to understand what constitutes a continuing offense for the sake of conceptual clarity. It is also important for ancillary reasons, such as determining how to apply the statute of limitations for a crime. The longer a crime continues, the longer a potential defendant will be at risk of prosecution. There are obviously competing values at stake in deciding how long a potential defendant should be vulnerable to state action; it is in the struggle of courts to reconcile those values that we can see some convergences with Kasper's notion of mercy. The courts recognize, for example, that statutes of limitations not only encourage efficiency and accuracy in prosecution but also protect the defendant's rights. Moreover, the courts actively favor the value of "repose," which legal scholar Jeffrey Boles defines as consisting of the "interrelated concepts of affording peace of mind, avoiding the disruption of settled expectations, and reducing uncertainty about the future in the lives of defendants."[42] By favoring the concept of repose, then, the courts recognize the need for parties to be able to move on with their lives, and (except in the case of very serious crimes, such as murder) not to be forever haunted by past mistakes. We can see here resonances of Kasper's understanding of the purpose of mercy.

In the United States, for many years no uniform approach existed to the definition of continuing offenses. In 1970, however, the U.S. Supreme

Court addressed the matter in *Toussie v. United States*.[43] Robert Toussie was required to register for the draft within five days of his eighteenth birthday, which occurred in 1959. He never registered with a draft board at any time, despite the fact that the law required every American man aged eighteen to twenty-six to do so. Toussie was indicted for evading the draft in 1967, and subsequently convicted of the crime. He argued on appeal that the indictment was barred by the five-year statute of limitations. In response, the U.S. government argued that the crime continued every day that he did not register until he reached age twenty-six.

The U.S. Supreme Court sided with the defendant and reversed his conviction.[44] The court set out a two-pronged test to identify continuing crimes. First, courts are to look at the intention of the lawmaker: Does the legislature intend to define the wrong as a continuing wrong or not? Second, courts are to look at the nature of the crime. The key factor here is whether the offense features "a harm that lasts as long as that course of conduct persists."[45] Precisely because it works to a greater disadvantage to the defendant, the Supreme Court maintains that there is a strong presumption against finding an offence to be continuing rather than completed.

So, for example, conspiracy, sometimes called a "criminal combination," is widely considered to be the paradigmatic continuing offense—two or more parties gather, often in secret, to plan other crimes. A conspiracy to rob banks, therefore, is a crime that is distinct from and additional to the specific robberies themselves. It continues until it is broken up by a distinct act, such as one of the co-conspirators going to the police to blow the whistle on his former partners or the police making an arrest. A criminal conspiracy is a powder keg of future criminal activity. Kidnapping is also generally seen as a continuing offense. "This is a crime of continuing force upon the person . . . while parents and family are kept in a constant state of anxiety."[46] Possession of prohibited items is also widely seen as a continuing offense. The very fact that dangerous and illegal items, such as bombs or drugs, are ready at hand, threatens the well-being of the community at large.

It is important to emphasize that one cannot draw the conclusion that an offense is a "continuing offense" simply because some of its aspects or effects carry on through time. The term "continuing offense" is a technical legal term, not merely a chronological term. The underlying situation in the *Toussie* case makes that fact abundantly clear. Although Robert Toussie was out of compliance with the draft registration requirement from five days after his eighteenth birthday until the time he turned twenty-six, the Supreme Court held that the actual offense was completed when he failed to register five days after his eighteenth birthday.

To qualify as a "continuing offense," from a legal perspective, the wrongdoing must involve continuing, legally cognizable harm. It is this point that helps us see why the better decisions have not treated every kind of extended, wrongful possession as a continuing offense.[47] For example, in *United States v. De La Mata*, the U.S. Court of Appeals for the 11th Circuit held that bank fraud is *not* a continuing offense.[48] The defendants had entered into fraudulent lease agreements, collecting payments on the leases until they were discovered and stopped by law enforcement agents. The prosecution maintained that the defendants were engaged in a continuing offense that did not terminate until they were caught. The court disagreed: "Taken to its logical conclusion, the collection of rents on a lease obtained by fraud, for a term of 99 years, would toll the statute of limitations for 99 years. We think this goes too far."[49] The court distinguished between the crime, which was the fraudulent scheme itself, and the working out through time of that crime, which was the collection of lease payments over the course of the lease term. The lesson of the *De La Mata* case, then, is this: The mere fact that the roll-out of the crime took place over time does not mean the crime itself was a continuing offense from a legal perspective. Unlike possession of dangerous weapons, the mere servicing of a fraudulent lease does not pose any further ongoing dangers to the community.

The secular law on continuing offenses offers lessons that can be applied by analogy to the situation of divorced and remarried Catholics, in two ways. First, in deciding whether or not an offense meets the technical legal definition of a continuing offense, the courts focus on whether the harm the law is designed to prevent continues throughout time. Let us assume for the sake of argument that a divorced person who has remarried has inflicted some wrong upon their first marriage. Is it correct, really, to say that the harm to the original spouse, their children, and the community continues to pile up indefinitely, year upon year? In the majority of cases, it seems to me that this is not the case. The harm is completed with the dissolution of the first marriage and all that it entails, such as the division of one household into two households. One could possibly make the counterargument that the second marriage ceremony causes some additional harm, as it is a definitive sign that the first marriage has no chance of being revivified. But even granting this counterargument, the harm does not extend throughout the second marriage. In fact, it may well be the case that the relationship between the parties to the original marriage is stabilized, and the well-being of their children is enhanced, if they both move on to stable second relationships. The parties to the sacramental marriage may be able to see each other without bitterness if they move on to partnerships in which they can flourish.

Second, the case law suggests that we might do well to adopt the distinction between the offense itself, on the one hand, and living out the consequences of the event, on the other. The current Catholic moral and canonical approach treats each sexual act in the second marriage as an ongoing betrayal of the first marriage—as the signposts of a continuing offense. In my judgment, this way of framing the situation is significantly distorted. In contrast, I think the life of the second marriage, including its sexual relationship, is best seen as a living out of the second wedding ceremony, which in most cases decisively ends the possibility of the resumption of the first marriage.[50]

Discerning the Intent of the Lawmaker—What Did Jesus Say and Do?

All the secular legal cases I have discussed make one important point: the intent of the legislator is a crucial factor in determining the nature and duration of an offense. The courts do not deny that it is within the power of a legislature to frame an offense as a continuing offense. Given the countervailing values, especially the value of repose, they insist that the intent of the legislature be clear before finding a particular offense to be a continuing offense. Within the Catholic community, the supreme lawgiver is God, as most perfectly revealed in Jesus Christ. What did Jesus teach regarding divorce and remarriage?[51] While a full examination of this topic is beyond the scope of this chapter, I think it is necessary to make a few observations.[52]

First, it is important to pay attention to the social context in which Jesus spoke. Divorce was a near-universal phenomenon in the ancient Near East, including among ancient Jews. As the distinguished New Testament scholar John P. Meier has pointed out, "Almost all the pre-70 Jewish texts known to us reflect a Judaism in which a man could divorce his wife for practically any reason."[53] The reverse was not true; in ancient Palestine, a woman could not divorce her husband for *any* reason. Furthermore, a divorced woman was in an extraordinarily precarious position in ancient societies; unless she could find another man to marry, she would be dependent upon her family of birth to take her in and protect her.[54]

In Luke and Matthew, therefore, the accounts of Jesus's statements on divorce reflect the vast disparity in power and vulnerability between husband and wife. It is the *man* who divorces his wife and marries another who commits adultery, and (in Matthew) *causes* his former wife to be involved in adultery. The moral fault is primarily his, not hers. In sharp contrast, Mark's Gospel and Paul's First Letter to the Corinthians also make the additional claim that a woman who divorces her husband commits adultery. Most commentators point out that the Gospel of Mark and Paul's First Letter to the Corinthians were written in the context of a Roman legal system, in which women as well as men had the legal right to divorce their spouses. Because this was not even an option for ordinary Jewish women in Jesus's era, Meier concludes that Mark 10:12 "almost automatically falls out of consideration as a saying coming from the historical Jesus."[55]

Is it logical to extend Jesus's words condemning divorce from a Palestinian context in which men can unilaterally divorce their vulnerable wives, to a Roman context in which women are more equal, and can also divorce their husbands? It depends, in my view, upon the point of the prohibition of divorce and remarriage. If the purpose is primarily to protect sexual purity, then the extension seems valid. If the purpose is to protect vulnerable people, especially vulnerable women, then the extension is more questionable, at least in some cases. As Jesus's conduct throughout Scripture reveals, his main concern is not to promote purity but instead to protect the vulnerable.

Second, it is important to pay attention to the audience to whom Jesus is speaking. The fullest synoptic account of Jesus's views on marriage and divorce are found in Mark 10:1–12. Jesus addresses the question in an academic way; we are told at the beginning of that passage that Jesus "left that place and went to the region of Judea and beyond the Jordan. And crowds again gathered around him; and, as was his custom, he again taught them. Some Pharisees came, and to test him they asked, "Is it lawful for a man to divorce his wife?"[56]

In response to the Pharisees, who pointed to Moses's permission to Jewish men to divorce their wives (for any reason), Jesus invokes God's original intention for marriage:

> He answered them, "What did Moses command you?" They said, "Moses allowed a man to write a certificate of dismissal and to

> divorce her." But Jesus said to them, "Because of your hardness of heart he wrote this commandment for you. But from the beginning of creation, 'God made them male and female. For this reason a man shall leave his father and mother and be joined to his wife, and the two shall become one flesh.' So they are no longer two, but one flesh. Therefore what God has joined together, let no one separate."[57]

Jesus is here giving an academic response to an academic question, posed by powerful and potentially hostile questioners who were "testing" him. Given their authority in the Jewish community, the Pharisees saw themselves in a position not only to test Jesus but also to judge him. Because their view on divorce was aligned with that of Moses, the Pharisees assumed it was aligned with God's own will regarding marriage. In his rejoinder, Jesus not only conveyed God's true position on marriage but he also demonstrated his own rank relative to Moses. Jesus claimed his own authority as the paramount interpreter of Jewish law.[58]

In his conversation with the Pharisees, therefore, Jesus was engaged in what we today would call an academic discussion with those who purported to be his equals or superiors in authority. He was not dealing with a pastoral situation, which called upon him to apply his teaching to particular human persons dealing with the consequences of human sin. Scripture also provides us with examples of Jesus's activity as a merciful healer, which helps us situate his more academic discussion of marriage in a broader context.

The story I find most helpful here is that of Jesus's encounter with the Samaritan woman at Jacob's well.[59] Jesus asks her for a drink, which astonished her, because Jews normally disdained interaction with Samaritans. In return, she asked him for the living water that only he could provide. The story continues:

> Jesus said to her, "Go, call your husband, and come back." The woman answered him, "I have no husband." Jesus said to her, "You are right in saying, 'I have no husband'; for you have had five husbands, and the one you have now is not your husband. What you have said is true!"[60]

Jesus reveals himself to the Samaritan woman as the Messiah. He makes known to her a great mystery: that he is the source of the waters of eternal life, and he calls upon her to "worship the Father in spirit and truth."[61] Yet Jesus does not impose a rigid, legal response upon her obviously irregular marital situation. Jesus does not tell her to return to her first husband, provided he is still living. He does not instruct her to leave her current consort. In short, he deals pastorally and constructively with the woman. He does not treat her situation in the same abstract manner that he conducted his academic discussion about marriage and divorce with the Pharisees.

Instead, Jesus makes creative use of the Samaritan woman's situation, turning her into her a disciple and a partner in his ongoing work of evangelization. He told her the truth about her situation; but he did it in love, in a way that made her marvel at his insight. And the truth was life-giving, not only to her but also to her entire community. "Many Samaritans from that city believed in him because of that women's testimony, 'He told me everything I have ever done.'"[62] He used his knowledge of her sins not to condemn her to death but to convert others to new life.

The Gospel of John also highlights the merciful tenderness in Jesus's treatment of sinners, in contrast with the sharpness that characterizes his more academic battles with religious teachers.[63] Seeking to trap Jesus yet again, the Pharisees used a woman caught in adultery as the bait. They brought her to Jesus, asking whether they should stone her in accordance with the law of Moses. Jesus not only evades the academic trap but also places himself pastorally squarely on the side of the terrified woman. He responds to their query by brilliantly deflecting its force: "Let anyone among you who is without sin be the first to throw a stone at her."[64] Everyone else drifts away, leaving Jesus alone with the woman. Yet the only sinless man does not condemn her, but tells her, "Go your way, and from now on do not sin again."[65]

What does Jesus's admonition mean? Would he require her to leave a second husband she married after her first husband divorced her? Why would Jesus deflect the condemnation of the Pharisees only to impose another legalism on her conscience? For Jesus to tell the woman to "go . . . and sin no more" means that it must be possible for her to go and sin no more—and to continue to live. Given the radical dependence of women upon their husbands for shelter and support, this woman would likely need to find a man to take her in as his wife; in all probability, it would not be the first man she had married, or even the man with whom she committed adultery.

Finally, it is important to pay attention to the overarching purpose of the law. No particular legal provision is self-interpreting; it must be understood and applied with reference to the good of the community it purports to guide and to serve. Jesus regularly reminds us that the commands and prohibitions of the Torah must be situated in a broader context. Confronting him with yet another test, a Pharisee asks him which commandment is the greatest; Jesus responds:

> "You shall love the Lord your God with all your heart, and with all your soul, and with all your mind." This is the greatest and first commandment. And a second is like it: "You shall love your neighbor as yourself." On these two commandments hang all the law and the prophets.[66]

As Walter Kasper has shown so well, the God whom we are to love is the God of mercy, the God who wills to save all human beings. We must therefore interpret Jesus's words about marriage and divorce in light of that overarching truth. It is clear that Jesus rejects divorce and remarriage as contrary to the original will of God. It is clear that he treats a man's divorce and remarriage as akin to adultery, and that from the earliest times in the Christian community, that judgment has been extended to a woman's divorce and remarriage. But nothing in Jesus's words or conduct demands that the sin involved in divorce and remarriage must be treated as a sin that continues indefinitely, without possibility of effective repentance as long as one's first spouse is still alive. To impose such a requirement in every case is not merciful, and mercy is the ultimate touchstone for the divine lawgiver.

The core of my argument can be summarized in this fashion: the parties to a failed first marriage may very well have harmed each other and that marriage during the course of their break-up and its immediate aftermath. In most cases, the contracting of a second civil marriage completely extinguishes any hope of reconciliation of the parties to the first marriage in this lifetime. Since in heaven there is no marrying or giving in marriage, the harm the parties have done to their first marriage is completed, not ongoing. Therefore, they should be able to repent of that harm and move on to fulfill the new responsibilities of their second marriage.

I have not addressed, however, one key objection. Someone might say that my analysis might be all well and good for natural marriage, but it does not accommodate the special concerns of sacramental marriage, which the church teaches is indissoluble. Addressing those concerns in detail is beyond the scope of this chapter. I will however, make a few brief points.

Note that the sharp distinction between natural and sacramental marriage is not supported by the biblical texts. It is an innovation of the canonical tradition itself. My own view is that it should be possible to see the bond created by the first sacramental marriage as continuing in some way (e.g., in the obligations of the parties to pray for each other), while not interpreting that continuing sacramental bond as excluding a second, natural marriage. Does the church have the power to develop its doctrine of sacramental marriage in this way, which the church holds is indissoluble? I believe so. In fact, there is precedent for such development within the tradition itself.

As John T. Noonan Jr. has demonstrated in his magisterial history of the canon law of marriage, the canonical tradition has long balanced a number of values in its definition of marriage.[67] Noonan explains that Catholicism viewed marriage as a symbol of the unbreakable union of Christ with the church—like the union of a bishop with his diocese. But from the beginning of church history, the symbolic value of both sorts of unions had always been balanced with other values. For example, the Gospel of Mathew, written for second-generation Christians, permits divorce for serious sexual immorality (*porneia*), such as adultery.[68] Christians have long debated how this passage should be treated. Since the Council of Trent, adultery has been treated in the Catholic tradition as grounds for permanent separation (although most Protestants, following Augustine, view it as grounds for divorce and remarriage). Earlier, in the first generation, Paul, confronted with situations in which one party to a pagan marriage desired to convert to Christianity, instructed the new convert to stay with his or her unbelieving spouse if possible. But Paul allowed divorce—and tacitly permitted remarriage—in cases where a pagan spouse was unwilling to remain in the marriage. He writes: "But if the unbelieving partner separates, let it be so; in such a case the brother or sister is not bound. It is to peace that God has called you."[69] To this day, canon law recognizes the papal power to dissolve a natural marriage between two unbaptized persons in order to enable a new convert to marry in the faith; it calls this power the "Pauline privilege."

Over the centuries, canon lawyers have found creative ways to preserve the ideal of lifelong union while dissolving many marriages in order to allow Catholics to participate more fully in the life of the church—or as the canonists say, "in favor of the faith." Many of these developments, such as the significant expansion of the Pauline privilege in the sixteenth century, were the consequence of missionary efforts to the Americas. Pius V (d. 1572) did not insist that a polygamous native man remain married to his first wife; such converts, he allowed, could choose the wife with whom they would be baptized. Gregory XIII (d. 1585) permitted slaves separated by great distances from their lawful spouses to remarry in the church, even if they could not say for sure that those lawful spouses would spurn Christianity. Moreover, canonists began to articulate the "Petrine privilege," which enabled the pope to undo a marriage between a baptized and a non-baptized person, in order to enable one of the parties to remarry in the church.

For a very long time, in other words, the church has claimed the power to dissolve marital unions: unions between the unbaptized; unions in which only one party is baptized; and unconsummated unions between baptized persons. So far, the church has stopped short only of dissolving valid, consummated marriages between two baptized Christians. And yet, in the rocky waters of modernity, these sacramental marriages break up, too. What about those who are shipwrecked, particularly those abandoned by their spouses—what can be done in favor of their faith?

As Cardinal Kasper has repeatedly noted, his proposal does not give such persons a second ship in the form of another sacramental marriage. It does, however, grant them a "plank of salvation"—namely, renewed admittance to the sacraments. Granting this renewal will bring the letter of canon law into harmony with its spirit. More important, it would reflect the merciful Spirit of God as revealed in Christ Jesus—the God who, as the apostle Paul states, has called us to peace.

9

Legalism and Christian Ethics

Engaging Grisez and Engelhardt

THE PRECEDING CHAPTERS have argued that concepts, approaches, and even substantive doctrines borrowed from secular law can assist the work of Christian ethicists in reflecting on the shape of a well-lived life, and in particular in pondering the relationship between love and justice in a community composed of believers and nonbelievers. Yet the cumulative effect of those arguments may provoke a word of resistance, if not an outright backlash. Some might ask: Isn't it dangerous for Christian ethicists to pay too much attention to law? In fact, doesn't incorporating the insights of law into the study of Christian ethics raise the specter of "legalism"?

This is not a concern to be lightly dismissed. It is inconceivable that any contemporary Christian moralist in his or her right mind, or at least in his or her enlightened *heart,* would admit to being a "legalist" or uncomplainingly accede to a description of his or her moral theological framework as "legalistic." But what, exactly, does it mean to call a Christian moral theory "legalistic"? The general consensus that legalism is unhelpful in a Christian moral framework is not matched by a corresponding consensus about either the exact definition of legalism or the precise impediments it poses to sound moral analysis. In part, this is because Christianity rejects not only legalism but also antinomianism.

In fact, from its very beginnings, Christianity expressed a complicated and ambivalent attitude toward the law, as its early leaders struggled to define its relationship with both Judaism and Greek philosophy. Chapter 3 of St. Paul's Letter to the Galatians furnishes us with a compact example. On the one hand, St. Paul tells us that "all who rely on the works of the law are under a curse."[1] On the other hand, after raising the rhetorical question "Is the law then opposed to the promises of God?," he emphatically responds "Certainly not!"[2] Distinguishing proper respect for the law, especially the moral law, from improper use of it or reliance upon it, especially with regard to salvation, has occupied the attention of many a Christian theologian from apostolic times until the present day.[3]

My aims in this chapter are modest. I do not pretend to resolve here the great questions about the role of law in Christian life, the relationship of the eternal law to the natural law, the influence of natural law on positive law, or the relationship of law and grace. I do hope to shed some light on the meaning and use of the charge of "legalism" in Christian ethics. I also hope to indicate why efforts to grapple with that charge are assisted rather than hindered by immersion in the secular legal tradition, particularly the common law. Paradoxically enough, wise lawmakers and judges need to avoid "legalism" just as much as good theologians and pastors do.

In order to make my case, I will use St. Thomas Aquinas's definition of law to structure a close comparison of the thought of H. Tristram Engelhardt Jr., an Eastern Orthodox thinker, and Germain Grisez, a Roman Catholic, on the role of law in the moral life.[4] Why Aquinas's definition of law? The charge of "legalism" cannot be fully understood without a clear understanding of the meaning of "law." Roughly speaking, to charge a moralist with "legalism" is to charge that he or she allows law, legal concepts, and characteristically legal ways of thinking unduly to influence his or her moral theory. What, then, does the concept of "law" entail? Manifesting his characteristic precision and nuance, Aquinas's definition offers a response to this question, and therefore a basis for gaining more precision about what the charge of "legalism" entails.

Why Engelhardt and Grisez? First, both are rigorous thinkers who have produced significant, lengthy, and wide-ranging articulations of their respective position on the relationship of Christianity and the moral life. Second, while Grisez and Engelhardt operate out of different traditions within Christianity, their positions are not difficult to bring into conversation with each other. Engelhardt, a former Roman Catholic, develops his argument for a "noetic" approach to theological ethics that emphasizes mystical union with God as the ultimate ground of moral knowledge, in critical conversation with Western Christian moral thought, particularly Roman Catholic moral casuistry. Grisez, in contrast, attempts to retrieve, reform, and refurbish the very tradition that Engelhardt has rejected. Third, while both Engelhardt and Grisez reject legalism, neither denies the relevance of norms, principles, and rules to Christian life. Neither is antinomian.

My plan is as follows. In the first section, I will briefly set forth the five components of the definition of law offered by Aquinas in his *Summa Theologiae* to serve as a framework for my comparative analysis. In the second section, I will attempt to flesh out precisely what Engelhardt and Grisez mean by "legalism" by analyzing their thought in light of Aquinas's definition of law. In the third section, I will examine some of the deleterious consequences that Engelhardt and Grisez believe a legalistic approach to morality entails for moral life and pastoral practice, and illustrate how those consequences also affect secular law.

Aquinas's Definition of Law

In the first question of his treatise on law, question 90 of the *Prima Secundae*, entitled, "Of the Essence of Law," Aquinas offers a multifaceted definition of law. It is "nothing else than an *ordinance of reason* for the *common good*, made by him *who has care of the community*, and *promulgated*."[5] In the four articles of that question, Aquinas systematically considers each element of that definition. Note, however, that the first element actually encompasses two components, not one: Aquinas tells us that law is an *ordinance* of *reason*. He takes it for granted that a law is fundamentally an *ordinance;* it is not simply a statement, as it makes a normative claim upon an agent subject to its jurisdiction. While Aquinas does not devote a separate article to an examination of this element of the definition of law, he does indicate what it involves in the course of explicating the other four elements. Since all five elements are relevant to my analysis of legalism, I will briefly describe Aquinas's treatment of each of them.

An ordinance. By its very nature, law has a normative, directive thrust. In article 1 of question 90, which discusses "whether law is something pertaining to reason," Aquinas clearly recognizes that "[i]t belongs to the law to command and to forbid."[6] Noting that the word *lex* (law) is derived from the word *ligare* (to bind), he writes that law "binds one to act."[7] Law operates as a constraint on human activity, either by mandating or by prohibiting certain particular actions. In fact, Aquinas takes it for granted that law orders human activity through its ordinances; on this basis, he goes on to ask what else must be true about law if it is to order human activity well and properly.

Of reason. The first and fundamental move that Aquinas makes is to shape, define, and qualify the type of ordinance that law is. It is not an ordinance of whimsy. It is not an demand based in pure desire, on the one hand, or pure fear on the other. It is not an arbitrary expression of power. Ordered as well as ordering, law is an ordinance of *reason*. Law is a "rule and measure" of human acts.[8] The ultimate rule and measure of human acts, however, is reason. Consequently, law must correspond to reason.[9] For Aquinas, therefore, it is necessary, but not sufficient, that law entails an ordinance or a command. He tells us that "in order that the volition of what is commanded may have the nature of law, it needs to be in accord with some rule of reason."[10]

For the common good. Practical reason is oriented toward achieving an end or a goal; that end or goal is in fact the starting point and first principle in its deliberations. To say, therefore, that law must be guided by practical reason is immediately to raise the question: What is the end or goal of the law? Aquinas tells us that the end of the law is "universal happiness," the flourishing not only of an individual but also of a perfect or complete community of individuals. The purpose of law is to direct individual actions with a view toward the good of that community—the common good. "[S]ince the law is chiefly ordained to the common good, any other precept in regard to some individual work, must needs be devoid of the nature of a law, save in so far as it regards the common good."[11]

Made by competent authority. If law is an ordinance of reason, whose reason counts? Can *any* reasonable person make law? Aquinas says no. Precisely because law pertains to the common good, only those responsible for the common good can make law. "Now to order anything to the common good, belongs either to the whole people, or to someone who is the vicegerent of the whole people."[12] Consequently, making law "belongs either to the whole people or to a public personage who has care of the whole people."[13] Moreover, Aquinas does not forget that law entails the coercive imposition of the lawgiver's will. "[C]oercive power is vested in the whole people or in some public personage, to whom it belongs to inflict penalties."[14]

And promulgated Finally, Aquinas maintains that law must be promulgated. Because "law is imposed on others by way of a rule and measure,"[15] those who are subject to the rule and measure must be given notice of its existence and application. "Wherefore promulgation is necessary for the law to obtain its force."[16] This requirement, while seemingly obvious, is in fact quite significant. It strongly suggests, for example, that *ex post facto* laws, which apply to actions that took place before they were promulgated, are not "laws" properly speaking.

HOW DOES AQUINAS'S multifaceted definition of law help us answer the question: What is legalism? My hypothesis is that moralists will label as "legalist" any view of moral norms that they believe gives disproportionate or otherwise inappropriate stress to one of the five elements of the definition of law given to us by Aquinas.

This way of understanding "legalism" has several advantages. First, it makes it clear that one's definition of legalism is (1) dependent upon one's understanding of the nature and function of law, and (2) integrally related to one's understanding of the way in which the norms of the moral life can helpfully be understood as laws. Second, it gives us a way to account for the fact that the various people who make the charge of legalism, and those who respond to it, frequently seem to be talking past one another, even while they seem to be loosely talking about the same thing—the moral law. This definition allows us to see how they are indeed talking about the same thing, but about different facets or aspects of it. Third, this definition makes clear that in some cases—perhaps in many cases—the charge of "legalism" within a Christian context can be more helpfully understood as a charge that a particular thinker or school of thought has incorporated one or more distorted elements into a proffered articulation or application of the moral law, rather than a charge that a thinker has wrongly extended the moral law into a sphere where it does not belong.

Engelhardt and Grisez: Competing Definitions of Legalism

We are now in a position to test the explanatory power of my hypothesis about legalism by considering the work of H. Tristram Engelhardt and Germain Grisez. The title of Engelhardt's book, *Foundations of Christian Bioethics*, needs some interpretation. It is not a book about biomedical ethical questions—or their foundations—narrowly construed; it is, rather, a book that situates biomedical questions within a broad articulation of an Orthodox Christian approach to the meaning and purpose of human life. Engelhardt clearly frames his objectives in the preface to his work:

> The cardinal philosophical and theological puzzle is: can one break through immanence to truth? And if so, how? By addressing this puzzle, this volume invites the reader to the Christianity of the first millennium, a Christianity rooted in mysticism, or better stated, in a noetic theology. It is here that the puzzle is solved and the door

> found in the horizon of immanence: Christianity's disclosure of an immediate experience of the uncreated energies of a radically transcendent, personal God.[17]

Engelhardt objects to the moral tradition of the Christian West on both political philosophical and religious grounds. Following Alasdair MacIntyre, he argues that the Western tradition in political philosophy has failed in its objective of identifying foundations for a common morality in a religiously pluralistic world.[18] Second, he maintains that Western Christianity has not even succeeded in providing a coherent, content-full morality that is uncontroversially acknowledged to be true by its own adherents.[19]

Engelhardt maintains that traditional Christianity, in contrast, is enabled, by the grace of God, to reach beyond the immanent in order truly to touch the transcendent—to touch the energies of God himself through a type of noetic experience. He argues that one virtue of his "traditional Christian" approach, which is rooted in the theological and liturgical traditions of Eastern Christianity, is that it avoids legalism. According to Engelhardt, Western Christian moral thought, particularly Roman Catholic moral thought, has long been plagued by legalistic modes of analysis. More specifically, his prototype of legalistic thinking seems to be the "manualist" model of moral theology that predominated in the Catholic Church from the time of the Council of Trent until the mid-twentieth century, and which was designed to allow confessors to evaluate the seriousness of the sins confessed by members of their flock and to set an appropriate penance.

Of course, as Engelhardt repeatedly observes, Catholic moral theology underwent a sea change after the Second Vatican Council. The moral manuals have all but disappeared from the scene. Are there any intellectually respectable, card-carrying legalists left within mainstream Roman Catholic thought? Or is Engelhardt's polemic against legalism nothing more than a quixotic battle with authoritarian ghosts of the past? It is hard to say, because Engelhardt does not support his accusations of Catholic legalism with citations of any contemporary Roman Catholic thinkers.

Germain Grisez seems to be an eminently plausible candidate for the role of an intelligent, contemporary, card-carrying legalist. Grisez has been a tireless defender of the Roman Catholic magisterium's affirmation of the existence of exceptionless moral rules, including an absolute prohibition against the use of drugs, devices, or surgical procedures for the purpose of preventing conception. At first glance, therefore, Grisez seems as likely as any post-Vatican II Catholic moralist to defend an explicitly and self-avowedly legalistic approach to moral theology. Nonetheless, he does not do so. In fact, in his three-volume moral treatise *The Way of the Lord Jesus* he devotes a great deal of explicit attention to combating what he defines as legalism and the abuses and distortions it introduces into the moral life of Christians.

How can both Engelhardt and Grisez be equally adamant in their condemnation of "legalism"? In fact, it turns out that they mean significantly different things—almost diametrically opposed things—by the term. By exploring their differences within the broader context of their respective theological commitments, I hope to shed some light on the more general question of when and how it is appropriate to understand Christian morality as a type of "law." The five-pronged definition of law offered by Aquinas offers us a way to organize and compare what the two thinkers mean by the term "legalism."

An Ordinance

To focus on the aspect of law as an *ordinance* is to focus on its nature as a command or an order given by the lawgiver to those subject to the law. To someone who concentrates on this aspect of the law, the content of the order is less decisive; it is the fact that it is valid *order* that is crucial for recognizing its binding legal character. Some Christian theologians have placed almost exclusive emphasis on God's role as lawgiver, conceiving of the moral life largely as obedience to a series of divine commands. Their heavy emphasis on the sovereignty of the divine will logically leads to the position that even a divine command to perform an evil action must be obeyed.[20] In one sense, such an approach is not different from that taken by theorists such as Aquinas, who also maintained that all divine commands should be obeyed. Aquinas took pains, however, to show that an apparently wrongful act (e.g., taking someone else's life) might not in fact be evil (because God is in command of life and death already).[21] Viewed narrowly, this endeavor may seem like an attempt at special pleading, an attempt to escape a difficult moral problem with a clever distinction. When viewed more broadly, however, Aquinas's goal is to ensure that the divine knowledge and the divine will are not set against one another.

For Grisez, the core mistake of legalism is placing too great an emphasis on the aspect of the moral law as primarily a product of the will of God, and only secondarily, rather than as something intelligible in itself, as an aspect of the divine intellect. He writes that voluntarism, "together with the isolation of moral from dogmatic theology, led classical moralists to pay less and less attention to intrinsic reasons for accepting Christian moral norms as true. Instead, they increasingly tended to treat moral norms as laws which members of the Church must obey because the Church insists upon them with divine authority."[22]

Grisez identifies four basic consequences of this voluntaristic legalism for the moral life. First, it concentrated too much on the "detailed specification of duties," without clarifying "the meaning of good and bad in terms of the total Christian vocation." Second, it meant that Catholic moral theology is primarily concerned with "the minimum required to avoid mortal sin." Third, it largely avoided addressing the responsibilities of personal vocation, because "it tended to suggest that what is not forbidden is thereby permitted, in the sense that one is free to do as one pleases in regard to it; thus it tended to ignore the responsibilities of personal vocation." Fourth, classical moral theology "tended to liken moral truths to Church laws," leading to the "suggestion that the Church might or should change its moral teaching, as if it were changeable law rather than unchangeable truth."[23]

Engelhardt would agree with Grisez about the undesirability—and the danger—of most of the consequences that the latter attributes to legalism. He would not, however, be likely to trace their source to an overemphasis on the moral law as an aspect of God's will, or of human willing in response to the will of God. According to Engelhardt, the basic move toward God is one of the will, rather than one of reason. "The impact of the Fall is not so much on man's will as often supposed in the West, but upon his intellect, his noetic capacity for non-discursive knowledge."[24] The knowledge of God's moral law follows upon, rather than leads to, an experience of God himself—what Engelhardt refers to as a noetic experience of God, which begins with a grace-inspired turning to God.[25] According to Engelhardt, our fundamental mistake is to attempt to come to know God through discursive reason before we are joined with him by grace. Consequently, as discussed below, for Engelhardt the key problem of legalism is a distorted emphasis on the powers of human reason to reach the mind of God by proceeding in a discursive manner.

Of Reason

For Aquinas, law is an ordinance of *reason;* it is not an arbitrary imposition expressing the whim of the lawgiver. In his account of morality, Grisez follows Aquinas in emphasizing the reasonableness of the moral law. In fact, it is in this emphasis on the reasonableness of the requirements of morality, and the reasonableness of expecting Christians to follow them, that Grisez locates the antidote to legalism. For example, he charges the "new moral theology" developed after Vatican II with remaining "as legalistic as the old," because "[i]t provides no account in Christian terms of why one should seek human fulfillment in this life, what the specifically Christian way of life is, and how living as a Christian in this life is intrinsically related to fulfillment in everlasting life."[26]

For Engelhardt, in sharp contrast, reason is not the solution, it is the problem. He believes that legalism results from distorted emphasis on the rational accessibility of divine law. As noted, the key for Engelhardt is the noetic experience of the uncreated energies of God, which is only made possible by union with God. The goal of the Christian life is "an intimate knowing between persons, most particularly an illumination of the creature by the Creator. It is only through this illumination that true knowledge becomes possible."[27] It is only by repenting of one's sins, joining with God, and living in accordance with God's will that one will be in a position to discern the requirements of the moral life.

Engelhardt contrasts "noetic knowledge"—the intimate, immediate, nondiscursive knowledge of the transcendent God made possible through this union with God—with "discursive knowledge," which is his name for human reasoning as it proceeds more or less autonomously. Discursive reason is helpful in dealing with the world of immanence, but absolutely useless in reaching the transcendent. In fact, by relying exclusively on discursive reason, human beings will move away from God rather than toward him. The sad history of Western debates over the establishment of rational foundations for morality demonstrates that discursive reason is not sufficient to produce a morality certain enough to provide a basis for living one's life. Relatedly, and perhaps more important, discursive reason remains trapped within the realm of immanence, according to Engelhardt. He would reject the effort to clarify and systematize moral norms that constitutes the heart of Grisez's project.[28]

A flash point revealing the difference in the approaches of the two theologians is their attitude toward the principle of double effect. At its core, the principle states that agents are responsible for the intended effects of their actions (whether they intend those effects as ends in themselves or merely as means to other intended ends) in a way different from their responsibility for the foreseen but unintended side effects of their actions. According to Grisez, this distinction between intended consequences and consequences that are merely foreseen is an essential tool of practical reason. Fundamentally, one constitutes one's character differently with respect to the intended effects of one's action (even those intended as means to other ends) than with respect to effects that are foreseen but unintended side effects of one's intentions. Consequently, Grisez believes that it is extremely important for deliberating agents to identify precisely which effects they are intending in their actions and which effects they are merely permitting as foreseen but unintended side effects.

Engelhardt rejects the principle of double effect, and its basic distinction between intended effects and side effects that are foreseen but unintended by the agent, as the tool of a legalistic, rationalist mentality. First, he believes that by exonerating certain types of unintentional killing, the distinction ignores the need for spiritual treatment in this type of case. He notes that in the church of the first millennium, even involuntary homicide required penance and purification. "One can become involved in an evil such as the death of a person, which even against one's will can have an effect on one's heart."[29] Second, he argues that the distinction is wrongly used to draw absolute distinctions between cases that should be treated as different in degree, not in kind. Engelhardt notes, for example, that according to traditional double-effect analysis, an indirect abortion should be justified and the direct abortion should be prohibited. In his view, both abortions can be permitted and both must be repented, in the sense that the spiritual harm they inflict upon both the physician and the mother should be recognized and treated in the context of spiritual direction.[30]

From one perspective, the difference between Engelhardt and Grisez on double effect may not be as great as it initially appears. Like Grisez, Engelhardt acknowledges that "differences in willing make a difference to the human heart,"[31] although obviously for him the difference is not as decisive as it is for Grisez. Moreover, although Engelhardt's approach might seem to be more permissive in theory, in practice the only cases of abortion that Engelhardt seems willing to allow are those designed to save the life of the mother. He categorically rules out other abortions, including in the stereotypical "hard cases" of rape and incest, although this position does not seem to be required by his theological commitments. For his part, Grisez's reformulation of the principle of double effect in order to focus on the purpose of the acting agent would likely permit the narrow range of actions permitted by Engelhardt but prohibited by many Catholic manualists (e.g., early delivery of a nonviable baby in the case of the mother's congestive heart failure).[32]

Yet significant divergences in opinion do remain. At bottom, Grisez believes that the distinction between intended effects and effects that are merely foreseen by the agent is an illuminating tool of moral discernment, separating unjustified actions from those that may, other things being equal, be justified for an agent to perform. For Engelhardt, this distinction, the core of the principle of double effect, functions to obscure more than it reveals. More specifically, it threatens to occlude the spiritual harm to an agent that can result from foreseeably causing certain effects—in particular, the death of another human being.

In identifying similarities and differences between Engelhardt and Grisez on the place of reason, it is important to avoid creating the impression that the two thinkers are as far apart as one might initially judge them to be on the basis of their rhetoric. Engelhardt, for his part, does not deny the usefulness of reason—it would be foolish for him to do so, given the analysis and argument that is the backbone of his four-hundred-page book.[33] His overriding goal is to downgrade the importance of discursive reason relative to the moral wisdom that stems from the noetic experience of God, which is a property more properly of the holy than of the analytically brilliant. More generally, he wants to affirm that the recognition and appreciation of moral norms are only possible within a life shaped by the liturgical and ascetic practices of the Orthodox Church.

Grisez, too, is sensitive to the need to situate morality within a well-lived Christian life. Moreover, he explicitly describes the moral life as leading to union with God, as God's decision to offer us divine life within the divine unity.[34] He notes, as well, that his position on this point "is very similar to the views of some theologians of the Eastern Church."[35] Furthermore, like Engelhardt, Grisez recognizes both that Christian morality is true morality, appropriate for all persons, and that a full account of that morality is only accessible with the help of the grace divinely provided to the church. He also acknowledges, like Engelhardt, that Christian commitment generates additional, specific norms binding only upon Christians.[36]

Nonetheless, there are significant differences in their understanding of the role of reason in identifying moral norms. Grisez certainly has more confidence than Engelhardt does in the power of a reasoning person, working with all the resources that the church has to offer, to identify moral norms and courses of action that correspond to them. It is not possible, with the texts at hand, to be more specific. However, it is not difficult to identify the point at which further conversation would need to begin. In describing his methodological approach, Grisez cites a passage from the First Vatican Council about the role of reason in the context of faith:

> It is, nevertheless, true that if human reason, with faith as its guiding light, inquires earnestly, devoutly, and circumspectly, it does reach, by God's generosity, some understanding of mysteries, and that a most profitable one. It achieves this by the similarity [*analogia*] with truths which it knows naturally and also from the interrelationship of mysteries with one another and with the final end of man.[37]

Grisez maintains that Vatican I should be understood here as implying that the appropriate method for theology is "dialectic," in Plato's sense of the term. "By this method, one considers truths of faith by comparison (*anologia*) with truths of reason, with one another, and with the ultimate fulfillment to which God calls us in the Lord Jesus."[38]

Does Grisez's dialectical method qualify as "discursive reason" in the sense condemned by Engelhardt? I am not sure. On the one hand, Engelhardt never gives a clear account of what he means by "discursive reason." At times, he seems to mean a process that stresses conceptual analysis as opposed to reflection on experience, an excessive concern for logical consistency, a desire for immediate certitude as opposed to dynamic progress in understanding eternal truths, and a total prioritization of unchanging human nature rather than the changing conditions of history. His account of discursive reason, in short, significantly resembles the "rationalism" of the pre-Vatican II Catholic Church that Grisez criticizes.[39] Moreover, admittedly with some glossing, Engelhardt's account of the practice of noetic theology, within the context of the ecclesial community of Orthodox Christians, could be encapsulated in Grisez's summary of the use of the dialectic method in Catholic thought. The use of that method "means that, accepting the truth of Catholic faith present in the living Church of which one is a member, one seeks a better understanding of this truth in which one already lives."[40]

On the other hand, Engelhardt might argue that the method that Grisez actually practices in his three-volume treatise, *The Way of the*

Lord Jesus, not infrequently seems more akin to discursive reason—or rationalism— than to dialectical reason. For example, he might suggest that the rhetorical tone, together with the exhaustively pursued question-and-answer format of the third volume, *Christian Moral Principles,* overwhelmingly conveys the impression of the author's certitude with regard to the answers he provides, rather than an invitation to the reader to engage in a dialogical pursuit of truth. One wag gave the title "Germain Grisez Explains it All (Well, Almost)" to a largely sympathetic review of *Difficult Moral Questions.*[41] In addition, Grisez's work bears more than a trace of the rationalist concern with true propositions. His most extensive and explicit discussion of truth in Scripture in *Christian Moral Principles,* for example, focuses largely on Scripture's role in transmitting true moral propositions to the faithful.[42]

For the Common Good

According to Aquinas, the purpose of law is to advance the common good. But what, exactly, is the "common good"? This is a notoriously elusive question. In *Gaudium et spes,* the common good is defined as "the sum of those conditions of social life which allow social groups and their individual members relatively thorough and ready access to their own fulfillment."[43]

In defining the common good, the precise relationship of the good of the individual person and the good of the community is a key issue. Christian thought has generally resisted the temptation to choose between the two, asserting that the common good is the good of all persons, who are by nature social creatures designed to flourish in community.

As I noted in chapter 1, according to Jacques Maritain, the common good "is therefore common *to the whole and to the parts,* to the parts, which are themselves wholes, since the very notion of *person* means totality; it is common to the whole and to the parts, over which it flows back and must all benefit from it."[44] On this basis, mainstream Christianity has rejected, for example, the idea that the community can sacrifice one innocent person to save many; any community that did so would actually be undermining its own common good, not merely the good of the sacrificed individual.[45] Nonetheless, many of the debates within Christian ethics can fruitfully be understood as rooted in a disagreement about the appropriate balance between protecting the good of the individual and safeguarding the good of the many in promoting the common good. These are debates with which the legal system is quite familiar, as explicated in chapter 4's exploration of Gene

Outka's work on love and justice in conjunction with the Wisconsin law of marriage and divorce in *Watts v. Watts*.[46]

In his articulation of the requirements of Christian morality, Engelhardt tends to emphasize the good of the individual over the broader concerns of the community. This emphasis appears first and foremost in his understanding of the point of the moral law: it is therapy for diseased souls, a way of preparing us to experience God. The moral law is intimately connected to a regime of personal asceticism, quelling our passions and enabling us to make life-giving contact with the energies of the divine being. For Engelhardt, "[t]he moral law is thus a means for the growth of an intimate connection between the creature and the Creator." In his view, "[m]orality must be lived so as to cure our souls from passions, to make us whole, and to unite us with God."[47] Like medicine, like therapy, the application of the moral law must be intensely personal, applied with discretion and judgment to each patient, taking into account his or her own particular strengths and weaknesses.

Engelhardt contrasts the notion of the moral law as therapy with a more legalistic notion of morality—one concerned not with promoting the well-being of the individual but with enforcing the requirements of "an impersonal codebook of divine law."[48] While he does not expand systematically on this contrast, it seems to me to include the following three components.

First, according to Engelhardt, the moral law should be applied and interpreted with the mindset of a healer—a spiritual physician, if you will. In contrast, he seems to believe that a legalistic conception of morality is applied and interpreted with the mindset of a judge. Second, of crucial importance for Engelhardt is his understanding of morality as *intensely personal*—grounded in and facilitating the relationship of a personal God with the persons created in his image and likeness. To subordinate the well-being of particular persons to the inexorable requirements of law is an aspect of what he means by "legalism."[49] Third, by combining his notion of the purpose of morality as being a type of healing with his understanding of morality's ground as a relationship between persons, Engelhardt develops a pastoral approach that gives great discretion to spiritual advisors to tailor moral advice to particular situations.

Grisez tends to focus more than Engelhardt does on morality's role in contributing to the well-being of the community as a whole, by providing a basis on which human beings can rightly structure their interactions with one another. In this vein, a striking difference between the two theorists is the way they conceptualize paradise and the human path to it. Engelhardt emphasizes the personal relationship between God and the believer, characterized by the communication of the divine energies to the human person. The social dimension of paradise is not developed in his analysis, which concentrates on the individual believer's union with God. In contrast, Grisez's notion of heaven, and our path to it, is much more essentially social—one could even say political, in the sense of having to do with a *polis*. He sees the task of earthly life as nothing less than building up the kingdom of God. Although the kingdom can only be brought to fruition with the second coming of Jesus Christ, Grisez maintains that believers are contributing to its construction here and now. In fact, every one of our morally acceptable actions contributes to the building up of the kingdom of God.[50]

A theory that sees morality as identifying the actions that contribute to the construction of the kingdom of God will have a significantly different understanding of the role of moral principles and rules than does a theory of morality that sees it as a type of therapy for sick souls. Grisez emphasizes that free choices are constitutive of both self and community.[51] His act analysis focuses on principles and rules, which pick out not the unique circumstances of agents and their lives but, rather, the generalizable features of action that are repeatable in a number of cases. Furthermore, he expresses far more concern than does Engelhardt for the maintenance of social practices in which large numbers of people may find their flourishing. For example, in analyzing the prohibition against divorce and remarriage in the Catholic Church, he stresses the importance of being able to make an absolute commitment for the creative unfolding of the lives of many Christians.

In responding to proportionalists—those who would make exceptions to some moral prohibitions (e.g., prohibitions against contraception, adultery, and divorce) in difficult circumstances for proportionate reason—Grisez is concerned with the impact of such exception-making upon moral and social practices in general; he thinks, for example, that proportionalism "undermines unconditional commitments, which are essential to Christian personal vocation."[52]

This is not to say that Grisez is insensitive to the needs of human beings who experience themselves constrained by moral rules and principles. A bedrock assumption of his approach is the ultimate compatibility of the flourishing of the individual with compliance with exceptionless moral rules, even in difficult situations. First, he emphasizes that such situations provide tremendous opportunities for evangelization.[53] Second, he emphasizes the self-constituting character of actions. "Human action is soul-making. Moral acts are ultimately most important insofar as they make a difference to the self one is constituting by doing the act. Ultimately, it would profit nothing if one saved the mortal lives of everyone in the world by committing one mortal sin."[54] Third, he believes that every Christian, by grace, has the power of avoiding mortal sin. Grisez rejects as incoherent the idea that there might be some circumstance under which one is required to commit a mortal sin. Fourth, and most generally, he believes that complying with the church's moral teaching is the only way to achieve genuine human fulfillment.[55]

Nonetheless, Engelhardt, in my view, would consider this analysis as verging dangerously close to his understanding of legalism. First, he would not accept the Roman Catholic tradition's clear division of sins into the categories of mortal and venial; he would argue that the failures of the human heart are deeper and murkier than that division permits. We all sin; in his terms, we all "fall short of the mark" and stand in need of some form of spiritual therapy. Engelhardt would likely consider any attempt to distinguish so sharply between fatal and nonfatal "falling short of the mark" to exemplify the rationalism he associates with legalism. Second, he would argue that it is simply unjustified to say that every human being is strong enough not to be morally or spiritually destroyed by bearing the burdens associated with acting in a morally courageous way. Third, he would contend that the Orthodox tradition allows for the possibility of maintaining the ideal, while permitting merciful exceptions to be made in individual instances. He could point, for example, to the Orthodox practice of allowing for divorce and remarriage in cases where it is simply impossible for the two parties to the first marriage to carry on in it. These exceptions do not endorse the less than optimal course of action *tout court*. They simply constitute a merciful recognition that the agents involved are not capable of doing more at the present time.[56] Grisez would likely respond that Engelhardt's view of morality is a logical muddle, particularly in its attempt to recognize that there some acts that are both permissible and morally forbidden. Engelhardt in turn would argue that Grisez's approach places too much emphasis on logical coherence.

Made by Competent Authority

Engelhardt and Grisez are in agreement that the source of the moral law is ultimately God, who has care of the universe. Both of them are worried, in some sense, that the moral law will be wrongly perceived as independent of the divine lawgiver. But the shape of that worry is very different in the two cases, which difference reflects back to other differences in their views of morality.

Engelhardt worries that the Roman Catholic tradition depicts the moral law as a constraint independent of God, and therefore as binding upon God in a way analogous to the way it binds human beings.[57] For him, the basic problem with this approach is that it will lead to an application of the moral law that does not take into account God's overriding purpose for it as a type of therapy for sinful and diseased souls. In contrast, Grisez worries that people will think of the law as independent of the divine law giver, for a different reason. If it is merely a product of divine will, then God, or divinely authorized representatives, can simply change the law or discount it as an arbitrary imposition by a divine bully. For Grisez, the basic separation at issue is that of divine will from divine intellect. The moral law is not an arbitrary imposition, but a constitutive element of God's rational plan for building the kingdom of God with the cooperation of human beings.

And Promulgated

Finally, of course, the different ecclesial commitments of Engelhardt and Grisez affect their assessments of legitimate and illegitimate moral law. For Engelhardt, as an Orthodox Christian, God's moral law is revealed preeminently in the theological reflections, liturgical practices, and ascetic disciplines that have been handed down by the Fathers of the Church. The true meaning of that law in difficult cases is revealed primarily to the holy, not primarily those skilled in discursive reasoning. The application of the law to one's own difficult case is to be done by engaging in prayer and appropriate liturgical and ascetic practices, and by consulting one's spiritual father or mother. For Engelhardt, therefore, the moral law of God is not definitively promulgated through the magisterium of the Roman Catholic Church. In fact, he argues that the widely secular culture which we have now has its roots in the rationalist understanding of the natural law perpetuated by the Catholic Church.[58] To Engelhardt's mind, the Roman Catholic moral tradition before the Second Vatican Council at least had the advantage of being coherent. Now, much of it simply follows the latest intellectual fashions, dictated by the concerns for liberal equality animating secular Western culture. It is post-traditional Christianity, which is nothing short of blasphemy to the traditional Christian.[59]

In contrast, for Grisez, the mind of Christ is closely identified, and at points virtually equated, with the authoritative teaching of the Catholic Church: "One ought to proceed with personal obedience of faith; one must submit one's experience, insights, and wishes to the judgment of the Church's teaching, prepared to reform oneself according to the mind of Christ."[60] While the Catholic tradition includes the possibility of the development of doctrine, and the revision of noninfallible church teaching, it is not a possibility upon which Grisez dwells. Instead, he emphasizes the need to bide one's time while living in a spirit of docility with respect to church teaching.[61] Consequently, for Grisez, when the church teaches authoritatively it is not legalistically imposing an arbitrary norm on the faithful; instead, it is communicating the will of God, which is ultimately inseparable from the mind of God. The point of the norm will therefore be accessible, in principle, to the mind of the believing Catholic "thinking" with the mind of the church.

Legalism and the Moral Life

The charge of legalism is not a solely theoretical charge, lodged against the plausibility or internal consistency of a moral theory in the abstract. It is a charge with a fierce practical bite; it is made with deep concern about the ramification that the legalism identified will have for the moral life of Christians. What are the consequences of legalism for the moral life? It is helpful to look at this question from two angles: how people apply the moral law to themselves in a legalistic framework, and how people in authority apply the moral law to others in such a framework.

One concrete problem often identified with legalism is the equation of the contents of the moral life with the application and extension of a discrete set of rules or principles—moral "laws," so to speak. This equation can have one of two consequences: moral minimalism and/or laxism, or moral maximalism and/or rigorism.

One could fear that a view of the moral life as a collection of rules or principles illegitimately reduces it to a *small* set of moral rules. Those who worry about this consequence focus on two aspects of legalism's effect on moral agents. First, a legalistic account of morality will create the impression that there are no moral norms applicable to situations falling outside these rules; if an agent follows the rules, then all other aspects of his or her life are matters of unfettered freedom. Second, such an account of morality will create the impression that the more difficult rules can be changed, provided enough pressure is exerted on the rule maker. Conjoined with the factual judgment that the most dangerous temptation in the contemporary world is to minimize the requirements of morality, a moralist could come to the conclusion that these two features of legalism will generate moral minimalism and/or laxism.[62]

In fact, this reasoning process encapsulates Grisez's most pressing worries about the practical consequences of legalism for moral life today.[63] At the end of his most extensive section discussing legalism at the beginning of *Christian Moral Principles,* he summarizes his concerns: "Legalism often causes the faithful to view the Church's moral teaching as an imposition. The suspicion grows that the Christian life itself is a kind of arbitrary test for which different rules could well be devised if only the test maker chose."[64]

In opposition to legalism, Grisez's major concern is to emphasize that every decision we make, every path we choose, is fraught with moral implications. We are never free to do as we choose in the sense that there are aspects of our lives that are unrelated to our overarching task to build up the kingdom of God by following "the way of the Lord Jesus." But we are generally free to do as we choose in the sense that every choice we make is an opportunity freely to constitute ourselves as the children of God whom we are called to be. In his view, the purpose of his book is to provide guidance to Catholics who realize, as adults and as believers, that "[i]n this passing world we make the selves and relationships which will endure forever."[65]

Like Grisez, Engelhardt wants to emphasize the radical, all-encompassing claim of Christianity on the lives of those who profess their faith in it. The goal is nothing short of holiness, which he repeatedly emphasizes cannot be achieved within the framework of a legalistic account of morality. For example, in articulating how a Christian should approach beginning-of-life ethics, he writes: "This focus on holiness transforms the question of how correctly to make reproductive choices from a merely legalistic engagement to the ascetic task of finding spiritual wholeness in a morally broken world."[66]

In contrast with Grisez, however, Engelhardt seems to be more worried about the maximalist rather than the minimalist tendencies of legalism. It is important to remember that Engelhardt's fundamental definition of legalism concentrates on an excessive rationalism, rather than on an excessive voluntarism. If we expand the sphere of operation of moral principles and rules and the demand for rational discernment to cover the whole of our lives, we will in his view lose the forest for the trees. More specifically, we will begin to think that holiness is virtually identical to, if not actually constituted by, the requirements of discursive rationality.

Engelhardt would say that a rationalist approach, even one as nuanced as Grisez's (or perhaps, especially one so nuanced), simply expands the requirements of immanence, when what is required is a turn to the transcendent. An analogy may be helpful here. The requirements of practical reasonableness are like a map. One can continue to mark landmarks, to fill in details, to add color and some texture to the map. Nonetheless, no matter how elaborate it becomes, the map remains two-dimensional. Finding the transcendent in life is fundamentally a matter of breaking the confines of the map itself; it requires a new movement into a third dimension, which transcends the map entirely.[67]

While rational argumentation has its place for Engelhardt, as do rules and principles, it is not fundamental. Instead, as I have noted, the fundamental source of knowledge is grace-filled participation in the liturgical rites and the way of life of traditional Christianity. The moral life and its rational regulation are preparatory means for the noetic experience of God.[68] Indeed, Engelhardt's major complaint against Roman Catholic thought is precisely that it has lost the forest for the trees: "In this century of intellectual energy [the 13th century, which saw the rise of the medieval university], theology came no longer to be regarded primarily as the fruit of holiness. Theology came instead to be understood more centrally as the fruit of scholarship."[69]

We apply the moral law not only to our own actions, both prospectively and retrospectively, but also to the actions of others. Often we do so informally, with respect to friends and acquaintances who seek our advice, with respect to the actions of public figures whose activities are reported by the media, and with respect to the actions of strangers who cross our paths. Some situations, however, present more formal occasions for evaluating the past acts of other persons or of giving counsel to them with respect to future acts. In Roman Catholicism, these occasions are most frequently associated with the priest–penitent relationship in the sacrament of penance; in Orthodoxy, they are found in the relationship between a spiritual father or mother and his or her spiritual children.

What special concerns arise in contexts where people apply the moral law to the lives and choices of other people? As I argued in chapter 1, John Noonan's *Persons and Masks of the Law* provides a good perspective on the problem, since the norms applied by the legal system are moral, as well as legal. Standing at the heart of any system of law are two entities: rules and persons.[70] Losing sight of either component creates grave moral and social risks. On the one hand, applying rules in a way that loses sight of the persons to whom they are applied can be ruthless. On the other hand, the abandonment of impartially formulated rules can replace justice with favoritism and arbitrariness.

Not surprisingly, Engelhardt is very concerned about the former possibility. His core concern is rooted in his conception of morality (and spiritual direction regarding moral concerns) as being a kind of therapy, designed to heal the soul and enable union with God. The task of the spiritual father or mother is always to keep this ultimate purpose of the moral law in sight when dealing with individual spiritual children.[71] Consequently, the spiritual parent has a significant amount of discretion in dealing with individual cases—serving as a guide and a healer, not as a judge. Fulfilling this role entails refusing to constrain one's evaluation of a spiritual child's actions within the law-oriented framework of "justified" or "unjustified," "innocent" or "guilty."

Sometimes, a spiritual father or mother must identify problematic aspects of situations that would not raise any question from the perspective of a more law-oriented framework focused on the culpability of the agent. Engelhardt recognizes, along with the Eastern tradition, the possibility of "involuntary sins," a manifestation of the brokenness of original sin in our lives. An example would be a woman who suffers a miscarriage, and who may face feelings of guilt, hopelessness, and despair because of it. If we recognize that repentance and spiritual therapy can be called for outside the narrow context of individual moral responsibility, then the Orthodox practice of providing for purification in such cases can be seen as a humane way of dealing with a situation that manifests human brokenness on an bodily level.[72] Furthermore, Engelhardt argues that some actions that may be morally justified from a legalist point of view (e.g., abortion to save the life of the mother)[73] are nonetheless fraught with spiritual danger. Persons who engage in these actions are at risk of spiritual harm, for which they should receive spiritual treatment.[74]

In other situations, Engelhardt believes that the strict requirements of the law should be modified to take into account the exigencies of the particular situation. Sometimes those modifications are designed to recognize that the application of the moral law in its full force will break a morally weak person, causing the individual to turn his or her back on the Christian message, or will cause harm to innocent third parties.[75] In some instances, a gradualist approach to Christian holiness is possible. For example, Engelhardt contends that prophylactics (and contraceptives) might be provided to unmarried persons "with regret, admonition, but without impropriety."[76]

Sometimes those modifications involve tailoring general moral concerns to specific situations. While Engelhardt recognizes the validity of many of the concerns identified in *Humanae vitae* about the consequences of widely available contraception,[77] he does not believe that these concerns justify an absolute prohibition against its use, even by married couples.[78] In these situations, the Orthodox tradition assigns the responsibility to spiritual fathers or mothers to help married persons make decisions in this regard in a way that will facilitate their journey to holiness. In some cases, that may mean abstaining from artificial contraception. In other cases, it may not.[79] Engelhardt writes: "The differences between the Orthodox and the Roman Catholic views regarding contraception lie in the first being primarily articulated in terms of an asceticism directed to approaching holiness and the second being directed to conforming to impersonal norms, including those rooted in a highly biological interpretation of natural law."[80]

Particularly important to Engelhardt is the difference between the notion of "economia" in the Orthodox Church and the notion of "dispensation" in the Western Church.

> A dispensation lifts the law for a particular person or class of persons. An economia recognizes that the purpose of the law, namely, to bring salvation, is best achieved by something other than the strict application of the law. An economia thus should not violate the spirit of the law; rather, it should focus better on the goal of the law by setting aside its letter. It is important to note that the notion of economia includes not only applying a canon less rigorously, but also applying it more rigorously, thus achieving the true purpose of the canon. At times, the spirit of the law is best served by acrivia, the strict application of the law.[81]

Grisez's concerns, in contrast, seem to be clustered more at the other end of Noonan's polarity: he is primarily worried about the monsters that strangle justice with arbitrariness and favoritism. Because he does not conceive of his approach to the moral life as the imposition of an arbitrary set of norms but, rather, as the fruits of the deliberation of practical reason (aided by the magisterium) about acts to be done and to be avoided, he would not share the worries about the impersonal application of the moral law expressed by Engelhardt. The idea that the requirements of practical reason should be bent to conform to the exigencies of particular situations would likely strike him as a deeply misguided claim. Within his framework, the danger that looms largest in our time with respect to the application of the moral law to others is precisely the temptation to distort the requirements of the moral law for irrational reasons (e.g., sympathy for the plight of a particular person).

Like Engelhardt, Grisez believes that Christians and the Christian community are called to perfect holiness, an ideal that is not possible immediately to achieve. At the same time, he firmly rejects any interpretation of Christian morality as an ideal that would reduce the claim that binding moral norms have upon us here and now.[82] While acknowledging that complying with some of those norms is difficult, he does not believe it is ever impossible, in congruence with Catholic belief that it is never impossible to refrain from sinning mortally. Consequently, moral gradualism, in the sense of only gradually bringing oneself to comply with difficult moral teaching (e.g., the teaching that using contraception is always wrong), is not acceptable to Grisez.

Unlike Engelhardt, Grisez struggles hard to demonstrate that there are no true moral dilemmas (i.e., situations in which one has no choice but to commit a wrongful act), at least for the morally upright, and sometimes even for those who have sinned. He emphasizes the possibility of always complying with the negative absolute norms, which by definition trump positive norms. He is less concerned about the specific effect of compliance with moral norms upon individuals, and more concerned with upholding the validity of the norm. In arguing that there are fewer moral conflicts than initially appear to be the case, Grisez writes:

> In many cases, apparent conflicts are removed when the morally right course, previously ignored because it is unappealing, is accepted as a practical possibility. For example, persons who have divorced and remarried need not really choose between committing adultery and renouncing their responsibilities to their second family. They can choose instead to live together in celibacy, in accord with the moral truth that they have no marital rights but do have familial responsibilities.[83]

For this reason, Grisez emphatically has rejected Cardinal Kasper's proposal to give communion to noncelibate divorced and remarried Catholics, a proposal which drew inspiration from the practices of the Orthodox.[84] In Engelhardt's view, however, Grisez's approach would likely epitomize an "impersonal" concern for the preservation of the moral law, rather than a "personal" concern for the well-being of the two parties. In some cases, a celibate marriage is likely to suffer immense strain, leading to a second divorce. In line with the Orthodox view, second marriages are permitted (regrettably) as a concession to the lingering effects of sin in human life. For Grisez, however, it would be triply wrong for a confessor to distort the requirements of practical reason by inappropriately responding to the emotionally appealing aspects of a particular situation. First, the priest would be conveying only illusory comfort to the penitent. Because the moral principles and rules at issue are rooted in reason, not in arbitrary will, they cannot be set aside in individual cases. Second, the priest would be undermining the social and religious fabric that allowed the faithful to recognize the truth. Third, he would be weakening his own moral character by choosing in a way that reflected and confirmed a distorted perception of the goods at stake.[85]

In short, Engelhardt and Grisez both condemn legalism, but mean significantly different things by the condemnation. Analyzing their use of the term reveals, I think, that legalism is not a conceptually self-sufficient idea. Instead, it is a derivative concept, drawing its meaning from a theologian's conception of the nature and proper function of the moral law in the Christian life. "Legalism" is a pejorative term, used by theologians to indicate what they believe are distorted elements in a competing understanding of the nature and function of the moral law for Christians. As Aquinas's definition reveals, however, the concept of law includes a number of components. Consequently, there are a number of trigger points in these components, each of which can attract a charge of legalism from one critic or another.

These trigger points touch on basic issues in Christian ethics, such as whether morality is more appropriately seen as an aspect of God's will or of God's reason; what relationship obtains among the individual, the community, and the common good; and what role various ecclesiastical authorities and theologians play in interpreting Christian moral teaching. Moreover, they have significant practical implications for how one addresses questions such as whether true moral dilemmas occur in the

Christian life, and whether some moral norms can be tailored to the exigencies of particular circumstances.

What does this mean for future conversation among Christian ethicists? In my view, it suggests that the charge of "legalism" generates more heat than light. To understand what precisely is meant by the charge, one has to understand the fundamental moral framework used by the theologian making it, in comparison to the framework of the theory against which the charge is being lodged. Once one understands the relevant frameworks, the charge itself loses its sting; it becomes situated within broader and more fundamental tensions about the nature and purpose of Christian life, and the role of the moral law within it. As previous chapters of this book have suggested, conversations with the secular law can help identify and manage those tensions, if not entirely resolve them.

Conclusion

The field of Christian ethics has had a long and complicated relationship to law. The complexities are both exemplified and fostered by the canonical writings of the apostle Paul, especially his Letters to the Galatians and Romans. Paul suggests that law is both thoroughly holy and utterly dangerous.[1] Law teaches us the paths of righteousness, while condemning us for our own lame inability to walk those paths.[2] Law keeps us safe when we are like children, but stifles our full flourishing once we have reached maturity.[3]

Paul helpfully warns us that we cannot expect the positive law, divine or human, to handle every problem in every aspect of human life. God's law cannot save us. Only God's self-communication in grace, which made possible our redemption in Christ Jesus, can fill the breach caused by sin. And neither divine nor human law can completely identify, much less prescribe, the particular acts made possible by a graced faith—the creative acts of neighbor love that acts that can be simultaneously self-sacrificial and the highest form of self-fulfillment.

At the same time, however, Paul's cautions and caveats about the limits of law have not eclipsed the positive aspects of law for generations of Christian theologians and pastors. Drawing on multiple roots in Jewish, Greek, and Roman sources, the Christian ethical tradition has long identified God's law with divine wisdom, and commended obedience to God's law as the surest path to human flourishing. Many important strands of Christian ethical reflection, spanning two millennia, have been organized around the Ten Commandments. In the first century after the death of Jesus, a community of Jewish Christians produced the *Didache*, also known as *The Teaching of the Twelve Apostles*, which integrated the commandments received by Moses with specifically Christian norms of ritual and morality to distinguish the Way of Life from the Way of Death. Since that time, Christian communities have not hesitated to make laws designed to structure the activities of their own members, frequently by detailed interpretations and applications of the Decalogue. Beginning with the Celtic penitential books and continuing through the present day, many Roman Catholic moralists have developed their normative positions by means of the nuanced application of the commandments to particular fact patterns.[4] The customary term for this process is "casuistry," or case-based reasoning. It is not, however, an exclusively Catholic practice. Protestant thinkers such as William Perkins (d. 1602) and William Ames (d. 1633) also developed methods and traditions of casuistry.[5]

The term "casuistry" has come to have a pejorative meaning, suggesting manipulative, twisted, or self-interested applications of rules to facts.[6] Without denying the possibilities of abuse (which can include mindless mechanical applications of law to facts, as well as hopelessly contorted applications), it is also important to retrieve and affirm a sense of the crucial role that case-based reasoning can play in both law and ethics.[7] As I hope to have demonstrated in *Ethics at the Edges of Law: Christian Moralists and American Legal Thought*, casuistry at its best encourages moralists to take into account the difficult particularities of peoples' lives and situations. It denies moralists the lazy luxury of speaking only in hazy generalities, untethered to the exigencies and realities of ordinary life. Good casuistry may foster sympathy, and perhaps even wisdom, about complicated and painful facets of human existence. If done right, casuistry does not deny the contingencies and ambiguities of life; it does, however, attempt to provide some guidance for avoiding moral paralysis and moving toward a constructive decision despite the fog of uncertainty.

Moreover, from the time of Constantine, Christian rulers rarely have been reluctant to infuse secular law with the normative commitments of their religious tradition. The leading figures of the English common law tradition, such as Edward Coke (d. 1634)) and William Blackstone (d. 1780), drew heavily on their Anglican Christian convictions in articulating common law doctrines.[8] When the Puritans left England to found a new colony in North America, they aimed to ensure that their polity conformed to the laws of God and the demands of Jesus Christ.[9] Until the mid-nineteenth century, criminal indictments in both America and England regularly charged the defendant with having committed a crime while "not having the fear of God before his eyes . . . but being moved and seduced by the instigation of the devil."[10] As I noted in chapter 2, in 1892, the U.S. Supreme Court declared that "we are a Christian people." The Court did not mean that Christianity was the nation's established religion but rather observed that "the morality of the country is deeply ingrafted upon Christianity."[11] As the country grew more pluralistic in the twentieth century, explicit references to the Christian roots of the American legal tradition became increasingly rare. Some of this reticence was doubtless due to the increasing secularization of the population. Yet it can also be attributed, in my view, to the increasing recognition on the part of American Christians that their own faith-based commitment to the equal dignity of all persons requires them to respect the integrity of citizens with different belief systems.[12]

At the same time, however, many continuing points of consonance between the Christian moral tradition and American legal categories remain to be explored. For example, the basic framework in which the criminal law analyzes a prohibited act bears significant resonances with the action theory of Thomas Aquinas, whose thought may well have indirectly influenced the common law tradition through the Anglican divine Richard Hooker.[13] It would be illuminating to compare Aquinas's framework for analyzing a moral act, including aggravating and mitigating factors, with the analyses of criminal acts in the contemporary Federal Sentencing Guidelines.[14] The topic of mercy, now so prominent in theological discussions, could be both clarified and tested by debates about the nature and limits of the presidential pardoning power.[15]

Moreover, as I hope to have shown in *Ethics at the Edges of Law*, the American legal tradition is in a unique position to highlight areas that beg for conceptual analysis and development *within* the field of Christian ethics, as well as the realm of religious ethics more generally. The legal doctrines of conspiracy and accessory liability have been well developed in both case law and scholarly commentary. They are useful, I think, in helping moralists think more deeply about problems concerning complicity with the wrongdoing of others—problems which are of increasing interest to those writing about global ethics.[16] Under certain circumstances, the tort doctrine of strict liability imposes legal responsibility on manufacturers for harmful products introduced into the stream of commerce—despite the fact that they were not in any way negligent in their production process.[17] One rationale for the doctrine is that it incentivizes continuous quality improvement by those who are in the best position to make such improvements. Another rationale is that it spreads the costs of accidents among all the parties who make and use the product, rather than forcing the unfortunate victim of the mishap to bear the entire burden. Those interested in religiously based social ethics might find some inspiration for thinking more deeply about risk, vulnerability, and solidarity in capitalist societies.

Of course, those possibilities of convergence between law and Christian ethics are meant to be illustrative, not an exhaustive list. My goal is to whet the appetite of religious moralists to mine the legal field for helpful points of consonance, just as they would mine the field of philosophy. More particularly, I want to encourage younger scholars, particularly those beginning their graduate studies, to consider pursuing legal studies as an ancillary conversation partner. It is not necessary to complete the course work for a law degree, any more than it is essential to obtain a second doctorate in philosophy in order to draw profitably on a range of philosophical writings in developing one's own position as a religious ethicist. A few carefully chosen law courses can provide the necessary foundation for years of fruitful work that crosses disciplinary boundaries. For example, a class in environmental law can enrich the substantive reflections of ethicists who work on climate change, while a course in administrative law can impart a sophisticated understanding of the powers and limits of the regulatory state in addressing any multifaceted social problem.

In my view, however, the ultimate benefits of studying secular law are theological and doxological in nature. Investigating both the significant achievements and the shameful failures of human legal systems can move believers to probe the depths of the divine law, which is ultimately identical with God's own loving wisdom and care for all of creation:

The law of the LORD is perfect,
reviving the soul;
the decrees of the LORD are sure,
making wise the simple;
the precepts of the LORD are right,
rejoicing the heart;
the commandment of the LORD is clear,
enlightening the eyes;
the fear of the LORD is pure,
enduring forever;
the ordinances of the LORD are true
and righteous altogether.
More to be desired are they than gold,
even much fine gold;
sweeter also than honey,
and drippings of the honeycomb.[18]

Notes

PREFACE

1. Paul Ramsey, *Ethics at the Edges of Life: Medical and Legal Intersections* (New Haven, CT: Yale University Press, 1978).
2. Paul Ramsey, *Nine Modern Moralists* (Englewood Cliffs, NJ: Prentice-Hall, 1962).
3. Ibid., 1.
4. *Roe v. Wade*, 410 U.S. 113 (1973).
5. *Citizens United v. Federal Election Commission*, 558 U.S. 310 (2010).

CHAPTER 1

1. Alasdair Maclntyre, *After Virtue*, 3rd ed. (Notre Dame, IN: University of Notre Dame Press, 2007).
2. John T. Noonan Jr., *The Scholastic Analysis of Usury* (Cambridge, MA: Harvard University Press, 1957).
3. MacIntyre, *After Virtue*, 222.
4. Pope Paul VI, *Humanae vitae* [Encyclical on Human Life] (1968).
5. John T. Noonan Jr., *Contraception: A History of Its Treatment by the Catholic Theologians and Canonists*, enl. ed. (Cambridge, MA: Belknap Press of Harvard University Press, 1986).
6. John T. Noonan Jr., *Power to Dissolve: Lawyers and Marriages in the Courts of the Roman Curia* (Cambridge, MA: Belknap Press of Harvard University Press, 1972).
7. John T. Noonan Jr., *The Antelope: The Ordeal of the Recaptured Africans in the Administrations of James Monroe and John Quincy Adams* (Berkeley: University of California Press, 1977).
8. John T. Noonan Jr., *Bribes* (New York: Macmillan, 1984).
9. John T. Noonan Jr., *The Believer and the Powers that Are: Cases, History, and Other Data Bearing on the Relation of Religion and Government* (New York: Macmillan, 1987), updated as John T. Noonan Jr. and Edward McGlynn Gaffney Jr., *Religious*

Freedom: History, Cases, and Other Materials on the Interaction of Religion and Government (New York: Foundation Press, 2001); John T. Noonan Jr., *The Lustre of Our Country: The American Experience of Religious Freedom* (Berkeley: University of California Press, 1998).

10. Noonan, *Contraception*, 107–39.
11. Noonan, *Power to Dissolve*.
12. Ibid., 80–122.
13. Noonan, *Bribes*.
14. Noonan, *The Believer and the Powers that Are*.
15. Noonan, *The Lustre of Our Country*.
16. Noonan, *Power to Dissolve*, 123.
17. Ibid., 125.
18. Noonan and Gaffney, *Religious Freedom*, 98.
19. Noonan, *Bribes*, 46–54.
20. Ibid., 375.
21. Ibid., 387.
22. Ibid., 382.
23. David Hollenbach, S.J., *The Common Good and Christian Ethics* (Cambridge: Cambridge University Press, 2002), 129–30.
24. John T. Noonan Jr., *Persons and Masks of the Law: Cardozo, Holmes, Jefferson, and Wythe as Makers of the Masks*, 2nd ed. (Berkley: University of California Press, 2002). Noonan quotes a passage from Jacques Maritain's *Humanisme Intégral* (1937) on the interweaving of masks and roles in the beginning of *Persons and Masks of the Law*.
25. Jacques Maritain, *The Rights of Man and Natural Law*, in Jacques Maritain, *Christianity and Democracy, and The Rights of Man and Natural Law*, trans. Doris C. Anson (San Francisco, CA: Ignatius Press, 2012), 66.
26. Ibid.
27. Ibid., 68.
28. Ibid., 70.
29. Noonan, *Persons and Masks of the Law*, xx.
30. Ibid., 12–13.
31. Ibid., 18.
32. Noonan, *Bribes*, xi.
33. Ibid., 61.
34. Noonan, *Persons and Masks of the Law*, 19.
35. Noonan, *The Antelope*, 1, 135.
36. Ibid., 141.
37. Ibid., 135.
38. Ibid., 51–68.
39. Noonan, *Persons and Masks of the Law*, 19–21.
40. Ibid., 26.

41. *Palsgraf v. Long Island Railroad* 248 N.Y. 339 (1928); see Noonan, *Persons and Masks of the Law*, 111–51.
42. Ibid., 144.
43. Ibid., 138.
44. Ibid., 137–39 (emphasis added).
45. Noonan, *Bribes*, 82.
46. Ibid., 65, 67.
47. Ibid., 16.
48. Noonan, *Power to Dissolve*, xvii.
49. Pope Leo XIII, *Rerum novarum* [Encyclical on Capital and Labor] (1891).
50. Vatican II, *Gaudium et spes* [Pastoral Constitution on the Church in the Modern World] (1965).
51. Noonan, *The Scholastic Analysis of Usury*, 170.
52. See John T. Noonan Jr., "Development in Moral Doctrine," *Theological Studies* 54, no. 4 (1993): 662–77. See also John T. Noonan Jr., *A Church that Can and Cannot Change: The Development of Catholic Moral Teaching* (Notre Dame, IN: University of Notre Dame Press, 2005). Building on his monumental study, Noonan uses usury as a key example of the development of doctrine in both the article and the book.
53. See, for example, Kenneth R. Himes, O.F.M., ed., *Modern Catholic Social Teaching: Commentaries & Interpretations* (Washington, DC: Georgetown University Press, 2005); David Matzko McCarthy, ed., *The Heart of Catholic Social Teaching: Its Origins and Contemporary Significance* (Grand Rapids, MI: Brazos Press, 2009); and Thomas Massaro, S.J., *Living Justice: Catholic Social Teaching in Action*, 2nd ed. (Lanham, MD: Rowman & Littlefield, 2012). Even an important official source, Pontifical Council for Justice and Peace, *Compendium of the Social Doctrine of the Church* (Washington, DC: USCCB Publishing, 2005), only mentions the word *usury* eleven times in 480 pages.
54. See, for example, John Mahoney, *The Making of Moral Theology: A Study of the Roman Catholic Tradition* (Oxford: Clarendon Press, 1987); John A. Gallagher, *Time Past, Time Future: An Historical Study of Catholic Moral Theology* (New York: Paulist Press, 1990). There are, however, important exceptions to my generalization. In his recent historical work, for example, Charles Curran has stressed the importance of the example of usury in making the case for development of doctrine. See, e.g., Charles E. Curran, *The Development of Moral Theology: Five Strands* (Washington, DC: Georgetown University Press, 2013).
55. Joseph A. DiNoia, O.P., "American Catholic Theology at Century's End—Postconcilliar, Postmodern, Post-Thomistic," *Thomist* 54, no. 3 (1990): 499–518. For broader accounts of the competing strands of the theology animating the Second Vatican Council, see John W. O'Malley, S.J., *What Happened at Vatican II* (Cambridge, MA: Belknap Press of Harvard University Press, 2008), and Richard R. Gaillardetz and Catherine Clifford, *Keys to the Council: Unlocking the Teaching of Vatican II* (Collegeville, MN: Liturgical Press, 2012).

56. Noonan, *The Scholastic Analysis of Usury*, 7.
57. Ibid., 14.
58. National Council of Catholic Bishops, *Economic Justice for All: Pastoral Letter on Catholic Social Teaching and the U.S. Economy* (Washington, DC: United States Catholic Conference, 1986); and Andrea Tornielli and Giacomo Galeazzi, *Pope Francis on Capitalism and Social Justice*, trans. Demetrio S. Yocum (Collegeville, MN: Liturgical Press, 2015).
59. Noonan's insights on this point bear some points of consonance with liberation theologians. See, e.g., Gustavo Gutiérrez, *A Theology of Liberation*, 15th anniv. ed. (New York: Orbis Books, 1988), xliv.
60. Noonan, *Contraception*, 533.
61. Ibid., 535–54.
62. See Lisa Sowle Cahill, "Catholic Sexual Ethics and the Dignity of the Person: A Double Message," *Theological Studies* 50, no. 1 (1989): 120–50, at 133–37.
63. Noonan, *Contraception*, 535.
64. John T. Noonan Jr., "Natural Law, the Teaching of the Church and the Regulation of the Rhythm of Human Fecundity," *American Journal of Jurisprudence* 25, no. 1 (1980): 16–37.
65. Noonan, *Contraception*, 554.
66. Noonan, *The Scholastic Analysis of Usury*, 200.
67. For a practical analysis of legal argumentation, see Wilson Huhn, *The Five Types of* Legal Argument, 2nd ed. (Durham, NC: Carolina Academic Press, 2008). See also James Boyd White, *Heracles' Bow: Essays on the Rhetoric and Poetics of the Law* (Madison: University of Wisconsin Press, 1985).
68. See, e.g., Christopher Kaczor, "Moral Theology, Development of Doctrine, and Human Experience," *Josephinum Journal of Theology* 10 (Summer/Fall 2003): 194–209 (taking usury as the example), and Joel S. Panzer, *The Popes and Slavery* (New York: Alba House 1996).
69. See, e.g., John Finnis, *Aquinas* (Oxford: Oxford University Press, 1998), §5.4 (esp. n. c) (disputing Noonan's account of Aquinas on the marital goods), and §6.4 (emphasizing the principled and context-dependent nature of Aquinas's theory of usury).
70. See, e.g., Avery Dulles, "Development or Reversal?," review of *A Church That Can and Cannot Change: The Development of Catholic Moral Teaching*, by John T. Noonan Jr., *First Things*, October 2005.
71. See, e.g., E. Christian Brugger, *Capital Punishment: Roman Catholic Moral Tradition* (Notre Dame, IN: University of Notre Dame Press, 2004).
72. See, e.g., Germain Grisez, *The Way of the Lord Jesus Volume 1: Christian Moral Principles* (Chicago, IL: Franciscan Press 1997), 891–94 (on development of doctrine and Noonan's account in *Contraception*).
73. It is, of course, only analogous. It is theoretically possible for the reader, unlike for the juror, to do the work necessary to come to his or her own independent

judgment. Nonetheless, that would require a prodigious amount of time and effort that not many readers are prepared to dedicate to the question.

74. M. Cathleen Kaveny, "A Response to John T. Noonan, Jr.," in *Proceedings of the Catholic Theological Society of America* 54 (1999): 57–64.
75. See John T. Noonan Jr., "Development in Moral Doctrine," *Theological Studies* 54, no. 4 (1993): 662–77, at 669.
76. Pope John Paul II, *Evangelium vitae* [Encyclical on the Gospel of Life] (1995). Capital punishment is discussed in paragraphs 55–57.
77. Noonan, "Development in Moral Doctrine," 662.
78. Arthur Vermeersch, S.J., "Usury," in *The Catholic Encyclopedia* (1913).
79. Ibid.
80. In assessing change or continuity in magisterial teaching, one has first to identify the *propositions* proposed to be true by the teaching in question. Theologians insist upon the difference between a proposition and a sentence; a proposition is not identical to the words in a sentence, but points to the meaning that the sentence conveys. See, e.g., Francis A. Sullivan, S.J., *Magisterium: Teaching Authority in the Catholic Church* (Mahwah, NJ: Paulist Press 1983), 15: "A sentence is a particular verbal expression, in a particular language: the proposition is the meaning which the sentence intends to express."
81. The conservative columnist Ross Douthat has acknowledged that conservative Catholics do not have a well-developed theory of development of doctrine. See Ross Douthat, "A Crisis of Conservative Catholicism" (2015 Erasmus Lecture), *First Things*, January 2016.
82. Paul Varnell, "How the Vatican Can Change," *IGF Culture Watch*, www.igfculturewatch.com/2000/09/27/how-the-vatican-can-change/. See also Patricia Beattie Jung with Joseph Andrew Coray, eds., *Sexual Diversity and Catholicism: Toward the Development of Moral Theology* (Collegeville, MN: Liturgical Press, 2001).
83. Varnell, "How the Vatican Can Change," citing Noonan, "Development in Moral Doctrine," 675.
84. Rachel Donadio, "On Gay Priests, Pope Francis Asks, 'Who Am I to Judge?,'" *New York Times*, July 29, 2013, A1.
85. Patrick M. O'Neil, "A Response to John T. Noonan, Jr. Concerning the Development of Catholic Moral Doctrine," *Faith & Reason* 22 (Spring–Summer 1996): 59. The article is available online at www.ewtn.com/library/THEOLOGY/FRNOONAN.htm.
86. See Vermeersch, *Usury*.
87. The process used to interpret ecclesiastical texts is not dissimilar to the process learned by law students to interpret legal texts. Francis A. Sullivan, S.J., *Creative Fidelity: Weighing and Interpreting Documents of the Magisterium* (Mahwah, NJ: Paulist Press, 1996).

88. MacIntyre, *After Virtue*, 188–89.
89. John Finnis, *Natural Law and Natural Rights* (Oxford: Clarendon Press of Oxford University Press, 1980), 232.
90. MacIntyre, *After Virtue*, 190.
91. MacIntyre defines "virtue" as "an acquired human quality the possession and exercise of which tends to enable us to achieve those goods which are internal to practices and the lack of which effectively prevents us from achieving any such goods." MacIntyre, *After Virtue*, 191.
92. In *Ex corde ecclesiae*, Pope John Paul II attempted to bring more order to this situation, in part by requiring that all Catholics teaching theology at Catholic colleges and universities request a mandate from the local bishop. Pope John Paul II, *Ex corde ecclesiae* [Apostolic Constitution on Catholic Universities] (1990). The document and the program of implementation became embroiled in the battles between progressive and conservative Catholics
93. For example, see John T. Noonan Jr., "Introduction" and "An Almost Absolute Value in History," in *The Morality of Abortion: Legal and Historical Perspectives*, ed. John T. Noonan Jr. (Cambridge, MA: Harvard University Press, 1970), ix–xviii and 1–59.
94. John T. Noonan Jr., *A Private Choice: Abortion in America in the Seventies* (New York: Free Press, 1979).
95. Beverly Wildung Harrison, *Our Right to Choose: Toward a New Ethic of Abortion* (Boston: Beacon Press, 1983), 267n25.
96. Vatican II, *Gaudium et spes*, §10.
97. Noonan, *The Scholastic Analysis of Usury*, 27.

CHAPTER 2

1. *Rector of Holy Trinity Church v. United States*, 143 U.S. 457, 471 (1892).
2. See Stanley Hauerwas, *The Peaceable Kingdom: A Primer in Christian Ethics* (Notre Dame, IN: University of Notre Dame Press, 1983).
3. Stanley Hauerwas, *With the Grain of the Universe: The Church's Witness and Natural Theology* (Grand Rapids, MI: Brazos Press, 2001).
4. John Blake, "How Obama's Favorite Theologian Shaped his First Year in Office," CNN Politics, February 5, 2010, www.cnn.com/2010/POLITICS/02/05/Obama.theologian/.
5. William James, *The Varieties of Religious Experience* (Cambridge, MA: Harvard University Press, 1985).
6. Hauerwas, *With the Grain of the Universe*, 80.
7. Ibid., 78–79.
8. Hauerwas claims that what matters for James in matters of religion is not intellectual beliefs, but "immediate and intuitive . . . assurance." Ibid., 71, quoting William James, *The Varieties of Religious Experience: A Study in Human Nature*,

foreword Jacques Barzun (New York: Mentor Book 1958), 214. Hauerwas goes on to object that this position is inconsistent with James's own pragmatism, which holds that "[t]he reasons why I find it satisfactory to believe that any idea is true, the *how* of my arriving at that belief, may be among the very reasons why the idea *is* true in reality." Ibid., 72 (emphasis in original), quoting William James, *Pragmatism and the Meaning of Truth*, intro. A. J. Ayer (Cambridge, MA: Harvard University Press 1996), 275. Hauerwas remarks, "It does not seem to occur to James that attending to the how of what it might mean to be forgiven is not separable from what Christians think God has done for the world in Christ." Ibid.

9. Ibid., 68.
10. "My concern at this point, however, is not why James thought he was justified to call his over-belief 'god.' Rather, my concern is to understand why James thought that what Christians believe about Christ, the Trinity, or the church are over-beliefs that can have no pragmatic justification." Ibid., 71.
11. See Stephen Prothero, "You Can't Reconcile Ayn Rand and Jesus," *USA Today*, June 6, 2011, 9A (noting that Ryan cites Rand as "the reason" for his involvement in public service). Ryan attempted to distance himself from Rand in response to public criticism. See, e.g., Jonathan Chait, "Here's What Paul Ryan's Latest Answer about Ayn Rand Really Means," *New York Magazine*, September 12, 2014, www.nymag.com/daily/intelligencer/2014/09/what-ryans-latest-answer-about-rand-means.html.
12. George Weigel, "The Pope, Chaplain to OWS? Rubbish," *National Review Online*, October 24, 2011, www.nationalreview.com/corner/281140/pope-chaplain-ows-rubbish-george-weigel.
13. See, e.g., Jeet Heer, "The Last Time Conservatives Dismissed a Major Encyclical, It Ended Terribly for Them," *New Republic*, June 17, 2015, https://newrepublic.com/article/122056/last-time-conservatives-dismissed-major-encyclical-it-ended-terribly.
14. Hauerwas, *With the Grain of the Universe*, 87.
15. Ibid., 88.
16. Ibid., 127
17. Ibid., 131.
18. Ibid., 137.
19. "Thus Niebuhr's account of original sin is his attempt to do natural theology. Christians may not be able to convince agnostics and nonbelievers that God exists, but Christians can convince nonbelievers that sin exists. Moreover, if sin exists, it makes some sense to think that God exists. Niebuhr's project is to provide an account of the human condition that is so compelling that the more 'absurd' aspects of 'orthodox Christianity'—such as the beliefs that God exists and that God is love—might also receive a hearing." Ibid., 120.
20. Ibid., 182–83.

21. Ibid., 182, quoting Martin Rumscheidt, "Epilogue" to Karl Church D, *Fragments Grave and Gay*, trans. Eric Mosbacher (London: Collins, 1971).
22. Ibid., 176.
23. Ibid., 180, quoting Karl Barth, *Church Dogmatics*, 2/2, ed. G. W. Bromiley and T. F. Torrance, trans. G. W. Bromiley et al. (Edinburgh: T. & T. Clark, 1957), 188.
24. See Hans W. Frei, *Types of Christian Theology*, ed. George Hunsinger and William C. Placher (New Haven, CT: Yale University Press, 1992).
25. Hauerwas, *With the Grain of the Universe*, 182.
26. Ibid., 191, quoting Karl Barth, *Church Dogmatics*, 2/1, ed. G. W. Bromiley and T. F. Torrance, trans. T. H. L. Parker et al. (Edinburgh: T. & T. Clark, 1957), 216.
27. Ibid., 196, quoting Karl Barth, *The Christian Life: Lecture Fragments* (*Church Dogmatics* 4/4), trans. Geoffrey Bromiley (Grand Rapids, MI: Eerdmans, 1981), 203–204.
28. Ibid., 198, quoting Karl Barth, *Church Dogmatics*, 4/3.2, ed. G. W. Bromiley and T. F. Torrance, trans. G. W. Bromiley (Edinburgh: T. & T. Clark, 1992), 623.
29. Ibid., 200 (emphasis in original).
30. Ibid., 200–201, quoting Barth, *Church Dogmatics*, 4/3.2, 494.
31. Needless to say, sociologists of religion (for example, those operating with a Weberian church–sect distinction) would offer a different analysis of what the term "church" means than an ecclesiologist working within a particular religious tradition.
32. Jean Bethke Elshtain, "Christian Contrarian," *Time*, September 17, 2001.
33. See Acts 17:22.
34. According to biblical scholars, the Areopagus, the "hill of Ares," was no longer the setting of the supreme Athenian council in Luke's day. Luke meant that Paul was invited to a learned disputation in the former setting of the council, not subpoenaed to appear at a trial. See Richard J. Dillon, "Acts of the Apostles," in *The New Jerome Biblical Commentary*, ed. Raymond E. Brown, S.S., Joseph A. Fitzmyer, S.J., and Roland E. Murphy, O.Carm (Englewood Cliffs, NJ: Prentice-Hall, 1990), 722–67, at 755.
35. See Manny Fernandez, "Perry Leads Rally at Stadium for a 'Nation in Crisis,'" *New York Times*, August 7, 2011, A12.
36. See, e.g., Harry S. Stout, *The New England Soul* (New York: Oxford University Press, 1986), chap. 4, "Days of Trouble and Thankful Remembrances."
37. See John Rawls, *A Theory of Justice* (Cambridge, MA: Belknap Press of Harvard University Press, 1971), 60–83.
38. See the following works by John Finnis: *Intention and Identity: Collected Essays Volume II* (Oxford: Oxford University Press, 2011), 85–86; *Natural Law and Natural Rights* (Oxford: Oxford University Press, 1980), 253–54; *Philosophy of Law: Collected Essays Volume IV* (Oxford: Oxford University Press, 2011), chap. 3, "Law as Coordination."

39. See, e.g., Karl Llewellyn, *The Bramble Bush: The Classic Lectures on the Law and Law School* (New York: Oxford University Press, 2008).
40. Jeffrey Stout, *Ethics After Babel: The Languages of Morals and Their Discontents* (Boston, MA: Beacon Press, 1988), 74–77.
41. For example, enforcement of the Civil Rights Act of 1866 was undermined by political factions and the actions of groups such as the Ku Klux Klan. See Eric Foner, *Reconstruction: America's Unfinished Revolution, 1863–1877* (New York: Harper & Row, 1988).
42. Paul Ramsey, *Nine Modern Moralists* (Lanham, MD: University Press of America, 1983), 195, quoting Edmond Cahn, *The Sense of Injustice* (New York: New York University Press, 1949) and *The Moral Decision: Right and Wrong in the Light of American Law* (Bloomington: Indiana University Press, 1955).
43. Karl Barth, *Church Dogmatics*, 3/1, ed. G. W. Bromiley and T. F. Torrance, trans. J. W. Edwards et al. (Edinburgh: T. &T. Clark, 1958), 42.
44. William Werpehowski, "Ad Hoc Apologetics," *Journal of Religion* 66, no. 3 (1986): 286–87 (emphasis in original).
45. Frei, *Types of Christian Theology*, 3–4.
46. For a careful examination of Frei's thought, see Jason A. Springs, *Toward a Generous Orthodoxy* (New York: Oxford University Press, 2010).
47. Frei, *Types of Christian Theology*, 4.
48. Ibid.
49. I am indebted to a conversation with William Werpehowski for crystalizing this point for me.
50. For Barth's debate on this topic with Emil Brunner, see Emil Brunner and Karl Barth, *Natural Theology: Comprising "Nature and Grace" by Professor Dr. Emil Brunner and the Reply "No!" by Dr. Karl Barth* (Eugene, OR: Wipf and Stock Publishers, 2002).
51. Ramsey, *Nine Modern Moralists*, 220–21.
52. Stanley Hauerwas and David B. Burrell, "From System to Story: An Alternative Pattern for Rationality Ethics," in Stanley Hauerwas, with Richard Bondi and David B. Burrell, *Truthfulness and Tragedy: Further Investigations into Christian Ethics* (Notre Dame, IN: University of Notre Dame Press, 1977), 15–39.
53. See John T. Noonan Jr., *Persons and Masks of the Law: Cardozo, Holmes, Jefferson and Wythe as Makers of the Masks*, 2nd ed. (University of California Press, 2002).
54. Ramsey, *Nine Modern Moralists*. In particular, see chap. 8, "Jacques Maritain and Edmond Cahn: The Egypt of the Natural Law," and chap. 9 "Jacques Maritain and Edmond Cahn: Man's Exodus from the Natural Law." Ramsey was one of the first American Protestants to engage the Catholic tradition in an interested, appreciative, and critical way. Ramsey recognizes that Maritain is attempting to reject the rationalistic, deductivist account of natural law that he himself associates with

Roman Catholicism. Ramsey does not, however, yet appreciate the variety in the Catholic tradition, although he does have an inkling that Aquinas himself is not subject to the criticisms he mounts. This book was written in the early 1960s; his interest and familiarity with Catholic moral theology grew over the next several decades.

55. Ibid., 221 (emphasis in original).
56. Ibid. (emphasis in original).
57. Ibid., 226, quoting Edmond Cahn, *The Sense of Injustice*, 11 and 6 (emphasis in original) .
58. Ibid., 224, quoting Edmond Cahn, *The Moral Decision*, 11 and 34 (emphasis in original).
59. Ibid., 213.
60. "The first distinctive feature of Protestant doctrines of the law of nature—though not only of Protestantism—is the separation of the natural law from the context of the authority of ecclesiastical positive law so that the inherent meaning of natural law might come to fulfillment in the progressive discovery of new and relevant truth through unlimited discussion." Ibid., 229.
61. Ibid., 213.
62. David Zaret, *The Heavenly Contract: Ideology and Organization in Pre-Revolutionary Puritanism* (Chicago, IL: University of Chicago Press, 1985), 168.

CHAPTER 3

1. Jeffrey Stout, *Democracy and Tradition* (Princeton, NJ: Princeton University Press, 2004), 11.
2. Ibid., 3.
3. Ibid.
4. Ibid., 7.
5. Ibid., 300–307.
6. Ibid., 270–78.
7. Ibid., 8, 164.
8. Ibid., 141–43, 170–71, citing Stanley Hauerwas and David B. Burrell, "From System to Story: An Alternative Pattern for Rationality in Ethics," in Stanley Hauerwas, with Richard Bondi and David B. Burrell, *Truthfulness and Tragedy: Further Investigations into Christian Ethics* (Notre Dame, IN: University of Notre Dame Press, 1977), 15–39.
9. Ibid., 170, citing Robert Musil, *The Man Without Qualities*, trans. Sophie Wilkins (New York: Alfred A. Knopf, 1995).
10. Ibid., 99. It is interesting that religious law schools, which present themselves as countercultural in significant ways, have expressed little difficulty in teaching the great common law courses in a conventional fashion with conventional materials.

11. For example, consider *Allegheny College v. National Chautauqua County Bank*, 159 N.E. 173 (N.Y. 1927). The case features an opinion written by the great jurist Benjamin Cardozo (1870–1938), who sat as a state court judge in New York before ascending to the U.S. Supreme Court. It has to do with the all too common situation of the failure to keep a charitable pledge. More specifically, it concerns the failure of a deceased woman's estate to keep her promise to give $5,000 to Allegheny College after her death "in consideration of my interest in Christian education." As Leon Lipson argues, Cardozo's virtuoso performance justifies enforcing the promise to the college by seamlessly interweaving two theories of contractual obligation: *agreement with consideration*, for which he had a solid legal rule but shaky facts; and *promissory estoppel*, for which he had solid facts but a shaky legal rule. Cardozo was able to demonstrate his extraordinary brilliance in this classic case only by taking seriously the problems of ordinary people. See Leon S. Lipson, "The Allegheny College Case," *Yale Law Report* 23, no. 2 (Spring 1977): 8–11.
12. Charles L. Knapp, Nathan M. Crystal, and Harry G. Prince, *Problems in Contract Law: Cases and Materials*, 7th ed. (New York: Aspen, 2012). An eighth edition was released in 2016; it eliminated some of these cases in order to make room for new ones.
13. Alasdair MacIntyre, *After Virtue: A Study in Moral Theory*, 3rd ed. (Notre Dame, IN: University of Notre Dame Press, 2007), 222.
14. Ibid., 223.
15. Alasdair MacIntyre, *Whose Justice? Which Rationality?* (Notre Dame, IN: University of Notre Dame Press, 1988), 7.
16. Ibid., 8.
17. Ibid., 9
18. Ibid.
19. Joseph M. Perillo, *Calamari and Perillo on Contracts*, 6th ed. (St. Paul, MN: West Academic Publishing, 2014), §16.2, pp. 553–54.
20. Restatement (Second) of Contracts, §90(1), in Charles L. Knapp, Nathan M. Crystal, and Harry G. Prince, *Rules of Contract Law: Selections from the Uniform Commercial Code, the CISG, the Restatement (Second) of Contracts, and the UNIDROIT Principles, with Material on Contract Drafting and Sample Exam Questions, 2012–2013* (New York: Wolters Kluwer Law & Business, 2012), 147 (emphasis added).
21. The development of the Restatement from an examination of the case law exemplifies Stout's view that "[m]oral principles . . . make explicit the material inferential commitments implicit in the practical reasoning that transpires when people hold one another responsible for their actions." Stout, *Democracy and Tradition*, 246.
22. Perillo, *Contracts*, §9.17, pp. 297–99.
23. MacIntyre, *Whose Justice? Which Rationality?*, 10.

24. Stout, *Democracy and Tradition*, 162.
25. See Alasdair MacIntyre, *After Virtue*, 216:

> [M]an is in his actions and practice, as well as in his fictions, essentially a story-telling animal. He is not essentially, but becomes through his history, a teller of stories that aspire to truth. But the key question for men is not about their own authorship; I can only answer the question "What am I to do?" if I can answer the prior question "Of what story or stories do I find myself a part?" We enter human society, that is, with one or more imputed characters—roles into which we have been drafted—and we have to learn what they are in order to be able to understand how others respond to us and how our responses to them are apt to be construed. It is through hearing stories about wicked stepmothers, lost children, good but misguided kings, wolves that suckle twin boys, youngest sons who receive no inheritance but must make their own way in the world and eldest sons who waste their inheritance on riotous living and go into exile to live with the swine, that children learn or mislearn both what a child and what a parent is, what the cast of characters may be in the drama into which they have been born and what the ways of the world are.

26. See, e.g., Hans W. Frei, *The Eclipse of Biblical Narrative: A Study in Eighteenth and Nineteenth Century Hermeneutics* (New Haven, CT: Yale University Press, 1974), and George A. Lindbeck, *The Nature of Doctrine: Religion and Theology in a Postliberal Age*, 25th anniv. ed. (Louisville, KY: Westminster John Knox Press, 2009).
27. See, for example, *Syester v. Banta*, 133 N.W.2d 666 (Iowa 1965). I discuss this case in detail later.
28. See, for example, the *Allegheny College* case and *King v. Trustees of Boston University*, 647 N.E.2d 1196 (Mass. 1995). Courts regularly used to bend the general rules regarding the criteria that must be met for a promise to be a legally enforceable promise, in order to enforce charitable subscriptions. In time, they created a new rule for charitable subscriptions.
29. See, for example, *Shoemaker v. Commonwealth Bank*, 700 A.2d 1003 (Pa. Super. Ct. 1997). In this Pennsylvania Superior Court case, a couple whose house had burned down sued the bank that held their mortgage, claiming that the bank had promised to obtain insurance on their behalf. The court ruled in favor of the plaintiffs, despite the fact that the bank had not made a straightforward promise, but had instead simply informed the couple that if they did not fulfill their contractual obligation to obtain homeowners' insurance, the bank would purchase it and add the cost of the premium to their monthly mortgage payment.
30. See, for example, *C & J Fertilizer, Inc. v. Allied Mutual Insurance Co.*, 227 N.W.2d 169 (Iowa 1975). In this Iowa Supreme Court case, a small business sued its insurance carrier, which had denied coverage for a burglary. Ruling in favor of the plaintiff, the court held that the parties were not bound by the clear meaning of the text of the contract, but instead by the reasonable expectations of the

small business owner, who did not read the contract before signing it. This result stands in sharp contrast with cases decided in accordance with the "duty to read" traditionally imposed by the courts.

31. See *Shoemaker v. Commonwealth Bank* (1997).
32. See, for example, *Hill v. Jones*, 725 P.2d 1115 (Ariz. Ct. App. 1986), which dealt with purchase and sale of a house that had at one time been infested with termites, and favored the disgruntled buyer by articulating a duty to disclose the infestation that stood in some tension with the older rule of *caveat emptor.*
33. Perillo, *Contracts*, §14.4(a), pp. 488–91.
34. Ibid., §14.15, pp. 506–509. For example, suppose the board of trustees of a charitable corporation decides to sponsor a fund-raising luncheon, hiring a caterer to provide the food at $10 per person. Assume that the trustees sell 200 tickets at $30 apiece. If the caterer breaches the contract one month before the event, telling the trustees that it will not be able to provide the food, then the corporation is entitled to sue the caterer for damages, in order to end up with the (say) $4,000 in profit that it would have earned had the contract been fulfilled ($6,000 gross receipts minus $2,000 in catering costs). The trustees cannot simply cancel the dinner and sue the caterer for $4,000 if they can find a comparable caterer to do the job for $2,500, which would mean an award of $500 in expectation damages.
35. *I. G. Katz v. Danny Dare, Inc.*, 610 S.W.2d 121 (Mo. Ct. App. 1980).
36. I think here of the case law interpreting various statutes of frauds, which specify that certain types of contracts must be evidenced by a writing in order to be enforceable, as well as the case law on the parol evidence rule, which governs when fact finders may consider prior or contemporaneous evidence in interpreting a contract that has been reduced to written form.
37. Jeffrey Stout, "Superpower View of Defense," in *Ethics after Babel: The Languages of Morals and Their Discontents* (Boston, MA: Beacon Press, 1988), 295, quoting Bernard Williams, *Ethics and the Limits of Philosophy* (Cambridge, MA: Harvard University Press, 1985), 84, and Robert Nozick, *Philosophical Explanations* (Cambridge, MA: Harvard University Press, 1981), 4–5.
38. Stout, *Democracy and Tradition*, 270.
39. Ibid., 274.
40. *Korematsu v. United States*, 323 U.S. 214 (1944).
41. Stout, *Democracy and Tradition*, 271.
42. Ibid., 275.
43. Ibid., 275–76.
44. Ibid., 276.
45. Jeffrey Stout, *The Flight from Authority: Religion, Morality, and the Quest for Autonomy* (Notre Dame, IN: University of Notre Dame Press, 1981), 2–3.
46. Stout, *Democracy and Tradition*, 281.
47. Ibid., 280.

48. Ibid., 262.
49. Ibid., 135, quoting Susan Moller Okin, *Justice, Gender, and the Family* (New York: Basic Books, 1989), 60–61 (Olkin's emphasis).
50. MacIntyre, *After Virtue*, 194.
51. Steven Alan Childress and Martha S. Davis, *Civil*, vol. 1 of *Federal Standards of Review*, 4th ed. (New Providence, NJ: LexisNexis, 2010), §§2.01–12, pp. 2-3–2-81.
52. Ibid., §§2.13–14, pp. 2-82–2-92.
53. Stout, *Democracy and Tradition*, 304.
54. Ibid., 277: "It is very important to see that in endorsing the view that norms are creatures of social practices, I am not endorsing a reduction of truth or objectivity to what some community takes to be true or objective. Our socially instituted conceptual norms do not in fact permit such a reduction."
55. Ibid., 255.
56. Knapp, Crystal, and Prince, *Problems in Contract Law*, 573–82.
57. *Syester v. Banta*, 133 N.W. 2d 666, 669.
58. I obtained this amount by plugging $29,000 in 1960 dollars into the "Measuring Worth" purchasing power calculator: https://www.measuringworth.com/uscompare/.
59. *Syester*, at 670.
60. *Syester*, at 671.
61. Ibid.
62. *Syester*, at 672.
63. *Syester*, at 673–74.
64. Perillo, *Contracts*, §4.4, pp. 154–56.
65. It would have been a violation of legal ethics for the studio's attorney to contact Mrs. Syester without her attorney's consent, let alone to encourage her to discharge him. But the pressure on Mrs. Syester to discharge her attorney came from the studio, not from its lawyer. As the court notes, this behavior was far "beyond the limits of propriety"; it was not, however, illegal. The court observes that the studio's own counsel "hesitated to participate" in the studio's attempts to convince Mrs. Syester to drop her lawsuit. *Syester*, at 672.
66. See *Syester*, at 674, and the Restatement (Second) of Contracts, §162, in Knapp, Crystal, and Prince, *Rules of Contract Law*, 152. The opinion glides over the "reasonableness" requirement.
67. *Syester*, at 670.
68. The defendant argued that these statements were not fraudulent, but instead were examples of a salesperson's "puffing."
69. *Syester*, at 672.
70. See Perillo, *Contracts*, §14.3, pp. 487–88.
71. *Syester*, at 676.
72. Ibid.

73. The court stressed its obligation to defer to the jury's factual findings. "It is not for us to say who should have prevailed with the jury. It is for us to determine the sufficiency of the admissible evidence to generate a jury question and the correctness of the instructions given the jury." *Syester*, at 668.
74. Unscrupulous dance studios continue to exploit the elderly, vulnerable, and lonely today. Lawmakers and policymakers on both the federal and the state level have begun to take measures to protect consumers against such practices. For example, the Federal Trade Commission issued a consumer warning pertaining to dance studios in 1992, available at www.web.archive.org/web/20090222062434/http://consumerlawpage.com/brochure/28.shtml. After several highly publicized scams against elderly members of its population, the state of Florida instituted measures to regulate dance studios, including adopting a Dance Studio Act in 2010, which was repealed in 2014. The text of the repealed law is available at http://archive.flsenate.gov/statutes/index.cfm?m&App_mode=Display_Statute&Search_String=&URL=0500-0599/0501/Sections/0501.143.html. For context, see Zac Anderson, "Florida Lawmakers Move to Repeal Buyer Protections," *The Ledger.com*, April 24, 2011, http://www.theledger.com/article/20110424/NEWS/110429701. The Florida attorney general's office continues to maintain a web page titled "How to Protect Yourself: Dance Studios," http://myfloridalegal.com/pages.nsf/main/0735bdd7a83ec7ca85256cc90055e9e7!opendocument.
75. Alasdair MacIntyre, *Dependent Rational Animals: Why Human Beings Need the Virtues* (Chicago, IL: Open Court, 1999).

CHAPTER 4

1. Luke 10:25–37.
2. Robert Wuthnow, *Acts of Compassion: Caring for Others and Helping Ourselves* (Princeton, NJ: Princeton University Press, 1991), chap. 6.
3. *Watts v. Watts*, 405 N.W.2d 305 (Wis. 1987).
4. Gene Outka, *Agape: An Ethical Analysis* (New Haven, CT: Yale University Press, 1972).
5. Gene Outka, "Universal Love and Impartiality," in *The Love Commandments: Essays in Christian Ethics and Moral Philosophy*, ed. Edmund N. Santurri and William Werpehowski (Washington, DC: Georgetown University Press, 1992), 1–103.
6. Ibid., 2.
7. Ibid., 2–3.
8. Anders Nygren, *Agape and Eros*, trans. Philip S. Watson (Chicago, IL: University of Chicago Press, 1982).
9. See Paul Ramsey, *War and the Christian Conscience* (Durham, NC: Duke University Press, 1961), chap. 3.
10. In addition to Wisconsin in *Watts*, other jurisdictions have considered these general issues. See, e.g., *Hewitt v. Hewitt*, 394 N.E.2d 1204 (Ill. 1979), *Kozlowski*

v. Kozlowski, 403 A.2d 902 (N.J. 1979). See also *Marvin v. Marvin*, 557 P.2d 106 (Cal.1976).

11. A full consideration of the underlying issues would require accounting for ways in which the law has recognized and protected the rights of women in stable heterosexual relationships that were nonetheless not *marital* relationships. For example, in the eighteenth and nineteenth centuries, the state of Louisiana recognized contracts of plaçage between white men and free women of color. The relationships were sometimes called "mariages de la main gauche," or left-handed marriages. See, e.g., Gwendolyn Midlo Hall, *Africans in Colonial Louisiana: The Development of Afro-Creole Culture in the Eighteenth Century* (Baton Rouge: Louisiana State University Press, 1992).
12. Outka, "Universal Love and Impartiality," 9.
13. Ibid., 71.
14. Ibid., 30, quoting Basil Mitchell, *Morality: Religious and Secular* (Oxford: Clarendon Press, 1980), 144.
15. For an introduction, see E. Allen Farnsworth, *Contracts*, 4th ed. (New York: Aspen, 2004).
16. Joseph Raz, *The Morality of Freedom* (Oxford: Clarendon Press, 1988), 204.
17. See, e.g., *Williams v. Walker Thomas Furniture*, 350 F.2d 445 (D.C. Cir. 1965). Rent-to-own arrangements saw resurgence in the Great Recession of 2007–2009. See, e.g., Jennifer Latson, "Many Buying into Rent-to-Own Idea during Recession," *Houston Chronicle*, July 13, 2009, www.chron.com/business/article/Many-buying-into-rent-to-own-idea-during-recession-1550537.php.
18. This is not to say that the law ought not to address the disparity in power between merchants and customers. Some scholars have suggested that the appropriate vehicle is consumer protection legislation rather than the common law. See, e.g., Stewart Macaulay, "Bambi Meets Godzilla: Reflections on Contracts Scholarship and Teaching vs. State Unfair and Deceptive Trade Practices and Consumer Protection Statutes," *Houston Law Review* 26, no. 4 (1989): 575–601. Others have suggested that the case for regulation is difficult to make. See, e.g., Jim Hawkins, "Renting the Good Life," *William and Mary Law Review* 49, no. 6 (2008): 2041–2117.
19. For good introductions to these areas of inquiry, see Nancy Levit and Robert R. M. Verchick, eds., *Feminist Legal Theory: A Primer*, 2nd ed. (New York: New York University Press, 2016), and Richard Delgado and Jean Stefancic, *Critical Race Theory: An Introduction*, 2nd rev. ed. (New York: New York University Press, 2012). For close analysis of the leading rent-to-own case using critical race and gender analysis, see Muriel Morisey Spence, "Teaching *Williams v. Walker-Thomas Furniture Co.*," *Temple Political and Civil Rights Law Review* 3 (1993–1994): 89–105. For a different perspective, see Russell Korobkin, "A 'Traditional' and 'Behavioral' Law-and-Economics Analysis of *Williams v. Walker-Thomas Furniture Company*," *University of Hawai'i Law Review* 26, no. 2 (2004): 441–68.

20. Lon L. Fuller and William R. Perdue Jr., "The Reliance Interest in Contract Damages: 1," *Yale Law Journal* 46, no. 1 (1936): 52–96, at 62.
21. Outka writes: "Often too, both my initiatives and responses are constrained and otherwise affected by interactions with others. In fact our lives are suffused with impure cases: unwanted decisions such as acceding to 'coercive offers' in corporate business transactions, firing incompetent employees in need, giving money under threat to drug addicts, plotting to bring down tyrannical governments, etc. Neither my situation as a recipient nor the complexity of these cases receive their due when we focus single-mindedly on autonomous initiatives." Outka, "Universal Love and Impartiality," 70.
22. See, e.g., Paul Ramsey, *The Patient as Person*, 2nd ed. (New Haven: Yale University Press, 2002), xlv–xlvi.
23. The first meaning of *covenant* offered in the *Oxford English Dictionary* is: "A mutual agreement between two or more persons to do or refrain from doing certain acts; a compact, contract, bargain; sometimes, the undertaking, pledge, or promise of one of the parties. Phrases, to make or enter into a covenant; to hold, keep, break covenant. (No longer in ordinary use, exc. when coloured by legal or theological associations.)" In the legal realm, the term "covenant" connotes a formal agreement, often an agreement under seal.
24. Outka, "Universal Love and Impartiality," 2.
25. Contract law does not require a promise to be explicitly made in order to be enforceable. The courts will ask whether one party's conduct would lead a reasonable person in the other party's shoes to infer that a promise had been made.
26. Some scholars are exploring the relationship between legal marriage and economic status. See, e.g., Linda C. McClain, "The Other Marriage Equality Problem," *Boston University Law Review* 93, no. 3 (2013): 921–70, and David Ray Papke, "Family Law for the Underlcass: Underscoring Law's Ideological Function," *Indiana Law Review* 42, no. 3 (2009): 583–609.
27. Outka, "Universal Love and Impartiality," 70.
28. Outka addresses this debate elsewhere, e.g., in chap. 4 of *Agape*.
29. John T. Noonan Jr., *Persons and Masks of the Law*, 2nd ed. (Berkeley: University of California Press, 2002), 4.
30. Ibid., chap. 2.
31. Ibid., 6–8.
32. Outka, "Universal Love and Impartiality," 7.
33. Paul Ramsey, *The Just War* (New York: Scribner, 1968), 143.
34. "Too often we focus on those cases of human interaction where actual or threatened physical violence looms as a definite possibility, to be either affirmed or rejected. We attend too little to the far more extensive number of cases where no one meaningfully envisages physical violence, not the agent, the recipient, or affected third parties, but where resistance in a wider sense looms as a definite possibility. To attend to the latter encourages us to

interpret the law of love comprehensively, in accordance with the claim noted earlier that moral principles do more than tell agents what they may or may not do; they also tell victims what sorts of treatment they may and may not object to, resist, or demand." Outka, "Universal Love and Impartiality," 39. Bringing a case to court is a form of nonviolent resistance to objectionable treatment.

35. *Watts*, at 308 (emphasis omitted), quoting the Wisconsin Family Code sec. 765.001(2). While not uncontroversial, this claim is supported by recent research in family law. See, e.g., Margaret F. Brinig and Steven L. Nock, "Marry Me, Bill: Should Cohabitation be the (Legal) Default Option?," *Louisiana Law Review* 64, no. 3 (2004): 403–42, and Margaret Brinig, *Family, Law, and Community: Supporting the Covenant* (Chicago: University of Chicago Press, 2010), chap. 1.
36. See, e.g., William Werpehowski, "'Agape' and Special Relations," in *The Love Commandments: Essays in Christian Ethics and Moral Philosophy*, ed. Santurri and Werpehowski (Washington, DC: Georgetown University Press, 1992), 138–56.
37. Outka, "Universal Love and Impartiality," 12.
38. One might object that this need not be the case; perhaps they saw themselves as deliberately misleading outsiders into thinking they were married, while preserving their own strong sense that they were merely living together. In my view, this objection fails to account for the fact that they held themselves as married to a wide variety of audiences, both public and private—apparently including their own children. Moreover, and more specifically, the fact that the Wattses held themselves out to the federal and state governments as married for some purposes ought to have led them to expect that those governments would treat them as married for other purposes as well.
39. The American Law Institute has advocated treating cohabiting couples who break up analogously to divorcing couples for purposes of property settlement. See *Principles of the Law of Family Dissolution: Analysis and Recommendations* (Philadelphia, PA: ALI, 2002). That position has been critiqued by a number of family law scholars. See Robin Fretwell Wilson, ed., *Reconceiving the Family: Critique on the ALI Principles of the Law of Family Dissolution* (New York: Cambridge University Press, 2006). It has also been argued that the ALI position has not been highly influential; see, e.g., Michael R. Clisham and Robin Fretwell Wilson, "American Law Institute's *Principles of the Law of Family Dissolution*, Eight Years After Adoption: Guiding Principles or Obligatory Footnote?" *Family Law Quarterly* 42, no. 3 (2008): 573–618.
40. Laura Pettreca, "Prenuptial Agreements: Unromantic but Important," *USA Today*, March 11, 2010, www.usatoday.com/money/perfi/basics/2010-03-08-prenups08_CV_N.htm. A recent survey suggests that attorneys are seeing an increase in requests for prenuptial agreements, especially by millennials. See American Academy of Matrimonial Lawyers, "Prenuptial Agreements on the

Rise Finds Survey," October 28, 2016, http://www.aaml.org/about-the-academy/press/press-releases/prenuptial-agreements-rise-finds-survey.

41. Wisconsin repealed its criminal prohibition of fornication in 1983.
42. *Watts*, at 311, citing *In Matter of Estate of Steffes*, 290 N.W.2d 697, 709 (Wis. 1980).
43. *Watts*, at 312.
44. See *Watts v. Watts*, 448 N.W.2d 292 (Wis. 1989). Why no award on the contract claim? On this second appeal, the Supreme Court found that neither party had the opportunity to argue that the contract had been breached, and remanded to the lower court for a new trial on this issue. After this point, however, the Wattses disappear from the official case reports.
45. James's expert, naturally, set this amount more cautiously; he estimated that James's net worth increased by $851,306.53 during the relevant time period.

CHAPTER 5

1. Hailey Branson-Potts, "Swedish Grad Students Who Pinned Down Stanford Sex Offender Speak Out," *Los Angeles Times*, June 8, 2016, http://www.latimes.com/local/lanow/la-me-ln-stanford-rape-witnesses-20160607-snap-htmlstory.html. See also Marina Koren, "Telling the Story of the Stanford Rape Case," *Atlantic*, June 6, 2016, http://www.theatlantic.com/news/archive/2016/06/stanford-sexual-assault-letters/485837/.
2. Superior Court of California, County of Santa Clara, *People v. Brock Allen Turner*, Felony Complaint, DA No. 150102055, filed January 28, 2015. This complaint and other documents are available at a website maintained by the *Los Angeles Times*, http://documents.latimes.com/stanford-brock-turner/.
3. Judge Persky, like most judges, relied heavily on the pre-sentencing report prepared by the probation officer assigned to Turner's case, which argued that the alcohol abuse mitigated Turner's culpability and predicted he was not likely to be a future danger to society. See Nick Anderson and Susan Svrluga, "In Stanford Sexual Assault Case, Probation Officer Recommended 'Moderate' Jail Term," *Washington Post*, June 10, 2016, https://www.washingtonpost.com/news/grade-point/wp/2016/06/10/probation-officers-report-for-brock-turners-sentencing/.
4. Ashley Fantz and Amanda Wills, "Stanford Rape Case: Who Is the Judge Who Gave Brock Turner 6 Months?," *CNN*, June 9, 2016, http://www.cnn.com/2016/06/08/us/aaron-persky-brock-turner-stanford-rape/.
5. Eliott C. McLaughlin, "One Million Sign Petition to Oust Judge in Brock Turner Case. Will It Matter?," *CNN*, June 10, 2016, http://www.cnn.com/2016/06/09/us/judge-aaron-persky-recall-petition-brock-turner-stanford-rape-trnd/.
6. Lindsey Bever, "'You took Away My Worth': A Sexual Assault Victim's Powerful Message to her Stanford Attacker," *Washington Post*, June 4, 2016, https://www.washingtonpost.com/news/early-lead/wp/2016/06/04/you-took-away-my-worth-a-rape-victim-delivers-powerful-message-to-a-former-stanford-swimmer/.

7. Emily Doe, victim impact statement, https://www.sccgov.org/sites/da/newsroom/newsreleases/Documents/B-Turner%20VIS.pdf.
8. "Read: Full Letter to the Judge by Dan Turner, Brock's Father," *Heavy*, June 8, 2016, http://heavy.com/news/2016/06/brock-turner-father-dad-dan-turner-full-letter-statement-stanford-rapist/. See also Michael E. Miller, "'A Steep Price to Pay for 20 Minutes of Action': Dad Defends Stanford Sex Offender," *Washington Post*, June 6, 2016, https://www.washingtonpost.com/news/morning-mix/wp/2016/06/06/a-steep-price-to-pay-for-20-minutes-of-action-dad-defends-stanford-sex-offender/
9. Aspen Matis, "'20 Minutes of Action' Is 20 Minutes for Brock Turner—For His Victim, It's a Lifetime," *Salon*, June 14, 2016, http://www.salon.com/2016/06/14/20_minutes_of_action_is_20_minutes_for_brock_turner_for_his_victim_its_a_lifetime/.
10. Margaret A. Farley, "The Role of Experience in Moral Discernment," in Margaret A. Farley, *Changing the Questions: Explorations in Christian Ethics*, ed. Jamie L. Manson (Maryknoll, NY: Orbis Books, 2015), 47–68, at 63.
11. As Farley notes: "If we are mistaken about the concrete reality of those for whom we care, then both our affective response and our caring actions can take mistaken forms." Margaret A. Farley, *Compassionate Respect: A Feminist Approach to Medical Ethics and Other Questions* (New York: Paulist Press, 2002), 33.
12. Ibid., 42.
13. "Again, while something is fundamentally contextual about the experience of embodiment, feminists have universalized bodily integrity as a reality and a value that ought not to be violated." Margaret A. Farley, "Feminism and Universal Morality," in Farley, *Changing the Questions*, 88–111, at 105.
14. Margaret A. Farley, "New Patterns of Relationship: Beginnings of a Moral Revolution," in Farley, *Changing the Questions*, 1–23, at 21.
15. Farley, *Compassionate Respect*, 37–38.
16. Elizabeth V. Spelman, *Fruits of Sorrow: Framing Our Attention to Suffering* (Boston, MA: Beacon Press, 1997).
17. Ibid., chap. 2, "Slavery and Tragedy," 34–58.
18. Ibid., chap. 5, "Changing the Subject: On Making Your Suffering Mine," 113–32.
19. Diana Tietjens Meyers, *Victims' Stories and the Advancement of Human Rights* (New York: Oxford University Press, 2016).
20. Ibid., chap. 1, "Two Victim Paradigms and the Problem of 'Impure' Victims," 26–64.
21. Emily Doe, victim impact statement.
22. Meyers, *Victims' Stories*, 60.
23. Ibid., 62.
24. Farley, *Compassionate Respect*, 79.
25. *Booth v. Maryland*, 482 U.S. 496, 502–503 (1987).
26. *South Carolina v. Gathers*, 490 U.S. 805, 812 (1989).
27. *Payne v. Tennessee*, 501 U.S. 808, (1991). *Booth* was a 5–4 decision: Justices Powell, Brennan, Marshall, Blackmun, and Stevens were in the majority, while Chief

Justice Rehnquist and Justices White, O'Connor, and Scalia dissented. *Payne* was decided in a 6–3 vote. The *Payne* majority comprised the four dissenting justices from *Booth*, along with more recently appointed justices Kennedy and Souter, who replaced Powell and Brennan. The dissent in *Payne* included Marshall, Blackmun, and Stevens—the three justices in the *Booth* majority still serving on the court.

28. Meyers, *Victims' Stories*, 154–56.
29. Ibid., 162.
30. Spelman, *Fruits of Sorrow*, 167.
31. Ibid., 132
32. Meyers, *Victims' Stories*, 63.
33. *Payne*, at 823–24.
34. *Payne*, at 814–15.
35. A well-known study of two thousand murder cases prosecuted by the state of Georgia in the 1970s showed that defendants convicted of killing white persons were more than four times more likely to be sentenced to death than those found guilty of killing black persons. David C. Baldus, Charles Pulaski, and George Woodworth, "Comparative Review of Death Sentences: An Empirical Study of the Georgia Experience," *Journal of Criminal Law and Criminology* 74, no. 3 (1983): 661–753.
36. See, e.g., Sonja B. Starr and M. Marit Rehavi, "Racial Disparity in Federal Criminal Sentences," *Journal of Political Economy* 122, no. 6 (2014): 1320–54.
37. *Booth*, at 507.
38. Aristotle, *On Rhetoric: A Theory of Civic Discourse*, trans. George A. Kennedy (New York: Oxford University Pres, 1991), book I, chap. 2.
39. *Booth*, at 505.
40. Meyers, *Victims' Stories*, chap. 2, "Narrative Structures, Narratives of Abuse, and Human Rights," 65–101.
41. Alasdair MacIntyre, *After Virtue*, 3rd ed. (Notre Dame, IN: University of Notre Dame Press, 2007), 193–96.
42. Reinhold Niebuhr, *Moral Man and Immoral Society: A Study in Ethics and Politics* (New York: Scribner, 1960).
43. John T. Noonan Jr., *Persons and Masks of the Law: Cardozo, Holmes, Jefferson, and Wythe as Makers of the Masks*, 2nd ed. (Berkeley: University of California Press, 2002), 19–28. See also John T. Noonan Jr., *Bribes* (New York: Macmillan, 1984), 61.
44. See, e.g., Irvin Waller, *Rights for Victims of Crime: Rebalancing Justice* (Lanham, MD: Rowman & Littlefield, 2011).
45. *Payne*, at 827, citing *Snyder v. Massachusetts*, 291 U.S. 97, 122 (1934) (citations omitted from quotation).
46. *Payne*, at 860 (Stevens, J., dissenting).
47. See, e.g., Elizabeth M. Schneider, *Battered Women and Feminist Lawmaking* (New Haven, CT: Yale University Press, 2000).

48. For an account of the efforts of Mothers Against Drunk Driving, as well as those who think their campaign is an overreaction, see Barron H. Lerner, *One for the Road: Drunk Driving Since 1900* (Baltimore, MD: Johns Hopkins University Press, 2011).
49. Waller, *Rights for Victims of Crime*, 108.
50. See, ibid., chap. 5, "Making Good the Loss: Reparation from Offender, State, and Civil Suits," 97–114.
51. Farley, *Compassionate Respect*, 75.
52. Ibid., 77–78.

CHAPTER 6

1. *Superintendent of Belchertown State School v. Joseph Saikewicz*, 370 N.E.2d 417, 431 (Mass. 1977).
2. *Saikewicz*, at 422.
3. Paul Ramsey, *Ethics at the Edges of Life: Medical and Legal Intersections* (New Haven, CT: Yale University Press, 1978), chap. 8, "The Strange Case of Joseph Saikewicz." See also his brief addendum, "The Final Decision in the Saikewicz Case," 335 (unpaginated).
4. Ibid., 304.
5. A sign of Ramsey's posthumous role in the culture wars is the use of his name by conservative combatants. For many years, the conservative monthly magazine *First Things* organized a "Ramsey Colloquium," which advanced religious and moral arguments against same-sex marriage and abortion and in favor of traditional Jewish and Christian sexual morality. The Center for Bioethics and Culture, which opposes most forms of artificial reproduction, as well as abortion, assisted suicide, and euthanasia, confers an annual "Paul Ramsey Award." The University of Notre Dame's Center for Ethics and Culture, which promotes a "culture of life" against a "culture of death," sponsors a "Paul Ramsey Fellow."
6. In my view, the best overview of Ramsey's extensive body of work is the "Introduction" by William Werpehowski and Stephen D. Crocco to the collection of Ramsey's writings that they co-edited. See Paul Ramsey, *The Essential Paul Ramsey: A Collection*, ed. William Werpehowski and Stephen D. Crocco (New Haven, CT: Yale University Press, 1994), vii–xxv. Particularly helpful on the themes discussed in this chapter is William Werpehowski, "Christian Love and Covenant Faithfulness," *Journal of Religious Ethics* 19, no. 2 (Fall 1991): 103–32.
7. Paul Ramsey, *Nine Modern Moralists* (Englewood Cliffs, NJ: Prentice-Hall, 1962). The chapters based on his NYU lectures are: "Jacques Maritain and Edmond Cahn: The Egypt of the Natural Law" (chap. 8) and "Jacques Maritain and Edmond Cahn: Man's Exodus from the Natural Law" (chap. 9).
8. Ibid., 5.
9. Ibid.

10. Ibid., 224.
11. Ibid., 217, quoting Jacques Maritain, *The Rights of Man and Natural Law* (New York: Scribner, 1943), 69.
12. Ibid., 224 (emphasis in original).
13. Ibid., quoting Edmond Cahn, *The Moral Decision: Right and Wrong in the Light of America Law* (Bloomington: Indiana University Press, 1955), 3.
14. Ibid., 226, quoting Edmond Cahn, *The Sense of Injustice* (New York: New York University Press, 1949), 6.
15. Ibid., 238.
16. Ibid.
17. Ibid., 236–38.
18. Ibid., 236. Ramsey writes on the same page: "It has to be said at once that only confusion can be the result of the *codification* of the revealed law of God . . . or for that matter the codification of any republished natural law, so long as the endeavor is made to bring these positive religious laws into *direct* relation to law-making in the modern age" (emphasis in original).
19. Ibid., 231 (emphasis in original).
20. Ibid., 244.
21. Paul Ramsey, *Christian Ethics and the Sit-In* (New York: Association Press, 1961); Paul Ramsey, *The Patient as Person: Explorations in Medical Ethics* (New Haven, CT: Yale University Press, 1970).
22. Paul Ramsey, "The Created Destination of Property Right," in Ramsey, *Christian Ethics and the Sit-In*, chap. 1, 17–39, at 25–26.
23. Ibid., 18.
24. Ibid., 21.
25. Ibid., 31 (emphasis in original).
26. Ibid., 37.
27. *Roe v. Wade*, 410 U.S. 113 (1973).
28. *Griswold v. Connecticut*, 381 U.S. 479 (1965).
29. *Eisenstadt v. Baird*, 405 U.S. 438 (1972).
30. *Planned Parenthood of Central Missouri v. Danforth*, 428 U.S. 52 (1976). Sixteen years later, the Supreme Court rejected the strict approach of *Danforth*, and permitted the states greater leeway in regulating abortion. See *Planned Parenthood v. Casey*, 505 U.S. 833 (1992). More recently, however, the Court has struck down some regulations for imposing an undue burden on a woman's right to seek a pre-viability abortion. See *Whole Woman's Health v. Hellerstedt*, 136 S.Ct. 2292 (2016).
31. Ramsey, *Ethics at the Edges of Life*, 42. The dissent Ramsey praises was authored by Byron White and joined by Warren Burger and William Rehnquist.
32. Ibid., 12.
33. Ibid., 139.
34. Ibid., 256.

35. Ibid., 34.
36. Ibid., chap. 2.
37. Quite strikingly, Ramsey also critically engages the concept of "cooperation with evil," which provides the Roman Catholic framework for assessing moral complicity. Ramsey argues that revisionist accounts of that concept that allow for more collaboration between Catholics and abortion providers are mistaken and even incoherent. Ibid., 80–93. Forty years later, the concept of "cooperation with evil" is at the center of debates about religious liberty and women's reproductive rights. Writing for the Court, Justice Samuel Alito invoked the concept in the course of deciding that the Religious Freedom Restoration Act required an exemption for closely held corporations objecting to providing contraception to employees. *Burwell v. Hobby Lobby Stores, Inc.*, 134 S.Ct. 2751, 2778n34 (2014). It was later invoked by Catholic religious orders in a similar lawsuit. See "Brief of 67 Catholic Theologians and Ethicists," http://www.becketfund.org/wp-content/uploads/2014/03/2014-03-03-67-Theologians-CA10-Amicus-LSP-v-Sebelius.pdf. (In my own view, the arguments in the brief are significantly flawed. See Cathleen Kaveny, "Law, Religion, and Conscience in a Pluralistic Society: The Case of the Little Sisters of the Poor," in *Conscience and Catholic Health Care: From Clinical Contexts to Government Mandates*, ed. David E. DeCosse and Thomas Nairn [Maryknoll, NY: Orbis, 2017], chap. 8.) The Supreme Court has now directed the parties to work out a mutually agreeable solution. *Zubick v. Burwell*, 136 S.Ct. 1557 (2016).
38. Ramsey, *Ethics at the Edges of Life*, 95.
39. In Ramsey's view, to argue that it harms some people to maintain their lives is to drastically alter fundamental tenets of Western morality. "[A]ll previous medical violations of the principle of 'do no harm,' all fallings short of a physician's covenant with his patient, all other departures from the *equality* of particular lives regardless of their state or condition, every past weakening of humanistic ethics, and all past practical atheisms that lost hold of the awesome claims of a human life and tried to rise above good and evil—all look puny by comparison." Ibid., 241.
40. Ibid., xv–xvi.
41. Ibid., xiii.
42. Pope John Paul II, *Evangelium vitae* [Encyclical on the Gospel of Life] (1995).
43. Ramsey, *Ethics at the Edges of Life*, 296 (emphasis in original).
44. *U.S. v. Holmes*, 26 F. Cas. 360 (C.C.E.D. Pa. 1842).
45. Ramsey, *Nine Modern Moralists*, 245–51.
46. Ibid., 249.
47. Ibid., 250.
48. Ibid., 251.
49. Ibid., 254. Ramsey is also speaking of lot-casting in the context of a dangerous pregnancy demanding the choice of mother or child.

50. The passage is from Reinhold Niebuhr, *The Children of Light and the Children of Darkness* (New York: Scribner, 1949), xi. On Ramsey's use of it in various contexts, see William Werpehowski and Stephen D. Crocco, "Introduction," in Ramsey, *The Essential Paul Ramsey*, xxi–xxii.
51. Paul Ramsey, *The Patient as Person*, 6.
52. Ramsey, *Christian Ethics and the Sit-In*, 20.
53. Ramsey, *The Patient as Person*, chap. 1, "Consent as a Canon of Loyalty with Special Reference to Children in Medical Investigations."
54. Ibid., 9.
55. Ibid., 14.
56. Richard A. McCormick, S.J., was Ramsey's most important interlocutor on the question of nontherapeutic research on children. For an overview of the debate, see Albert R. Johnsen, "Nontherapeutic Research with Children: The Ramsey versus McCormick Debate," *Journal of Pediatrics* 149, no. 1 (Suppl.; July 2006): S12–S14.
57. Ramsey, *The Patient as Person*, 7.
58. Ramsey, *Ethics at the Edges of Life*, 156–66. In *The Patient as Person*, Ramsey treats the consent requirement in the case of competent patients as something that "holds without exception for ordinary medical practice" (7). In *Ethics at the Edges of Life*, he worries that the requirement "enthrones . . . an arbitrary freedom" (157). See also pp. 197–98n15: "To date both Western law and morality favor pro-life decisions—unless one refuses treatment for oneself, and that too reaches its moral limit at suicidal refusals of ordinary treatment."
59. Ramsey, *Ethics at the Edges of Life*,chap. 1.
60. Ibid., chap. 3.
61. Ibid., chaps. 4–9.
62. Ibid., chap. 4.
63. Ibid., 317.
64. Cathleen Kaveny, *Law's Virtues* (Washington, DC: Georgetown University Press, 2012).
65. Margaret A. Farley, *Changing the Questions: Explorations in Christian Ethics*, ed. Jamie L. Manson (Maryknoll, NY: Orbis Books, 2015).
66. Other scholars also omitted any discussion of the scandals at Belchertown State School. See, e.g., "The Incompetent's Right to Die: The Case of Joseph Saikewicz," *Hastings Center Report* 8, no. 1 (February 1978): 21–23. John J. Paris, S.J., is a notable exception: in his article on the case, he detailed the steps taken by the school to consult with specialists, noting that "[t]here is no question that the staff was concerned with Saikewicz's welfare." John J. Paris, S.J., "Withholding of Life-Supporting Treatment from the Mentally Incompetent," *Linacre Quarterly* 45, no. 3 (August 1978): 237–48.
67. Robert Hornick, *The Girls and Boys of Belchertown: A Social History of the Belchertown State School for the Feeble-Minded* (Amherst, MA: University of Massachusetts

Press, 2012), 84, citing James Shanks, "The Tragedy of Belchertown," *Springfield (Mass.) Sunday Republican*, March 15, 1970. This was the Sunday edition of the *Springfield Union*.

68. Ibid., 86, citing Shanks, "The Tragedy of Belchertown."
69. Ibid., 104–116. The lawsuit was *Ricci v. Greenblatt*, Civil Action #72-469-T (U.S. Dist. Ct. Mass.). The plaintiffs contended that the conditions at the school violated statutory and constitutional rights of the residents, including the right to adequate care and treatment.
70. Benjamin Ricci was a tireless advocate for the mentally handicapped. See Ricci's book about his struggles to improve the conditions at Belchertown State School: Benjamin Ricci, *Crimes Against Humanity: A Historical Perspective* (Lincoln, NE: iUniverse, 2004).
71. Hornick, *The Girls and Boys of Belchertown*, 113, citing Joan Axelrod-Contrada, "Resort Spa May Replace Closed State Institution, *Boston Globe*, February 11, 2006.
72. After parents of children at other state facilities brought suit, the consent decrees were later expanded to cover five Massachusetts facilities for the mentally retarded: Belchertown, Wrentham, Dever, and Fernald State Schools, as well as the Monson Development Center. A good overview of the litigation can be found at "Ricci v. Okin," Civil Rights Litigation Clearinghouse, University of Michigan Law School, http://www.clearinghouse.net/detail.php?id=454.
73. Hornick, *The Girls and Boys of Belchertown*, 126.
74. Beth Schwartzapfel, "The Judge," *Brown Alumni Magazine*, January/February 2015, http://www.brownalumnimagazine.com/content/view/3838/40/.
75. Hornick, *The Girls and Boys of Belchertown*, 4–5.
76. Ibid., 70–71.
77. John F. Kennedy Presidential Library and Museum, "John F. Kennedy and People with Intellectual Disabilities," https://www.jfklibrary.org/JFK/JFK-in-History/JFK-and-People-with-Intellectual-Disabilities.aspx.
78. Hornick, *The Girls and Boys of Belchertown*, 117–18.
79. Ibid., 119–27.
80. Ramsey, *The Patient as Person*, 155, quoting Karl Barth, *Church Dogmatics* 3/4, ed. G. W. Bromiley and T. F. Torrance, trans. A. T. Mckay et al. (Edinburgh: T. & T. Clark, 1961), 427.

CHAPTER 7

1. Thomas L. Shaffer, "The Christian Jurisprudence of Robert E. Rodes, Jr.," *Notre Dame Law Review* 73, no. 3 (1998): 737–72, 738, quoting a recorded conversation of the symposium on March 25, 1995.
2. Robert E. Rodes Jr., *Pilgrim Law* (Notre Dame, IN: University of Notre Dame Press 1998), 11.
3. Ibid., 11–12.

4. For example, Rodes's understanding of the way in which social structures, including legal structures, ought to incorporate an "option for the poor" is deeply influence by socialist political philosophy; see Milovan Djilas, *The New Class: An Analysis of the Communist System* (New York: Praeger, 1957); it was also influenced by Christian liberation theology; see Gustavo Gutiérrez, *A Theology of Liberation: History, Politics, and Salvation* (Maryknoll, NY: Orbis Books, 1973).
5. Most impressively, he has produced a massive and detailed historical study of the established church in England, which has given him a tremendous factual background upon which to draw in formulating his own normative reflections on the relationship of the church and society, particularly as that relationship is instantiated through the law, both civil and canonical. See Robert E. Rodes Jr., *This House I Have Built: A Study of the Legal History of Establishment in England,* a three volume series: *Ecclesiastical Administration in Medieval England: The Anglo-Saxons to the Reformation* (Notre Dame, IN: University of Notre Dame Press,1977); *Lay Authority and Reformation in the English Church: Edward I to the Civil War* (Notre Dame, IN: University of Notre Dame Press, 1982); and *Law and Modernization in the Church of England: Charles I to the Welfare State* (Notre Dame, IN: University of Notre Dame Press, 1991).
6. See, e.g., Robert E. Rodes Jr., "What O'Clock I Say: Juridical Epistemics and the Magisterium of the Church," *Journal of Law and Religion* 14, no. 2 (1999–2000): 285–311; Robert E. Rodes Jr., "On Juridical Elements in Theology," *Louvain Studies* 28, no. 2 (2003): 113–42.
7. Rodes, "On Juridical Elements in Theology," 114.
8. Rodes, "What O'Clock I Say," 286.
9. Rodes, *Pilgrim Law,* 6–10.
10. Ibid., 140–43.
11. *Obergefell v. Hodges,* 576 U.S. ___, 135 S. Ct. 2584 (2015).
12. Rodes, "On Juridical Elements in Theology," 122.
13. Ibid.
14. Ibid.
15. Ibid., 125.
16. Ibid., 123.
17. Ibid.
18. Ibid., 130.
19. Ibid.
20. Ibid.
21. Ibid., 131.
22. Ibid.
23. Ibid., 131–32.
24. Ibid., 123.
25. Ibid.
26. Ibid., 125.

27. Ibid., 126.
28. Ibid.
29. Ibid.
30. Ibid., 126–27.
31. Rodes, *Pilgrim Law*, 6–7.
32. Ibid., 7.
33. Ibid., 6.
34. Ibid.
35. Rodes notes that a good example of such harmony is civil rights legislation. "The same statutes and judicial decisions that produced injunctions, contempt citations, reinstatement with back pay, and cease and desist orders made people who practiced discrimination with impunity ashamed of themselves or at least defensive; made victims of discrimination assertive; encouraged people who believed in equality to make their presence felt; and brought home the moral objections to discrimination to people who had not previously thought about the matter one way or the other." Ibid., 7.
36. Ibid.
37. Ibid., 8.
38. Ibid.
39. Ibid., 9.
40. Rodes describes the origin of this label in the following way: "The vision of the church as sharing the historical vicissitudes of the rest of society I call Erastian. Erastus (1524–83) was a Swiss theologian who taught that the church had no proper coercive jurisdiction independent of the civil magistrate. His name became attached to those Anglicans who were content with the substantial role played by Crown and Parliament in the affairs of their church." Ibid., 141.
41. Robert E. Rodes Jr., "Pluralist Christendom and the Christian Civil Magistrate," *Capital University Law Review* 8, no. 3 (1979): 413–28, at 418.
42. Rodes, *Pilgrim Law*, 141.
43. Ibid., 142.
44. Ibid.
45. Rodes notes that "[t]he term was originally applied to those Anglicans who saw the polity and autonomy of the church as divinely established, or who stressed the sacramental and liturgical aspects of the Christian life rather than the personal and evangelical aspects." Ibid., 141.
46. Ibid.
47. Ibid., 142.
48. Rodes, "Pluralist Christendom," 418.
49. Rodes, *Pilgrim Law*, 143.
50. For a succinct summary of the influence of Djilas on Rodes's work, see Schaffer, "The Christian Jurisprudence of Robert E. Rodes, Jr.," 742–46.

51. Rodes, *Pilgrim Law*, 153.
52. Ibid., 153–54.
53. Ibid., 157.
54. Ibid., 154.
55. Thomas Aquinas, *Summa Theologica*, trans. Fathers of the English Dominican Province (New York: Benzinger Bros., 1947–48), I-II, q. 91, art. 1.
56. Ibid., I-lI, q. 91, art. 2.
57. Ibid., I-II, q. 95.
58. Ibid.
59. Rodes, "Pluralist Christendom," 417.
60. It seems to me that the position of Anthony Fisher, O.P., now the Archbishop of Sydney, Australia, reflects this sensitivity to the moral stance of the broader culture. See Anthony Fisher, O.P., "Cooperation in Evil: Understanding the Issues," in Helen Watt, ed., *Cooperation, Complicity and Conscience: Problems in Healthcare, Science, Law and Public Policy* (London: Linacre Centre, 2005), 27–64.
61. As a technical term of moral theology, "cooperation with evil" is generally used to describe a situation in which one agent (the "cooperator") faces a situation in which his or her act will somehow contribute, in a subordinate way, to a morally unacceptable action plan designed and controlled by someone else (the "principal agent"). For a good introduction to the categories of the matrix used by traditional moralists, see Anthony Fisher, "Co-operation in Evil," *Catholic Medical Quarterly* 44, no. 3 (February 1994): 15–22.
62. Compare Fisher, "Cooperation with Evil: Understanding the Issues," with M. Cathleen Kaveny, "Tax Lawyers, Prophets, and Pilgrims: A Response to Anthony Fisher," in Helen Watt, ed., *Cooperation, Complicity and Conscience: Problems in Healthcare, Science, Law and Public Policy* (London: Linacre Center, 2005), 65–88. In Rodes's terms, Bishop Fisher could be understood as adopting more of a High Church approach to cooperation with evil, while I could be seen as adopting more of an Erastian approach to the question of cooperation with evil.
63. For a modified Erastian viewpoint that makes this argument, see Mary Ann Glendon, *Abortion and Divorce in Western Law: American Failures, European Challenges* (Cambridge, MA: Harvard University Press, 1987), chap. 3.
64. For a passionate High Church viewpoint that makes this argument, see Colin Harte, *Changing Unjust Laws Justly: Pro-Life Solidarity with the "Last and Least"* (Washington, DC: Catholic University of America Press, 2005).
65. Patricia Wen, "Archdiocesan Agency Aids in Adoptions by Gays," *Boston Globe*, October 22, 2005, A1.
66. Ibid.
67. Agencies that provide adoption services need a license from the Massachusetts Department of Early Education and Care. 102 Mass. Code. Regs. 1.03 (1) (2005)

provided that "[t]he licensee shall not discriminate in providing services to children and their families on the basis of race, religion, cultural heritage, political beliefs, national origin, marital status, sexual orientation or disability. A statement that the program does not discriminate on these bases shall be made part of the written statement of purpose where required." Operating without a license was not an option. §1.03 (2) provides: "No persons shall operate or purport to operate a program licensable by the Office of Child Care Services without a license or approval issued by the Office."

68. Congregation for the Doctrine of the Faith, *Considerations Regarding Proposals to Give Legal Recognition to Unions Between Homosexual Persons*, June 3, 2003, www.vatican.va/roman_curia/congregations/cfaith/documents/rc_con_cfaith_doc_20030731_homosexual-unions_en.html. See part III, §7, para. 3:

> As experience has shown, the absence of sexual complementarity in these [homosexual] unions creates obstacles in the normal development of children who would be placed in the care of such persons. They would be deprived of the experience of either fatherhood or motherhood. Allowing children to be adopted by persons living in such unions would actually mean doing violence to these children, in the sense that their condition of dependency would be used to place them in an environment that is not conducive to their full human development. This is gravely immoral and in open contradiction to the principle, recognized also in the United Nations Convention on the Rights of the Child, that the best interests of the child, as the weaker and more vulnerable party, are to be the paramount consideration in every case.

69. Patricia Wen, "Church Reviews Role in Gay Adoptions," *Boston Globe*, November 4, 2005, B2.

70. Statement of the Massachusetts Catholic Conference on Behalf of Archbishop Seán P. O'Malley (Boston), Bishop George W. Coleman (Fall River), Bishop Timothy A. McDonnell (Springfield), and Bishop Robert J. McManus (Worcester), February 28, 2006, available at www.bostoncatholic.org/uploadedFiles/News_releases_2006_statement060228.pdf. The key paragraph reads as follows:

> Because of the Church's teaching, Catholic agencies may not provide adoptions to same sex couples. Hence we intend to seek relief from the regulatory requirements of the Commonwealth on this issue. We do this in the hope that we will be able to continue focusing our attention on serving children in need of adoption, and to do so in a way which does not conflict with Catholic teaching and practice. We are asking the Commonwealth to respect the Constitutional guarantee of religious freedom and allow the Catholic Church to continue serving children in need of adoption without violating the tenets of our faith.

71. Patricia Wen, "Seven Quit Charity Over Policy of Bishops," *Boston Globe*, March 2, 2006, A1. Later, an eighth member resigned as well. Patricia Wen, "In Break from Romney, Healey Raps Gay Adoption Exclusion," *Boston Globe*, March 3, 2006, B4.

72. Patricia Wen, "Bishops Dealt Setback in Pursuit of Gay Adoption Exemption," *Boston Globe*, February 17, 2006, B3.
73. Patricia Wen, "Bishops' Gay Ban May Cost Millions: Private Donors Wary of Adoption Policy," *Boston Globe*, March 5, 2006, A1.
74. Patricia Wen, "Catholic Charities Stuns State, Ends Adoptions," *Boston Globe*, March 11, 2006, A1.
75. J. Bryan Hehir and Jeffrey Kaneb, Statement of Catholic Charities, Archdiocese of Boston, On Adoption Programs, March 10, 2006, http://www.bostoncatholic.org/uploadedFiles/News_releases_2006_statement060310-2.pdf.
76. Viewed from a financial perspective, adoption services constituted only a small portion of the portfolio of Boston Catholic Charities. In the fiscal year 2005, its total revenue was $37 million; its reimbursement for adoption services was only $1 million. "Catholic Charities of Boston to Discontinue Adoption Services," March 10, 2006, http://www.bostoncatholic.org/uploadedFiles/News_releases_2006_statement060310-1.pdf.
77. Patricia Wen, "'They Cared for the Children': Amid Shifting Social Winds, Catholic Charities Prepares to End its 103 Years of Finding Homes for Foster Children and Evolving Families," *Boston Globe*, June 25, 2006, A1.
78. "A Globe Conversation with Archbishop O'Malley," transcript, *Boston Globe Question*, March 19, 2006, www.boston.com/news/local/massachusetts/articles/2006/03/19/omalley_transcript/.
79. *Goodridge v. Mass. Dept. Pub. Health*, 798 N.E.2d 941 (Mass. 2003).
80. From this perspective, same-sex marriage is not so much wrong as *impossible*—a contradiction in terms. See, e.g., William E. May, "On the Impossibility of Same-Sex Marriage: A Review of Catholic Teaching," *National Catholic Bioethics Quarterly* 4, no. 2 (2004): 303–16.
81. Editorial, "Abandoned Children," *Commonweal*, March 24, 2006, 5. It claims that "[b]oth the bishops and the Massachusetts legislature are wrong"—the legislature for not granting an exemption to Catholic Charities in the first instance, and Catholic Charities for not continuing to provide adoption services despite the refusal of the exemption.
82. Rodes, *Pilgrim Law*, 12–13.
83. Ibid.

CHAPTER 8

1. Pope Francis, *Amoris laetitia* [Apostolic Exhortation on Love in the Family] (2016).
2. Joshua J. McElwee, "Francis: 'New Concrete Possibilities' for Remarried after Family Exortation, *National Catholic Reporter*, April 16, 2016, http://ncronline.org/news/vatican/francis-new-concrete-possibilities-remarried-after-family-exhortation.

3. Gerald O'Connell, "'Amoris Laetitia' Represents an Organic Development of Doctrine, 'Nota Rupture,'" *America*, April 8, 2016, http://americamagazine.org/content/dispatches/pope-francis-exhortation-family-organic-development-doctrine.
4. "Cardinal Baldisseri's Intervention at Presentation of Amoris Laetitia," *Zenit*, April 8, 2016, https://zenit.org/articles/cardinal-baldisseris-intervention-at-presentation-of-amoris-laetitia/. Baldisseri is citing Pope Francis, *Evangelii gaudium* [Encyclical on the Joy of the Gospel], §§ 222–25, and Pope Francis, *Amoris laetitia*, §3, §261.
5. Ibid. Baldisseri is citing *Amoris laetitia*, § 297.
6. See, e.g., David Gibson, "Cardinal Kasper is the 'Pope's Theologian,'" *National Catholic Reporter*, June 3, 2014, http://ncronline.org/news/vatican/cardinal-kasper-popes-theologian.
7. Walter Kasper, *Mercy: The Essence of the Gospel and the Key to Christian Life*, trans. William Madges (New York: Paulist Press, 2013), 9.
8. Ibid., 45.
9. Ibid., 55. See also page 56: "Thus, God's mercy is the power of God that sustains, protects, promotes, builds up, and creates life anew. It burst the logic of human injustice, which entails the punishment and death of the sinner. God's mercy desires life. In fidelity to the covenant with his people, God mercifully reestablishes the relationship with him that was destroyed by sin and he grants dependable living conditions anew. Mercy is God's option for life."
10. Ibid., 83. Kasper argues that mercy is a mirror of the self-communicative love of the Trinity. Ibid., 91–97.
11. Ibid., 89. Needless to say, working out the relationship of mercy and justice is extremely difficult. Justice is generally defined as giving each person is her due, of respecting the moral fundamental order of the world. Yet it is also a virtue oriented toward the common good of the community. Divine mercy, one might say, is the quality by which God enables sinners to continue to exist, in a situation where justice, by itself, would call for their destruction as punishment for their sins.
12. Ibid., 97.
13. Ibid., 109.
14. Ibid., 157.
15. Pope John Paul II, *Dives in misericordia* [Encyclical, Rich in Mercy] (1980).
16. Kasper, *Mercy*, 159.
17. Ibid., 169.
18. Ibid., 179.
19. Ibid., 177.
20. Ibid., 180.
21. Walter Kasper, *The Gospel of the Family* (New York: Paulist Press, 2014). This is his lecture to the extraordinary consistory of cardinals on the topic of family life, which took place February 20–21, 2014, in Vatican City.

22. Ibid., 25.
23. Ibid., 26.
24. Ibid.
25. Ibid.
26. Ibid., 29.
27. Ibid., 30.
28. Ibid., 31.
29. Ibid., 32.
30. Ibid.
31. See, e.g., Samuel Gregg, "Cardinal Kasper, Communion, and Divorce—Again," *Catholic World Report*, June 4, 2014, www.catholicworldreport.com/Item/3173/cardinal_kasper_communion_and_divorceagain.aspx; "Cardinal Caffarra Expresses Serious Concerns About Family Synod DeBates," *Zenit*, March 24, 2014, www.zenit.org/en/articles/cardinal-caffarra-expresses-serious-concerns-about-family-synod-debates; Robert Spaemann, "Divorce and Remarriage," *First Things*, August/September 2014; and John Corbett, O.P., et al., "Recent Proposals for the Pastoral Care of the Divorced and Remarried: A Theological Assessment," *Nova et Vetera* 12, no. 3 (2014): 601–30.
32. The definition of "adultery" in the *Catechism of the Catholic Church* focuses on the sexual component of the act. Yet there is precedent in both the Catholic moral tradition and in the legal traditions of the West for the developments of more nuanced understandings of the wrong targeted by specific moral prohibitions. We no longer view adultery as a property crime, for example.
33. See, e.g., James Fitzjames Stephen, *A History of the Criminal Law of England*, 3 vols. (London: Macmillan, 1883). For a brief overview, see Charles E. Moylan Jr., "A Brief History of Criminal Homicide and its Exponential Proliferation," in *Criminal Homicide Law* (Baltimore: Maryland Institute for Continuing Professional Education of Lawyers, 2002), chap. 2. For an account of how factors that initially triggered a sovereign's pardon (a concept related to but not identical with mercy) were incorporated into nuanced systems of justice, see Kathleen Dean Moore, *Pardons: Justice, Mercy, and the Public Interest* (New York: Oxford University Press, 1989).
34. William H. Theis, "The Double Jeopardy Defense and Multiple Prosecutions for Conspiracy," *Southern Methodist University Law Review* 49, no. 2 (1996): 269–307. See also Jeffrey M. Chemerinsky, "Counting Offenses," *Duke Law Journal* 58, no. 4 (2009): 709–46, to whom these examples are indebted.
35. Theis, "Double Jeopardy Defense," 280, citing *Commonwealth v. Robinson*, 126 Mass. 259 (1879), which held that keeping a tavern is a single continuing offense.
36. *In re Snow*, 120 U.S. 274 (1887); see Theis, "Double Jeopardy Defense," 280–81.
37. *In re Nielsen*, 131 U.S. 176 (1889); see Theis, "Double Jeopardy Defense," 280–81.
38. There is a separate question about the status of the second marriage, as legitimating sexual activity. Fully addressing this question is beyond the scope of this

chapter. I think it is possible to say that after a civil divorce from a sacramental marriage, it is possible for a man or woman to enter into a new, natural (not sacramental) marriage, in which a sexual relationship is morally permissible.

39. See the helpful analysis in Jeffrey R. Boles, "Easing the Tension between Statutes of Limitations and the Continuing Offense Doctrine," *Northwestern Journal of Law and Social Policy* 7, no. 2 (2012): 219–56. I am deeply indebted to his article for both for his own insights and his valuable collection of sources and citations, which I draw upon in this chapter.
40. *United States v. Yashar*, 166 F.3d 873, 875 (1999), quoting *Toussie v. United States*, 397 U.S. 112 at 122.
41. *United States v. McGoff*, 831 F.2d 1071, 1079 (D.C. Cir. 1987).
42. Boles, "Easing the Tension," 225.
43. *Toussie v. United States*, 397 U.S. 112 (1970).
44. As the *Toussie* dissent notes, most courts had previously considered draft evasion to be a continuing offense.
45. Boles argues that the *Toussie* test should be refined to direct courts to investigate whether each element of the crime continuously causes harm. Boles, "Easing the Tension," 253–55.
46. *United States v. Garcia*, 854 F.2d 340, 343, quoting *Parnell v. Superior Court*, 173 Cal. Rptr. 906, 915 (Ct. App. 1981).
47. As Bole notes, not all lower courts have applied the *Toussie* test in this manner; see his essay for an account of cases taking the less adequate approach.
48. *United States v. De La Mata*, 266 F.3d 1275 (11th Cir. 2001).
49. *De La Mata*, at 1289.
50. In fact, modern case law dealing with bigamy appears to be moving in that direction. In 1991, a military court found that bigamy was *not* a continuing offense. "We hold that, under the allegations contained in the pleadings of this case, the bigamy offense ... is not a continuing offense ..." *United States v. Lee*, 32 M.J. 857, 861 (1991). Instead it was an on offense that took place at the time the second marriage was solemnized. Most American states also do not treat bigamy as a continuing offense. See, e.g., *People v. Hess*, 146 N.Y.S.2d 210, 211 (App. Div. 1955), where the New York appellate court reaffrimed that "bigamy is not a continuing offense; the crime is committed the instant the second ceremonial marriage is consummated" (citation omitted). Consequently, the court held that "a person is not guilty of bigamy because he lives in this State with the partner to an illegal second marriage contracted elsewhere."
51. The key synoptic texts are: Matt. 5:31–32 and Luke 16:18 (the Q tradition), as well as Mark 10:2–12. See also Matt. 19:1–9 and 1 Cor. 7:10–11.
52. I am indebted to John P. Meier, *A Marginal Jew: Rethinking the Historical Jesus*, vol. 4, *Law and Love* (New Haven, CT: Yale University Press, 2009). His bibliography is exhaustive.

53. Ibid., 126.
54. Ibid., 106.
55. Ibid., 110.
56. Mark 10:1–2.
57. Mark 10:3–9.
58. Meier believes that this contest story is "a literary and theological creation of Mark, welded together out of various traditions and motifs and shaped by Mark's theological agenda and literary style." Meier, *Law and Love*, 123.
59. John 4:1–42.
60. John 4:16–18.
61. John 4:23–24.
62. John 4:39.
63. John 8:1–11.
64. John 8:7.
65. John 8:11.
66. Matt. 22:37–40.
67. John T. Noonan Jr., *Power to Dissolve: Lawyers and Marriages in the Courts of the Roman Curia* (Cambridge, MA: Belknap Press of Harvard University Press, 1972).
68. Matt. 5:32.
69. 1 Cor. 7:15.

CHAPTER 9

1. Gal. 3:10.
2. Gal. 3:21.
3. After the Reformation, St. Paul tended to be pervasively misread as a proto-Lutheran. Recent scholarship has corrected this misreading by situating him in his own historical and social context of late Second Temple Judaism. See, e.g., E. P. Sanders, *Paul, the Law, and the Jewish People* (Philadelphia, PA: Fortress Press, 1983); and Markus Bockmuehl, *Jewish Law in Gentile Churches: Halakhah and the Beginning of Christian Public Ethics* (Grand Rapids, MI: Baker Academic, 2003).
4. I will focus on the following works: H. Tristram Engelhardt, Jr. *The Foundations of Christian Bioethics* (Lisse: Swets & Zeitlinger, 2000); and Germain Grisez, *Christian Moral Principles*, vol. 1 of *The Way of the Lord Jesus* (Quincy, IL: Franciscan Press, 1983); *Living a Christian Life*, vol. 2 of *The Way of the Lord Jesus* (Quincy, IL: Franciscan Press, 1993); and *Difficult Moral Questions*, vol. 3 of *The Way of the Lord Jesus* (Quincy, IL: Franciscan Press, 1997).
5. Thomas Aquinas, *Summa Theologica*, trans. Fathers of the English Dominican Province (Westminster, MD: Christian Classics, 1981), I-II, q. 90, a. 4 (emphasis added). I draw more broadly on Aquinas's understanding of the nature, purpose, and limits of law in Cathleen Kaveny, *Law's Virtues: Fostering Autonomy and*

Solidarity in American Society (Washington, DC: Georgetown University Press, 2012).

6. Ibid., I-II, q. 90, a. 1.
7. Ibid.
8. Ibid., I-II, q. 90, a. 1.
9. Ibid.
10. Ibid., rep. ob. 3.
11. Ibid., I-II, q. 90, a. 2.
12. Ibid., I-II, q. 90, a. 3.
13. Ibid.
14. Ibid., I-II, q. 90, a. 3, rep. ob. 2.
15. Ibid., I-II, q. 90, a. 4.
16. Ibid.
17. Engelhardt, *The Foundations of Christian Bioethics*, xiii.
18. Ibid., xi–xii.
19. Ibid., 127–29.
20. For an overview, see Janine Marie Idziak, *Divine Command Morality: Historical and Contemporary Readings* (New York: Edwin Mellen Press, 1979); Philip L. Quinn, *Divine Commands and Moral Requirements* (Oxford: Clarendon Press, 1978); and Paul Helm, ed., *Divine Commands and Morality* (New York: Oxford University Press, 1981). See also Richard J. Mouw, *The God Who Commands: A Study in Divine Command Ethics* (Notre Dame, IN: University of Notre Dame Press, 1991).
21. Aquinas, *Summa Theologica*, II-II, q. 64, a. 6, rep. ob. 1.
22. Grisez, *Christian Moral Principles*, 12–13.
23. Ibid., 13.
24. Engelhardt, *The Foundations of Christian Bioethics*, 174.
25. Ibid., 176.
26. Grisez, *Christian Moral Principles*, 15.
27. Engelhardt, *The Foundations of Christian Bioethics*, 163.
28. Ibid., 209.
29. Ibid., 278.
30. Ibid., 279–80.
31. Ibid., 279.
32. Grisez, *Christian Moral Principles*, 299. The manualists tended to describe the object of the agent's action from a purely external perspective. They also considered the timing of the two effects to be significant; if the undesired effect precedes the desired effect, they considered it to be a means to the desired effect.
33. Engelhardt, *The Foundations of Christian Bioethics*, 180.
34. Grisez, *Christian Moral Principles*, 580–86.
35. Ibid., 597n24.

36. Ibid., 606–609.
37. Ibid., 31, citing Henricus Denzinger and Adolfus Schönmetzer, S.I., *Enchiridion symbolorum definitionum et declarationum de rebus fidei et morum*, 34th ed. (Freiburg in Breisgau: Herder, 1967), 3016/1796.
38. Grisez, *Christian Moral Principles*, 31.
39. Ibid., 27–31.
40. Ibid., 7.
41. Mark Brumley, "Germain Grisez Explains It All (Well, Almost)," *The Catholic Faith*, March–April 1999.
42. Grisez, *Christian Moral Principles*, 831–35, 861–63.
43. Vatican II, *Gaudium et spes* [Pastoral Constitution on the Church in the Modern World] (1965), para. 26.
44. Jacques Maritain, *The Rights of Man and Natural Law*, in Jacques Maritain, *Christianity and Democracy and The Rights of Man and Natural Law* (New York: Scribner, 1943), 8–9.
45. Aquinas does come disturbingly close to the notion of sacrificing one to save many in the case of a guilty person. He justifies the killing of wicked individuals by analogy to the situation in which one cuts off a gangrenous limb in order to save the body as a whole. See Aquinas, *Summa Theologica*, II-II, q. 64, a. 3.
46. *Watts v. Watts*, 405 N. W.2d 303 (Wis. 1987).
47. Engelhardt, *The Foundations of Christian Bioethics*, 171.
48. Ibid., 169.
49. Ibid., 209: "Persons are central. Moral principles are at best chapter headings and rules of thumb. Too much attention to general principles can even divert attention from the personal character of the communion with God to which all theology and all bioethics should lead."
50. Grisez, *Christian Moral Principles*, 1–2.
51. Ibid., 56–58.
52. Ibid., 155.
53. Ibid.
54. Ibid.
55. Ibid., 329.
56. I am extrapolating from Engelhardt, *The Foundations of Christian Bioethics*, 237.
57. Ibid., 173.
58. Ibid., 6.
59. Ibid., 144–48.
60. Grisez, *Christian Moral Principles*, 18–19.
61. Ibid., 871.
62. Grisez would no doubt acknowledge that in other circumstances, of course, these features of legalism could generate rigorism: the web of rules fixing the

moral life could conceivably be large, not small; changes in the teaching of the church could be more restrictive, not less restrictive.

63. On the basic question is whether the person is bound by law or free to do as he or she pleases, see, e.g., Grisez, *Christian Moral Principles*, 13, 86–87, 293–94, 304–305, 370, 375, and 514. See also Grisez, *Living a Christian Life*, 9, 34, 250–51, 535, 544, 672, and 876. In Grisez, *Difficult Moral Questions*, see xvii, xxv, 44, 250, 452, 607–608, and 645. On the idea that moral rules are changeable laws rather than unchangeable truths, see, e.g., Grisez, *Christian Moral Principles*, 13, 21–22, 74, 85, 101, 107, 154, 283, 382. See also Grisez, *Living a Christian Life*, 249.

Grisez believes that many people today pick and choose from a legalistic world view, in order further to minimize their moral responsibilities. (Grisez, *Christian Moral Principles*, 307). By contrast, I have found only two places where Grisez interprets legalism as the use of authority to impose a morally unjustified burden: *Christian Moral Principles*, 535–36 (discussing Jesus's interaction with the Pharisees), and *Difficult Moral Questions*, 64–68 (tithing).

64. Grisez, *Christian Moral Principles*, 13.
65. Ibid., xxix.
66. Engelhardt, *The Foundations of Christian Bioethics*, 6.
67. See, e.g., ibid., 170: "Only if truth veridically communicates with us can we break out of the horizon of immanence."
68. See, e.g., ibid., 179–80: "Because the goal par excellence of human life is holiness, union with God, then the moral life, the keeping of the commandments, the acquisition of virtue, along with the articulation of a Christian bioethics, are not ends in themselves. They are means to carry us to the other side of natural knowledge." Grisez would not deny that these things are means to that end; he would emphasize that they are constitutive means, and not instrumental means. Consequently, we cannot legitimately decide to follow them or depart from them on a case-by-case basis.
69. Ibid., 203.
70. John T. Noonan Jr., *Persons and Masks of the Law: Cardozo, Holmes, Jefferson, and Wythe as Makers of the Masks*, 2nd ed. (Berkeley: University of California Press, 2002), 18.
71. See, e.g., Engelhardt, *The Foundations of Christian Bioethics*, 283–84.
72. Ibid., 277.
73. Grisez would say that no action taken with the intent of destroying the baby is ever justified, even to save the mother. However, some actions which foreseeably result in the death of the baby are allowable for this purpose, if the purpose is not to kill the baby, under the principle of double effect. Grisez, *Living a Christian Life*, 499–507. As noted, Engelhardt rejects the principle of double effect as a legalistic strategy used to evade responsibility.
74. Engelhardt, *The Foundations of Christian Bioethics*, 278, 325–27.

75. See ibid., 284: "The Church is uncompromising in her demand that we open our hearts to God, that we become perfect, that we become saints. She is therapeutic in her approach to making us perfect. She recognizes that she must begin by treating us where she finds us in our sins."
76. Ibid., 274.
77. Ibid., 267.
78. Ibid., 267–68.
79. Ibid., 299n101.
80. Ibid., 300n102.
81. Ibid. Engelhardt clearly thinks that some moral prohibitions function as "real moral boundaries" (ibid., 236) while other prohibitions are more flexible. Grisez would no doubt press him to articulate more fully the distinction between the two categories.
82. Grisez, *Christian Moral Principles*, 684–85.
83. Ibid., 297.
84. Germain Grisez, "The Unsoundness of Synod 2015's 'New Way,'" *The Catholic World Report*, December 7, 2015, http://www.catholicworldreport.com/Item/4422/the_unsoundness_of_synod_2015s_new_way.aspx.
85. Grisez, *Christian Moral Principles*, 154.

CONCLUSION

1. "I was once alive apart from the law, but when the commandment came, sin revived and I died, and the very commandment that promised life proved to be death to me. For sin, seizing an opportunity in the commandment, deceived me and through it killed me. So the law is holy, and the commandment is holy and just and good. Did what is good, then, bring death to me? By no means! It was sin, working death in me through what is good, in order that sin might be shown to be sin, and through the commandment might become sinful beyond measure." Rom. 7:9–13.
2. "For all who rely on the works of the law are under a curse; for it is written, 'Cursed is everyone who does not observe and obey all the things written in the book of the law.'" Gal. 3:10.
3. "Now before faith came, we were imprisoned and guarded under the law until faith would be revealed. Therefore the law was our disciplinarian until Christ came, so that we might be justified by faith. But now that faith has come, we are no longer subject to a disciplinarian, for in Christ Jesus you are all children of God through faith." Gal. 3:23–26.
4. See, e.g., John Mahoney, *The Making of Moral Theology: A Study of the Roman Catholic Tradition* (Oxford: Oxford University Press, 1987), chap. 1.

5. See, e.g., Joel R. Beeke, "The Puritans on Conscience and Casuistry," *Puritan Reformed Journal* 4, no. 2 (July 2012): 95–114; James F. Keenan, S.J., "William Perkins (1558–1602) and the Birth of British Casuistry," in *The Context of Casuistry*, ed. James F. Keenan, S.J., and Thomas A. Shannon (Washington, DC: Georgetown University Press, 1995), 105–30.
6. See, e.g., Albert R. Jonsen and Stephen Toulmin, *The Abuse of Casuistry: A History of Moral Reasoning* (Berkeley: University of California Press, 1988).
7. See M. Cathleen Kaveny, "Retrieving and Reframing Catholic Casuistry," in *The Crisis of Authority in Catholic Modernity*, ed. Michael J. Lacey and Francis Oakley (New York: Oxford University Press, 2011), 225–58, and M. Cathleen Kaveny, "Law and Christian Ethics: Signposts for a Fruitful Conversation," *Journal of the Society of Christian Ethics* 35, no. 2 (2015): 3–32.
8. See, e.g., Augusto Zimmermann, "A Law above the Law: Christian Roots of the English Common Law," *Global Conversations* 1, no. 1 (November 2013): 85–98.
9. See Cathleen Kaveny, *Prophecy without Contempt: Religious Discourse in the Public Square* (Cambridge, MA: Harvard University Press, 2016), chaps. 4–5.
10. See, e.g., the indictment of Aaron Burr (August 1807), University of Missouri-Kansas City Faculty Projects, http://www.famous-trials.com/burr/159-indictment.
11. *Rector, Holy Trinity Church v. United States*, 143 U.S. 457, 471 (1892). The sentence goes on to refer to adherents of the Muslim faith in derogatory terms.
12. For Roman Catholics, the Second Vatican Council's Declaration on Religious Liberty provided ample justification for such efforts. See Vatican II, *Dignitatis humanae* [Declaration on Religious Freedom] (1965).
13. The indirect influence of Aquinas on the English common law tradition particularly merits further investigation. On Aquinas's influence on Hooker, see, e.g., A. J. Joyce, *Richard Hooker and Anglican Moral Theology* (Oxford: Oxford University Press, 2012).
14. Compare, for example, Thomas Aquinas, *Summa Theologica*, trans. Fathers of the English Dominican Province (New York: Benzinger Bros., 1947–48), I–II, qq. 6–21, with United States Sentencing Commission, *Guidelines Manual 2016*, http://www.ussc.gov/sites/default/files/pdf/guidelines-manual/2016/GLMFull.pdf. The Guidelines analyze the crime of homicide in ways that converge with the Aristotelian-Thomistic framework of act analysis, defining the act in terms of its object or immediate purpose, and qualifying its moral character in terms of its motive or end, as well as aggravating and mitigating circumstances.
15. Pope Francis declared an "Extraordinary Jubilee of Mercy" which ran from December 8, 2015 to November 20, 2016. See, e.g., Vatican Radio, "Pope Francis to Prisoners: Never Lose Hope in God's Mercy," November 6, 2016, http://en.radiovaticana.va/news/2016/11/06/pope_francis_to_prisoners_never_lose_

hope_in_god%E2%80%99s_mercy/1270460. For a helpful discussion of the history and practice of the presidential pardoning power, see Kathleen Dean Moore, *Pardons: Justice, Mercy, and the Public Interest* (New York: Oxford University Press, 1989).

16. For a legal philosophical perspective, see, e.g., Christopher Kutz, *Complicity: Ethics and Law for a Collective Age* (Cambridge: Cambridge University Press, 2000); for a theological perspective, see Albino Barrera, *Market Complicity and Christian Ethics* (New York: Cambridge University Press, 2011).
17. For an introduction to the relevant law, see David G. Owen, *Products Liability in a Nutshell*, 9th ed. (St. Paul, MN, West Publishing, 2014).
18. Ps. 19:7–10.

Index

www.ingramcontent.com/pod-product-compliance
Lightning Source LLC
Chambersburg PA
CBHW070046221025
34366CB00003B/71